4

Paul Dummett

John Hughes

Helen Stephenson

Life Level 4 Student Book

Paul Dummett

John Hughes

Helen Stephenson

Publisher: Sherrise Roehr

Executive Editor: Sarah T. Kenney

Associate Development Editor:
Nathan A. Gamache

Editorial Assistant: Patricia Giunta

Director of Global Marketing: Ian Martin

Senior Product Marketing Manager:
Caitlin Thomas

Director of Content and Media Production:
Michael Burggren

Production Manager: Daisy Sosa

Senior Print Buyer: Mary Beth Hennebury

Cover Designers: Scott Baker and Alex Dull

Cover Image: Jim Richardson / National
Geographic Creative

Compositor: MPS Limited

Cover Image

Gondolas docked by the Piazza San Marcos in
Venice, Italy. *Photograph by Jim Richardson.*

Student Book
ISBN-13: 978-1-305-25620-0

Student Book + CD-ROM
ISBN-13: 978-1-305-25629-3

Student Book + Online Workbook
ISBN-13: 978-1-305-26038-2

National Geographic Learning/Cengage Learning
20 Channel Center Street
Boston, MA 02210
USA

Cengage Learning is a leading provider of customized learning solutions
with office locations around the globe, including Singapore, the United
Kingdom, Australia, Mexico, Brazil, and Japan.

Cengage Learning products are represented in Canada by Nelson
Education, Ltd.

Visit National Geographic Learning online at **NGL.cengage.com**
Visit our corporate website at **www.cengage.com**

Printed in the United States of America
6 7 8 9 10 20 19 18 17 16

UNIT 1
COLOR

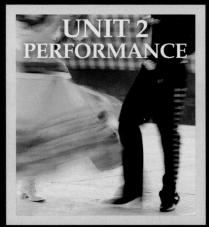

UNIT 2
PERFORMANCE

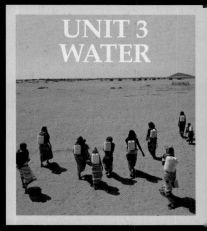

UNIT 3
WATER

UNIT 4
OPPORTUNITIES

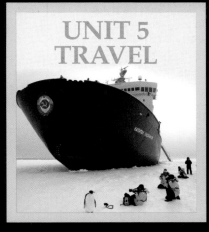

UNIT 5
TRAVEL

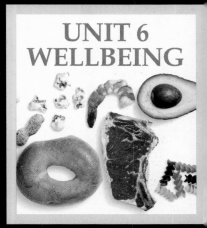

UNIT 6
WELLBEING

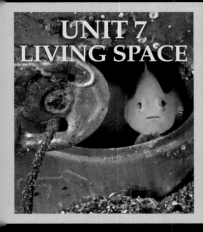

UNIT 7
LIVING SPACE

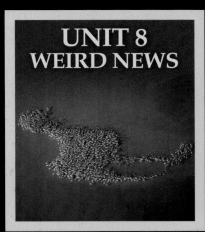

UNIT 8
WEIRD NEWS

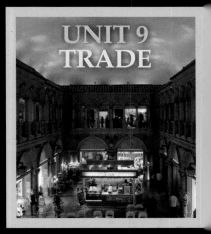

UNIT 9
TRADE

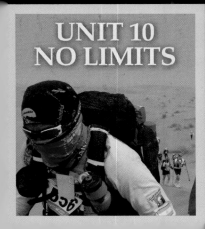

UNIT 10
NO LIMITS

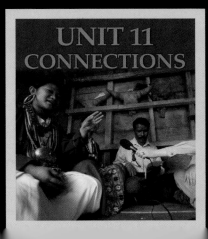

UNIT 11
CONNECTIONS

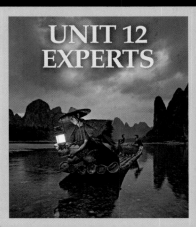

UNIT 12
EXPERTS

Contents

LISTENING	READING	CRITICAL THINKING	SPEAKING	WRITING
two people doing a quiz about colors and their meaning	an article about how we use color an article about the color red	conclusions	routines and leisure activities personal questions the roles we play	text type: a website profile writing skill: criteria for writing
a radio show about world fusion music	an article about why we dance an article about globalization	sources	new releases performing changes	text type: a profile writing skill: linking ideas (1)
two people talking about what happened next	an interview about underwater discoveries an article about an unforgettable experience	reading between the lines	the first time puzzles it happened to me	text type: a blog post writing skill: interesting language
three young women talking about their future	an article about India's new superhighway an article about the economic boom in China	arguments	predictions planning your work pay and conditions	text type: a cover letter writing skill: formal style
part of a radio show about a wildlife conservationist three conversations about vacation activities	a profile of a wildlife conservationist an article about vacation destinations an article about tourism and conservation	close reading	travel experiences what makes a good vacation green activities	text type: a postcard writing skill: informal style
two people discussing the power of the mind	a news item about traditional dishes a news item about imaginary eating an article about modern lifestyles	language clues	your favorite dish a healthy lifestyle modern life	text type: a formal letter writing skill: explaining consequences

LISTENING	READING	CRITICAL THINKING	SPEAKING	WRITING
podcast replies about homes around the world four people talking about where they live	an article about what New York used to be like an article about a little town in Puerto Rico	descriptions	house or apartment? your town wish you were here!	text type: a description of a place writing skill: organizing ideas
some clips from a website about mysteries in nature part of a radio show about the Nazca lines	an article about the Nazca lines an article about one of aviation's greatest mysteries	opinion or fact?	missing captions speculating about the past give your opinion	text type: a news story writing skill: structuring a news story
a radio show about banking with cell phones	a website about producers and products an article about how to negotiate a price	testing a conclusion	saving money brands negotiating	text type: an eBay ad writing skill: relevant and irrelevant information
part of a TV preview show about bionic bodies	a webpage about life on Mars two stories about feats of endurance	reading between the lines	medicine I'd love to live in… inspirational people	text type: a personal email writing skill: linking ideas (2)
four conversations about news headlines	a news item about the last "uncontacted" tribe an article about social networking	summarizing	news stories personal communication digital media	text type: a report of a meeting writing skill: using notes to write a report
two stories about uncomfortable experiences	a review of a book about Arctic expeditions an article about the samurai	relevance	where did I go wrong? what if… ? going back in time	text type: a website article writing skill: revising

Life around the world

Unit 2 Taiko master

The history of Taiko drumming from its origins in Japan to modern-day San Francisco.

Unit 7 A special kind of neighborhood

Stories from the Mission District of San Francisco.

Unit 8 Killer bees

Discover why killer bees are damaging the future of the Latin American rain forests.

Unit 9 Making a deal

Learn how to bargain in Morocco.

Unit 3 One village makes a difference

Solving the problems of India's water shortage.

Unit 4 Confucianism in China

Learn more about the famous Chinese philosopher Confucius.

San Francisco
USA

Pacific Ocean

Mexico

Morocco

China

Japan

India

Panama

Ethiopia

Gabon

Unit 12 Shark vs. octopus

What happens when a shark and an octopus meet.

Peru
Bolivia

Argentina

Unit 5 A disappearing world

A scientific expedition to record data about the rain forests of the Congo Basin.

Unit 10 High-altitude people

Why research into people living at high altitude gives us a better understanding of human evolution.

Antarctica

Unit 1 Peruvian weavers

A weavers' cooperative managed by the women of Chinchero.

Unit 11 Crossing Antarctica

The amazing story of two women's ambition to ski across Antarctica.

Unit 6 Dangerous dining

Find out why people eat the most dangerous fish on Earth: fugu.

Unit 1 Color

Two girls at a family event in Brunei
Photograph by Adam Hanif

FEATURES

1 Work in pairs. Look at the photo. What do the colors tell you about where the girls are? How do you think they feel?

2 Work in pairs. How do these colors make you feel? What do they make you think of? When do you see them or use them?

red	purple
black	green
yellow	blue
white	gray

3 Discuss these questions with your partner. Are your answers similar or different?

1 What color is your house / your kitchen / your car / your cell phone?
2 What is your favorite color? Why?
3 Which color do you normally wear? Why?

1a Life in color

Reading

1 Read the article *Life in color*. How is color important to the people in the photos?

2 Read the article again and find the following information:

1 three ways we use color
2 one example of each way we use color

3 Work in pairs. Compare your answers from Exercise 2. Then think of examples for the three uses of color from your own culture.

Grammar simple present and present continuous

4 Underline the simple present and circle the present continuous forms in the article. Which verb form do we use for these things?

1 things that are always or generally true?
2 things that are in progress at the time of speaking?
3 things that are regular actions?

> ▶ **SIMPLE PRESENT and PRESENT CONTINUOUS**
>
> **Simple present**
> *The "in" color changes every season.*
> **Present continuous**
> *This fall, women are wearing shades of purple and lilac.*
>
> For more information and practice, see page 156.

Huli villager, Papua New Guinea
Photograph by Tim Laman

Quechua high-school student, Peru
Photograph by Michael S Lewis

Life in *color*

We live our lives in color from our earliest days. For example, in Western cultures, pink is for baby girls and blue is for baby boys. Color plays a big part in everything we do. We use it both as a badge of identity and a way of expressing our individuality through decoration. And we use different colors to send out very different messages.

IDENTITY People need a sense of group identity. Look at the schoolboy in the photo. From his colorful traditional dress, other people in Peru know he comes from the Quechua community. We wear uniforms at school and work, and we dress in our favorite sports teams' colors to say the same thing: we belong to this group.

DECORATION The Huli villager in the photo is getting ready for a local festival. He's applying the traditional colors of red, black, and white in his own personal pattern. Face painting is an important part of the celebrations, and these days people are starting to experiment with brightly colored synthetic paints as well as traditional hues. In fashion-conscious Western cities, the "in" color changes every season. This fall, for example, women are wearing shades of purple and lilac.

MESSAGES Marketing experts understand the power of color very well. Packaging and labels in eye-catching colors stand out on the supermarket shelf. And companies always select the color of their brand very carefully—a calm blue for a bank you can trust, dark green to suggest quality and sophistication, or brown and green to indicate eco-friendliness.

hue (n) /hju/ a shade of a color
packaging (n) /ˈpækɪdʒɪŋ/ a container for a product

5 Complete the comments with the simple present and present continuous forms of the verbs.

Feng, IT student
We ¹ _____ (dress) casually at my college. But today my tutor ² _____ (wear) bright blue bike shorts! I know everyone ³ _____ (say) IT people are "different," but I think it's a little much!

Leo, finance assistant
My boss often ⁴ _____ (get) crazy ideas. At the moment, we ⁵ _____ (try) out a new color coding system in shades of pink!

Mina, sales assistant
I usually ⁶ _____ (get) take-out for lunch. I ⁷ _____ (not /eat) inside because the bright yellow and red tables are horrible!

▶ **STATIVE VERBS**

We use stative verbs to talk about states. These verbs are not normally used in the continuous form. Some verbs, for example *love*, can have both stative and dynamic meanings.
Jinous loves clothes. Jinous is loving her new job.

For more information and practice, see page 156.

6 Complete the table with these stative verbs. Can you add more?

| belong | contain | know | love | mean |
| need | sound | suppose | taste | understand |

Categories	Stative verbs
thoughts / mental processes	believe, _____ , _____ , _____ , _____
the senses	hear, _____ , _____
emotions	want, _____ , _____
possession	have, _____ , _____

7 Complete the sentences with the simple present or present continuous forms of the verbs. Are they stative or dynamic?

1 a I _____ (think) this color is OK.
   b We _____ (think) about moving.
2 a The Quechua people _____ (come) from South America.
   b A lot of people _____ (come) to the city to live these days.
3 a I _____ (love) purple flowers.
   b My sister is on vacation in Peru. She _____ (love) it!

Vocabulary time expressions

8 Find these time expressions in the article and in the comments in Exercise 5. Then complete the table with the expressions and add more.

| always | at the moment | often | this fall |
| today | usually |

Simple present	Present continuous
on weekends	right now
every day	this month
never	this week

9 Write questions with these verbs using the simple present or present continuous and time expressions. Then work in pairs. Ask and answer your questions.

| buy | dress | eat | try out | wear | work |

Do you usually dress differently on weekends?

Not really, no.

Speaking

10 Work in pairs. Ask and answer the questions like the ones below about these activities. Find three things you have in common.

cook a meal
decorate your house
do housework
dress up
go online
go out with friends
go shopping
go to evening classes
go to an exercise class
learn a new skill
make something with your hands
read a new book
spend time with your family

How often do you cook a meal?

Are you cooking a meal at the moment?

When do you usually cook meals?

What are you cooking these days?

1b Culture and color

Vocabulary feelings and personal states

1 Work in pairs. Which color do you associate with the words *love* and *anger*?

2 Choose the correct word for each definition. Check that you understand the meaning of the other words. Use a dictionary if necessary.

1 *passion / prosperity* financial success
2 *love / luck* what happens by chance
3 *courage / anger* the ability to face dangerous situations without being afraid
4 *happiness / wisdom* the ability to make good decisions based on experience
5 *knowledge / sorrow* information you get from experience or education
6 *power / sadness* unhappiness
7 *joy / mourning* great sadness when someone dies
8 *pride / envy* wanting what someone else has

Listening

3 🎵 1 Work in pairs. Take the quiz *Colors and their meaning*. Then listen and check your answers.

4 🎵 1 Listen again and complete the notes.

Color	Place	Meaning
red	Western cultures	love, passion, ¹ ....
	Eastern cultures	luck, prosperity, courage
yellow	China India	power wisdom, ² ....
orange	Japan	happiness, ³ ....
⁴	international Western cultures	environmentalism envy

5 Do these colors mean the same in your culture?

Colors and their meaning

1 Look at the photo. Where are the women going?
a to a birthday party
b to a wedding

2 Does red have different meanings in Eastern and Western cultures?
a yes   b no

3 Where does yellow symbolize wisdom?
a China   b India

4 Which color means "happiness" in Japan?
a orange   b pink

5 Who uses green as their symbol?
a the environmental movement
b paint manufacturers

6 Pronunciation questions

a 🔊 2 Listen to the questions and repeat them. Notice how the speaker's voice rises at the end of questions that begin with verbs, and rises then falls for questions that begin with *Wh-* words.

1 Do you want to do this quiz?
2 Where are the women going?

b 🔊 3 Listen and repeat these questions.

1 Where does yellow symbolize wisdom?
2 Is it China?
3 What's the next question?
4 Are there any more questions?
5 Do you want to give it a try?

Grammar question forms

7 Match the questions in the quiz with these statements (a–c).

a We use *do* and *does* to make questions in the simple present.
b When we make questions with *be* or modal verbs (like *can*), we invert the subject and the verb.
c When the question word is the subject of the question, we don't invert the subject and the verb.

> **▶ QUESTION FORMS**
>
> | (why /
where /
how /
what
etc.) | are
can

does
is | you
you

it
she

who /
what |
find

work ?
doing?

uses | happy?
this
word?

this
color? |
> |---|---|---|---|---|
>
> For more information and practice, see page 156.

8 Look at the grammar box. Complete the *blue* and *yellow* quiz questions with verbs or question words.

9 Work in two pairs in groups of four.

Pair A: Turn to page 153 and follow the instructions.

Pair B: Turn to page 154 and follow the instructions.

Quiz

1 Where _____ the Tuareg—or "blue people" —originally come from?
2 _____ lives in the Blue House in South Korea?
3 What _____ the name of the country where the Blue Nile begins?
4 Which part of the US _____ famous for "the blues" (music)?

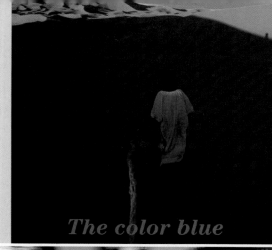

The color blue

The color yellow

1 Which fruit _____ the California Yellow Fruit Festival celebrate?
2 _____ sport gives a yellow jersey to the winner?
3 Where _____ yellow taxi cabs come from originally?
4 Where _____ you see the house that inspired Van Gogh's *Yellow House* painting?

Writing and speaking

10 You are going to learn about your classmates. First, prepare some questions. Match questions 1–4 with the follow-up questions (a–d). Then write four more follow-up questions of your own for questions 5–8.

1 What do you do?
2 Do you live near here?
3 Are you from a large family?
4 How many languages do you speak?
5 Why are you learning English?
6 What do you think of the course?
7 Are you taking any other classes at the moment?
8 Do you have any hobbies?

a How well do you speak _____ ?
b How many _____ do you have?
c Can you walk home from here?
d Do you enjoy your job?

11 Now use your questions to learn about three or four classmates. Be prepared to share what you learn with the class.

1c Red is for winners

Reading

1 How many sports teams can you write down in one minute? What are their team colors? Which are the most successful?

2 Work in pairs. Read the article headline on page 15 and discuss what you think it means. Choose one of these options (a–c).

   a Traditional gold medals are now red.
   b Teams with the word "red" in their names win more often.
   c Red sports clothes lead to more success.

3 Read the article quickly. Check your ideas from Exercise 2.

4 Find information about these people in the article and correct the factual mistakes in these sentences.

   1 Russell Hill and Robert Barton are athletes.
   2 Joanna Setchell studies African birds.
   3 Jonathan Blount is an anthropologist.

5 Match the research topics (1–4) with the scientists' conclusions (a–d).

   1 Results at the Olympic Games
   2 African mandrills' success with the opposite sex
   3 Male and female zebra finches
   4 The color of birds' beaks

   a The color red gives some male monkeys an advantage.
   b The color red makes some male birds more successful.
   c Brightly colored beaks are indicators of healthier birds.
   d The color red can give some athletes an advantage.

Critical thinking conclusions

6 Read Hill and Barton's conclusion carefully. Which statement (a–c) means the same thing?

> When sports competitors are equally matched, the team dressed in red is more likely to win, according to a new study.

   a The color red can make a weak athlete successful against a strong athlete.
   b The color red is only an important factor when there is very little difference in the athletes' skill.
   c The color red does not affect results when there is very little difference in the athletes' skill.

Vocabulary and speaking the roles we play

7 Look at the list of roles people can have. Which of these roles are mentioned in the text?

anthropologist	athlete	biologist	colleague
competitor	contestant	friend	manager
mentor	opponent	parent	primatologist
researcher	scientist	teacher	

> ▶ **WORDBUILDING activity → person**
> We can change the ending of some nouns to make words that describe what people do.
> *anthropology → anthropologist*
> *win → winner*

8 Work in pairs. Take turns choosing one of the words and describing what a person in that role does. Your partner will guess the word.

> *This person helps you at work, but is not your boss.*

> colleague

9 How many different roles do you play in your life? Compare with your partner.

> *Well, I'm participating in a photography competition, so I suppose I'm a competitor.*

When sports competitors are equally matched, the team dressed in red is more likely to win, according to a new study.

That is the conclusion of anthropologists Russell Hill and Robert Barton, after studying the results of one-on-one boxing, tae kwon do, Greco-Roman wrestling, and freestyle wrestling matches at the Olympic Games. Their study shows that when a competitor is equally matched with an opponent in fitness and skill, the athlete wearing red is more likely to win.

Hill and Barton report that when one contestant is much better than the other, color has no effect on the result. However, when there is only a small difference between them, the effect of color is sufficient to tip the scale. The anthropologists say that the number of times red wins is not simply by chance, but is statistically significant.

Joanna Setchell, a primate researcher, has found similar results in nature. She studies the large African monkeys known as mandrills. Mandrills have bright red noses that stand out against their white faces. Setchell's work shows that the dominant males—the ones who are more successful with females—have a brighter red nose than other males. Setchell says that the finding that red also has an advantage in human athletics does not surprise her, and she adds that "the idea of the study is very clever."

Hill and Barton got the idea for their research because of the role that the color red plays in the animal world. "Red seems to be the color, across species, that signals male dominance," Barton says. They thought that "there might be a similar effect in humans." Setchell, the primatologist, agrees: "As Hill and Barton say, humans redden when we are angry and go pale when we're scared. These are very important signals to other individuals."

Red seems to be the color… that signals male dominance.

In a study demonstrating the effect of red among birds, scientists put red plastic rings on the legs of male zebra finches and found an increase in the birds' success with female zebra finches. Zebra finches already have bright red beaks, so this study suggests that, as with Olympic athletes, an extra flash of red is significant. In fact, researchers from the University of Glasgow say that the birds' brightly colored beaks are an indicator of health. Jonathan Blount, a biologist, says that females of many species choose to mate with the brightest males. Blount and his colleagues think that bright red or orange beaks attract females because they mean that the males are healthier. Nothing in nature is simple, however, because in species such as the blue-footed booby, a completely different color seems to give the male birds the same advantage with females.

… bright red or orange beaks attract females because they mean that the males are healthier.

Meanwhile, what about those athletes who win in their events while wearing red? Do their clothes give them an unintentional advantage? Maybe it's time for new regulations on team colors?

Team color red

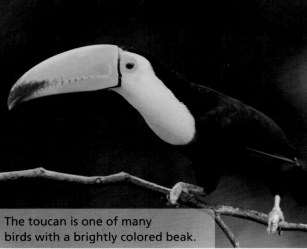
The toucan is one of many birds with a brightly colored beak.

The blue-footed booby's feet are the main attraction.

fitness (n) /ˈfɪtnɪs/ health and strength
indicator (n) /ˈɪndɪˌkeɪtər/ sign
regulations (n) /ˌregyəˈleɪʃənz/ rules
significant (adj) /sɪɡˈnɪfɪkənt/ 1 not by chance 2 with an important meaning
unintentional (adj) /ˌʌnɪnˈtenʃən(ə)l/ not planned

1d First impressions

Real life opening and closing conversations

You never get a second chance to make a good first impression.

- ☐ Dress appropriately. A dark blue suit is great for a business meeting, a red tie or scarf suggests power and energy. But what if you work in the arts?
- ☐ Be punctual, courteous, and positive.
- ☐ Make sure you know the other person's name. Use it!
- ☐ Make the other person the focus of your attention. Sound interested! Ask questions!
- ☐ Know what you want to say and say it effectively!
- ☐ Don't forget to follow up on your meeting with a phone call or an email.

1 Work in groups. Discuss the text above with respect to your own country.

1 Do the colors and clothes mean the same thing?
2 What does *punctual* mean?
3 Do you use first or last names?
4 Which advice is appropriate in your country?
5 Which advice is not appropriate in your country?

2 🎵 4 Listen to four participants at a business skills seminar. They are role-playing "first meetings." Mark the points on the handout above that the speakers follow.

3 🎵 4 Look at the expressions for opening and closing conversations. Listen again and mark the expressions you hear. Which pair of participants do you think gave the best performance?

▶ **OPENING AND CLOSING CONVERSATIONS**

Opening a conversation
May I introduce myself?
Allow me to introduce myself.
Hi, how are you? I'm…
It's a pleasure to meet you.
Nice meeting you.

Closing a conversation and moving on
Thanks for your time.
It's been good talking to you.
Let me give you my card.
Let's stay in touch.
Why don't I give you my card?
How about meeting again?

---

4 Pronunciation short questions

a 🎵 5 Listen to these exchanges. Notice how the speakers use short questions to show interest.

1 —I mostly work on web advertising.
  —Do you?

2 —I'm in sales.
  —Oh, are you?

3 —Oh yes, my brother goes to your gym.
  —Does he?

b Work in pairs. Practice the exchanges.

5 Look at the audioscript on page 173. Practice the conversations with your partner.

6 Imagine you are a participant at a business skills seminar. Complete the profile information card and then do the seminar task. Use the expressions for opening and closing conversations to help you.

Name _____
Company
_____
Position
_____
Responsibilities
_____
Current projects you
are involved in
_____

First Impressions
Task: You are at a networking event. Introduce yourself to as many people as you can and arrange to follow up useful contacts. You only have two minutes with each person.

---

networking [n] /'net,wɜrkɪŋ/ making useful business contacts

7 Work in pairs. Compare the information you found out about different people in Exercise 6.

1e About us

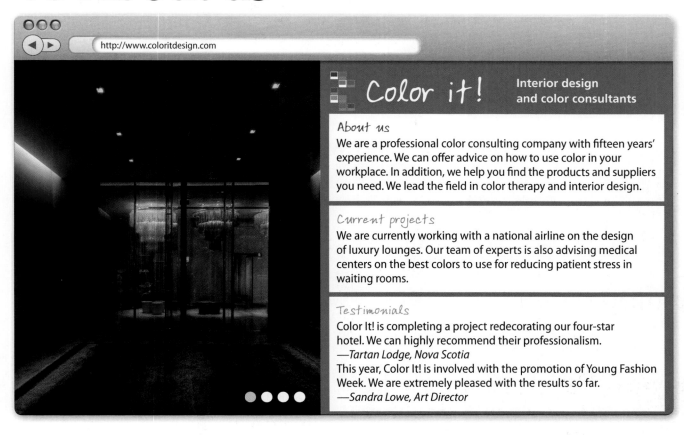

http://www.coloritdesign.com

Color it!
Interior design and color consultants

About us
We are a professional color consulting company with fifteen years' experience. We can offer advice on how to use color in your workplace. In addition, we help you find the products and suppliers you need. We lead the field in color therapy and interior design.

Current projects
We are currently working with a national airline on the design of luxury lounges. Our team of experts is also advising medical centers on the best colors to use for reducing patient stress in waiting rooms.

Testimonials
Color It! is completing a project redecorating our four-star hotel. We can highly recommend their professionalism.
—*Tartan Lodge, Nova Scotia*
This year, Color It! is involved with the promotion of Young Fashion Week. We are extremely pleased with the results so far.
—*Sandra Lowe, Art Director*

Writing a website profile

1 Read the information about the Color It! consulting company. Who (a–d) do you think would be interested in their services?

  a a nursery school with a new location
  b a newlywed couple buying their first home
  c a paint manufacturer
  d a fashion store opening new branches

2 Writing skill criteria for writing

a Read the information again. Choose the correct option.

  1 text type: *website / letter*
  2 style: *neutral / formal / informal*
  3 reader: *current clients / potential clients*
  4 purpose: *to promote the company / to advertise a product*

b Which features of the text helped you decide your answers in Exercise 2a?

3 Underline these expressions and verbs in the text.

  1 time expressions
  2 expressions that signal additional information
  3 verbs describing the company's work

4 Complete the sentences with some of the expressions you underlined in Exercise 3.

  1 We are _____ carrying out market research into cell phone use for a large telecommunications company. _____ , we are advising a fast food company on a new logo.
  2 _____ our company is opening four new offices in major cities in the US. We are _____ expanding to Latin America.

5 Work in groups. Imagine you run a small business together. Decide on your company name, field of work, and some current projects.

6 Work on your own. Write a website profile to promote your business. Use the Color It! profile and the categories in Exercise 2 to help you.

7 Work in your groups again. Read your profiles and choose the one that best promotes your company. The best profile should have no spelling mistakes and should make readers understand exactly what your company does.

Peruvian weavers

These villagers are part of something new.

Before you watch

1 Work in groups. Look at the photo and discuss these questions.

   1 Where do the people come from?
   2 What are they doing?

2 Complete the summary with these words.

business	cooked	farming	self-sufficient
shawls	traditions	village	visitors	weavers

The video is about a group of women ¹ _____ in a small ² _____ in Peru. Traditionally in this village, women ³ _____ , looked after the children, and made cloth, and men farmed. But now ⁴ _____ is not enough to support a family, and some women have formed a new type of ⁵ _____ : a weavers' cooperative. The women use traditional methods to weave blankets, ⁶ _____ , and ponchos that they sell to ⁷ _____ . In this way, they preserve their identity and ⁸ _____ but also make some money that helps them become ⁹ _____ .

While you watch

3 Watch the video and check your answers from Exercise 2.

4 Put these statements in the order you hear them.

  a Farming has long been a tradition in Chinchero.
  b Now, in Chinchero, weaving isn't just a tradition. It's a way to make money.
  c A few people from the village… catch the sheep and prepare the knife.
  d I learned when I was in the third grade.
  e The methods they use are traditional, but these villagers are part of something new.
  f They want to keep the Peruvian weaving traditions alive.

5 Answer the questions.

   1 Who is Nilda Cayanupa?

   2 Why did she start the cooperative?

   3 What was her dream?

   4 How did one man get involved in the weaving?

   5 How much money can the women make?

After you watch

6 **Roleplay an interview with Nilda**

Work in pairs.

Student A: You are a journalist for *National Geographic*. Prepare to ask Nilda:

- how the cooperative started.
- what is special about the cooperative.
- what the women have learned to do.
- what the women do with the money they make.
- how life is changing in the village.

Student B: You are Nilda. Look at the ideas above and think about what you are going to say to the journalist.

Act out the interview, then change roles.

7 At the end of the video, the narrator says: "Many threads together are stronger than one alone." How is this true for the women of Chinchero? Do you think this is always true?

8 Work in groups. Ask and answer the questions with other people in your group and write down their answers. Then report the results to the class.

   1 Do you like the clothes the women make?
   2 Have you ever worn traditional clothes? When?
   3 Do your clothes express who you are?
   4 Which is more important to you: brand or color and design?

blanket (n) /ˈblæŋkɪt/ a covering that keeps you warm in bed
cloth (n) /klɔθ/ material used for making clothes, etc.
cooperative (n) /koʊˈɑpərətɪv/ a business or organization owned by the people who work in it and who all profit from it
poncho (n) /ˈpɑntʃoʊ/ a traditional South American coat made from a single piece of cloth, with a hole in the middle for the head
self-sufficient (adj) /ˈself səˈfɪʃənt/ able to provide everything you need for yourself
shawl (n) /ʃɔl/ an article of clothing worn around the shoulders
spin (v) /spɪn / twist fibers of a material into thread to make cloth
thread (n) /θred/ a long thin line of fiber
weave (v) /wiv/ make cloth by crossing threads over and under each other
weaver (n) /ˈwivər/ a person who weaves
wool (n) /wʊl/ a material made from the hair of sheep and other animals
yarn (n) /yɑrn/ a long thick line of fiber made by twisting threads together

UNIT 1 REVIEW

Grammar

1 Work in pairs. Discuss the questions.

1   What do you think the life of an Olympic athlete is like?
2   How do athletes prepare for top-level competitions?
3   How do you think it feels to compete in major competitions?

2 Jiao Liuyang is a gold-medal winning swimmer for China. Complete the interview that she gave a reporter.

1   Q: What _____ (this championship / mean) to you?
    A: Actually, I _____ (not / think) too much about it. I _____ (concentrate) on what I _____ (do) now.
2   Q: _____ (what / influence) you during a race?
    A: When you _____ (hear) people cheering your name, it _____ (make) it more exciting.
3   Q: _____ (you / train) every day?
    A: At the moment, I _____ (do) a little more than usual. I only _____ (get) Sundays off.
4   Q: So this competition _____ (affect) your training routine?
    A: Yes, the routine _____ (change) before a major championship. And this time, we _____ (try) different methods for training.

3 Work in pairs. Compare your answers from Exercise 2. Then act out the interview.

I CAN	
ask and answer questions about things that are always and generally true, and routines (simple present)	
ask and answer questions about things happening now (present continuous)	
talk about possessions and states: thoughts, etc. (stative verbs)	

Vocabulary

4 Tell your partner about something you do or are doing at these times. Then choose one activity of your partner's that you don't know very much about and ask follow-up questions.

always	on weekends	every day
never	often	right now
this month	this week	today
usually		

5 Race your partner to figure out what these words for people's roles are by filling in the missing vowels. Do you know people who have these roles? Tell your partner about them.

thlt	cntstnt	prnt
blgst	mngr	rsrchr
cllg	mntr	scntst
cmpttr	ppnnt	tchr

I CAN	
talk about feelings and personal states	
use time expressions with the simple present and present continuous	
talk about the roles people have	

Real life

6 Work in small groups. You are at a reception for a local sports charity. Choose one of the roles from Exercise 5. Then act out conversations with different partners using these pairs of expressions to begin and end the conversation.

1   "May I introduce myself?"
    "Let's stay in touch."
2   "Hi! My name's…"
    "Let me give you my card."
3   "Hi, how are you? I'm…"
    "How about meeting again?"

I CAN	
introduce myself in formal and informal situations	
open and close a conversation	
ask for and give personal information	

Speaking

7 Choose a role: a successful athlete, movie star, politician, etc. Then work in pairs and tell each other who you are.

8 Work on your own. Prepare questions to interview your partner about their success in their career. Use the ideas from Exercise 2. Then take turns asking and answering your questions.

Unit 2 Performance

Mexican dancers

FEATURES

1 Look at the photo of a traditional dance from Mexico. With a partner, discuss: what other types of traditional dances do you know about?

2 Which word is the odd one out in each group? Why?

1 actor audience dance director
  dance – all the others are people
2 choreographer conductor musician play
3 concert dancer musical show
4 act comedian entertainer magician
5 band choir orchestra singer
6 ballet clown drama opera
7 blues jazz drummer flamenco
8 dancing acting hiking singing

3 Work in pairs. Are you interested in the arts? Discuss these questions.

1 How often do you go to concerts, shows, or the theater?
2 What are your favorite types of entertainment?
3 What traditional events in your country or region do you enjoy?
4 Do you like taking part in performances or do you prefer being in the audience?

2a A world of music

Vocabulary musical styles

1 What kind of music do you like? Write a list of as many types of music as you can in two minutes. Then work in pairs and discuss your lists. Use the expressions below to help you. Do you have similar tastes?

> *What do you think of rap?*

> *I hate it. It's so repetitive.*

> I love/hate/enjoy/adore it.
> I'm (not) into it.
> I can't stand it.
> I kind of like / don't mind it.

2 Work in pairs. Match the music genres (1–8) with their countries of origin (a–h). Check your answers with your instructor.

1 blues US	a Jamaica
2 bossa nova d	b Cuba
3 charanga b	c US
4 fado g	d Brazil
5 flamenco F	e Mongolia
6 hoomii e	f Spain
7 reggae a	g Portugal
8 taiko drumming h	h Japan

3 Work in pairs. Describe as many of the music genres in Exercise 2 as you know. Use these words.

catchy	cheerful	lively	melancholy
melodic	moving	repetitive	rhythmic
tuneless	unusual		

Listening

4 💿 6 Listen to a radio show about world fusion music. Complete the sentences.

1 World fusion mixes several different _influences_
2 Manu Chao sings in _6_ languages.
3 Paul Simon has worked with _Zulu_ artists Ladysmith Black Mambazo.
4 Peter Gabriel is a _British_ musician.
5 Youssou N'Dour is a Senegalese _singer_.
6 Zap Mama are a world fusion group from _Belgium_

While waiting for their meal to cook, a group in Darhan, Mongolia, enjoys a song.
Photograph by Christopher De Bruyn

5 💿 6 Listen again. Correct the factual errors in the sentences.

1 Manu Chao has not been successful in the French-speaking world. _(English)_
2 World fusion has become better-known since the release of Paul Simon's film *Graceland*. _album_ _many since 1980_
3 Peter Gabriel has been part of WOMAD for two years.
4 Zap Mama have had several hits in Belgium. _International_

6 Work in pairs. What did you learn from the radio show?

Grammar present perfect

7 Look at the sentences in Exercise 5. Which one of these statements is false?

1 The activities or situations started at some time in the past.
2 The activities or situations continue into the present.
3 The activities or situations ended in the past.
4 We use *since* with the starting point of an activity.
5 We use *for* with a period of time long ended.

8 Look at the grammar box. Complete the sentences with the present perfect form of the verbs. Which verbs are <u>regular</u>? Which are irregular?

1 Manu Chao _has lived_ (live) in France for most of his life.
2 Youssou N'Dour _has become_ (become) very popular since working with Peter Gabriel.
3 Young musicians _have mixed_ (mix) folk with punk.
4 What _has happened_ (happen) to world fusion since the 1980s?
5 We _have heard_ (hear) lots of great music in the past few years.
6 How many albums _has_ Zap Mama _Made_ (make)?

put custom
play custom
dress up: dress formally

▶ PRESENT PERFECT

I/you/we/they	have (not)	past participle been
he/she/it	has (not)	had
What	has	happened?

For more information and practice, see page 157.

---

take off: go   take up: start
+ take over: dominate

9 Complete the paragraph with the present perfect form of the verbs.

The number of online music sites ¹ _has grown_ (grow) enormously since Internet connections became cheaper. In many (ways) these sites ² _have taken_ (take over) the _over_ traditional roles of both radio stations and music stores. Buying music online ³ _has become_ (become) more popular than many music companies imagined: you can now download music files directly to your music player. It ⁴ _has also gotten_ (also / get) much easier to listen to different kinds of music on blogs and sites. Artists ⁵ _have started_ (start) uploading their music directly to the Internet and some ⁶ _have found_ (find) mainstream success that way.

10 Are these expressions used with *for* or *since*? Write two lists.

for a couple of days   *since* 1986   *for* a while
for a few months   *for* ages   *for* centuries
since I was a child   *since* July   *since* last Monday
since my last vacation   *since* lunchtime   *for* some time
since the day before yesterday   *for* years

---

11 Write the present perfect form of the verbs. Then complete the sentences so that they are true for you. Work in pairs and compare your sentences.

1 I _have lived_ (live) here for _2 years_ .
2 I _have been_ (be) at my current job since _2016_ .
3 I _have known_ (know) my best friend since _I moved here_ .
4 I _haven't_ (not / listen to) _listened to this music_ for ages.
5 I _have always_ (always / want) to _wanted to travel to_ . Japan since I was teenager
6 I _have never_ (never / have) _had a dog since I was a kid_
7 I _have studied_ (study) English since _I was 5 yrs old_
8 I _have been_ (be) in this class for _2 years_ .

▶ ALREADY, JUST, and YET

They've already had several international hits.
You've just heard a [...] track from Manu Chao's latest album.
He hasn't had a big impact in this country yet.

For more information, see page 158.

---

12 Match the comments (1–4) with the responses (a–d). Complete the sentences with *already*, *just*, and *yet*. Check your answers with your instructor.

D 1 Have you heard Shakira's new single? _I have already heard_
A 2 Do you want to borrow this DVD of Matt Damon's latest movie? _No, I have just seen the movie_
B 3 Have you seen *Gone with the Wind* _already_ ?
C 4 The National Ballet has _just_ announced its new season.

a No, thanks. I've _already_ seen it.
b Yes, we have. It's even better than the book.
c They have? Which ballets are they doing?
d No, not _yet_ . Is it as good as her last one?

Speaking

13 Work in pairs. Act out conversations like the ones in Exercise 12. Use these words.

a new album / song / band
a musical / show / play / concert / movie
an exhibit / a festival

The new Arctic Monkeys album has just come out. Have you heard it?

No, I haven't. What's it like?

take in : make it smaller

2b Dance across America

Reading

1 Work in pairs. Answer the questions.

1 What kind of dances are traditional in your country?
2 Have you ever been to a dance class or learned a dance?
3 Do you dance at special occasions? Which ones?
4 How does dancing make you feel?

2 Read the article *Dance across America*. What is the article about? Choose the correct option (a–c).

a professional dancers
b ordinary people
c professional dancers and ordinary people

3 Underline three reasons why people dance. Circle three effects dancing has on people.

4 The article talks about the role of dancing in people's lives. Can you think of other activities people do to:

1 make them feel young?   *keep in shape*
2 meet people?
3 have a social life?
4 change their mood?

DANCE ACROSS AMERICA

Before there was the written word, there was the language of dance. Dance expresses love and hate, joy and sorrow, life and death, and everything else in between.

Dance in America is everywhere. We dance from Florida to Alaska, and from coast to coast. We dance to celebrate or just to fill the time.

"I adore dancing," says Lester Bridges, the owner of a dance studio in Iowa. "I can't imagine doing anything else with my life." Bridges runs dance classes for all ages. "Teaching dance is wonderful. My older students say it makes them feel young. It's marvelous to watch them. For many of them, it's a way of meeting people and having a social life."

So why do we dance? "I can tell you about one young couple," says Bridges. "They're learning to do traditional dances. They arrive at the class in a bad mood and they leave with a smile. Dancing seems to change their mood completely."

So, do we dance to make ourselves feel better, calmer, healthier? Andrea Hillier, a choreographer, says "Dance, like the rhythm of a beating heart, is life. Even after all these years, I want to get better and better. I keep practicing even when I'm exhausted. I find it hard to stop! Dancing reminds me I'm alive."

Grammar verb patterns: *-ing* form and *to* + infinitive

5 Look at the grammar box. Choose the correct option in these sentences.

1 We use the *-ing* form of the verb after certain verbs, as the subject of a sentence and after *adjectives / prepositions*.

2 We use the infinitive of the verb (*to* + base form) after certain verbs and after *adjectives / prepositions*.

▶ VERB PATTERNS: *-ING* FORM AND INFINITIVE			
-ing form	I/you/we/they/he/she	adore(s)	dancing.
	It's a way	of	meeting people.
	Dancing	is	wonderful.
infinitive	I/you/we/they/he/she	want(s)	to get better.
	It's	marvelous	to watch.
For more information and practice, see page 158.			

6 In the article, underline examples of the patterns above. Then complete the lists with the verbs in the article.

1 verb + *-ing* form: adore, _____ , _____

2 verb + infinitive: learn, _____ , _____

7 Each option in these sentences is grammatically possible. Which one is not logically possible?

1 Andrea Hillier *agrees / expects / intends* to get better.
2 Some students *need / hope / pretend* to make new friends.
3 One student *involves / keeps / practices* doing the steps every day.
4 All our best students *choose / promise / refuse* to practice regularly.
5 Few students *decide / help / plan* to give up.

8 Complete the sentences with the *-ing* form and infinitive form of the verbs. Which sentences are true about you? Which do you agree with? Then work in pairs. Tell your partner.

1 I enjoy _____ (do) creative activities.
2 _____ (paint) is one of my favorite hobbies.
3 It's hard _____ (be) completely original.
4 I often imagine _____ (change) my lifestyle.
5 I'm too old _____ (learn) something new.
6 I'm learning _____ (play) the piano.
7 I'm thinking about _____ (try) folk dancing.
8 I never seem _____ (find) time to meet people.

Vocabulary emotions

9 What kind of things can change your mood? Match the two parts of the sentences.

1 Going out dancing
2 Every time I hear a sad song, I want
3 That music is so cheerful—it always
4 It's a really funny movie. I can't stop
5 Seeing horror movies makes me

a feel scared.
b laughing when I think about it.
c makes me smile.
d really energizes me up.
e to cry.

10 Think of specific examples for each sentence in Exercise 9. Then work in pairs. Tell your partner about them.

> *I don't go out dancing every week, maybe a couple of times a month. I always have a good time. It puts me in a good mood.*

Speaking

11 Use these phrases or your own ideas to make sentences that are true for you. Write sentences with the *-ing* form and the infinitive form of the verbs.

act	perform in public
be behind the scenes	play an instrument
be in the spotlight	sing
be on stage	tell jokes
go to dances	give a speech

1 I really enjoy _____
2 I can't imagine _____
3 I hate _____
4 _____ makes me feel great.
5 It's not easy _____
6 I'm learning _____

12 Work in pairs. Compare your sentences from Exercise 11 and find things you feel the same way about. Ask follow-up questions.

> *So, you enjoy performing in public. What kind of performances do you do?*

> *Well, I like singing karaoke at parties! And it makes my friends laugh!*

2c A world together

Reading

1 Work in groups. What does the term *globalization* mean to your group? Give examples.

2 Read the first two paragraphs of the article. Compare your answer from Exercise 1 with the information.

3 Read the rest of the article. Which paragraph talks about:

1 American products in other countries?
2 globalization in the future?
3 the speed of the globalization process?

4 What examples of globalization does the author give for these things?

1 dance   4 the English language
2 food   5 American TV shows
3 dolls

5 Which of these statements (a–d) agree with the article?

a It's hard to find examples of globalization in everyday life.
b Globalization is not a new phenomenon, but the speed of change these days is new.
c Some people think that globalization is a negative thing.
d The author thinks that world cultures cannot resist Western influences.

Critical thinking **sources**

6 Find these phrases in the article. Why does the author put some words in quotation marks? Match the phrases (1–4) with the reasons (a–b).

1 These are "globalization" moments. (paragraph 2)
2 …"is a reality, not a choice." (paragraph 3)
3 …one big "McWorld." (paragraph 3)
4 "We've taken an American box,"… (paragraph 4)

a The author is reporting someone else's actual words.
b The author wants to emphasize an idea.

7 Which statement best reflects the text? Choose one option (a–c).

a The author thinks globalization is a good thing.
b The author thinks globalization is a bad thing.
c The author does not express her opinion about globalization.

8 What is your opinion? Is globalization a good or a bad thing? Tell your group.

Vocabulary **global culture**

> ▶ **WORDBUILDING adjective + noun**
>
> Some adjectives and nouns often go together.
> *outside world   popular culture*

9 Complete the sentences with these words from the article.

connections	culture	influences	market	world

1 Television is a good example of **popular** _____ .
2 There's a **growing** _____ for reality TV.
3 We're trying to encourage **cultural** _____ between our two countries.
4 Many societies have been open to **Western** _____ .
5 Do they have any contact with the **outside** _____ ?

Speaking

10 Work in pairs. Make notes about how things have changed since the year 2000. Use some of these ideas and ideas of your own.

- Popular culture: reality TV, social networking, international movies and music
- Technology: digital photography, phone technology, the Internet
- The economy and work: where things are made, working abroad

11 Work in groups. Compare your ideas and discuss how things have changed in your area or country. Decide which are the biggest changes at the local and national level. Then present your conclusions to the class.

Digital photography has become much more popular.

Yes, a lot of people use digital cameras these days.

A world together

Goods move. People move. Ideas move. And cultures change.

BY ERLA ZWINGLE

Once I start looking for them, I realize these moments are everywhere. One day, I'm sitting in a coffee shop in London having a cup of Italian espresso served by an Algerian waiter, listening to the Beach Boys playing in the background. Another day, I'm eating in a restaurant in New Delhi that serves Lebanese food to the music of a Filipino band, in rooms decorated with a vintage poster for a blues concert in New Orleans.

These are "globalization" moments. We are in the middle of a worldwide change in cultures—a transformation of entertainment, business, and politics. Popular culture has crossed borders in ways we have never seen before. According to social scientists, our world is shrinking. In Japan, people have become flamenco fanatics and there are hundreds of dance schools around the country. In the last few years, dozens of top Spanish flamenco artists have given performances there. It's a huge and growing market. Meanwhile, in Denmark people have discovered a new interest in Italian food, and pasta imports have grown 500% over the last decade. And the classic American blonde Barbie doll now comes in about 30 national varieties, including Austrian and Moroccan.

How do people feel about globalization? It depends to a large extent on where they live and how much money they have. However, globalization, as one report has stated, "is a reality, not a choice." Humans have always developed commercial and cultural connections, but these days computers, the Internet, cell phones, cable TV, and cheaper air transportation have accelerated and complicated these connections. Nevertheless, the basic dynamic is the same:

Goods move. People move. Ideas move. And cultures change. The difference now is the speed and extent of these changes. Television had 50 million users after thirteen years; the Internet had the same number after only five years. But now that more than one-fifth of all the people in the world speak at least some English, critics of globalization say that we are one big "McWorld."

But I have discovered that cultures are as resourceful, resilient, and unpredictable as the people they include. In Los Angeles, I saw more diversity than I thought possible at Hollywood High School, where the student body speaks 32 different languages. In Shanghai, I found that the television show *Sesame Street* has been redesigned by Chinese educators to teach Chinese values and traditions. "We've taken an American box," one told me, "and put Chinese content into it." In India, where there are more than 400 languages and several very strict religions, McDonald's serves lamb instead of beef and offers a vegetarian menu acceptable to even the most orthodox Hindu.

So what's next? It's the eve of the millennium and the remote Himalayan country of Bhutan has just granted its citizens access to television—the last country on the planet to do so. The outside world has suddenly appeared in stores and living rooms across the country. What will happen now—when an isolated and deeply conservative society is exposed to hip-hop and MTV?

eve (n) /iv/ the night before a significant date or day
vintage (adj) /ˈvɪntɪdʒ/ from an earlier time or era

2d What's playing?

Real life choosing an event

1 Work in pairs. Look at the ads. Which event appeals to you the most—and the least?

2 🎧 **7** Read the comments. Then listen to the conversation and write the number of the ad (1–3) next to the comments. Which event do they decide to go and see?

1   It sounds really awful.
2   That sounds really interesting.
3   Apparently, it's absolutely superb.
4   It looks pretty good.
5   Jackie Chan is absolutely hilarious.
6   He's not very funny.

3 🎧 **7** Look at the expressions for choosing an event. Listen again and mark the expressions Lesley and Richard use.

> **CHOOSING AN EVENT**
>
> **Suggestions and responses**
> Do you feel like going out tonight?
> Do you want to go to the movies?
> Would you like to see a movie?
> Do you like the sound of that?
>
> Sure, why not?
> Yeah, sure.
> I like the sound of that.
> I'm not crazy about him.
> I'm not in the mood for anything depressing.
> It doesn't really appeal to me.
> It sounds great.
>
> **Details of the event**
> What's playing?
> Who's in it?
> What else is playing?
> Who's it by?
> Where / When / What time is it at?
> What's it about?

Vocabulary describing performances

4 Look at the sentences in Exercise 2. Write the words used before these adjectives. Which adjectives have stronger meanings?

1   .... : awful, superb, hilarious
2   .... , ... , ... : interesting, good, funny

5 Which words (absolutely, pretty, really, very) do you use with each group of adjectives?

> **A** fantastic   fascinating   spectacular
> terrible   terrific   thrilling   unforgettable

> **B**   boring   depressing   disappointing   dull
> entertaining

6 **Pronunciation intonation with *really*, *absolutely*, *pretty*, and *very***

a 🎧 **8** Listen to these sentences from Exercise 2 again. Notice how the speakers stress both the adverb and adjective in the affirmative statements.

b Work in pairs. Practice these exchanges paying attention to your intonation.

1   A: What was the movie like?
    B: It was really awful.

2   A: Do you like flamenco?
    B: Yes, I think it's pretty interesting.

3   A: Was it a good festival?
    B: Yes, it was absolutely superb.

4   A: How was the show?
    B: Oh, very entertaining!

7 Work in pairs. Invite your partner to see the event that most appealed to you in Exercise 1. Include words from Exercises 4 and 5. Use the expressions for choosing an event to help you.

2e A portrait of an artist

Writing a profile

1 Work in pairs. Who is your favorite performer or artist? Tell your partner about this person and why you like him/her.

2 Read the portrait of Baz Luhrmann. What kind of information about him does it include? Choose the correct options (a–d).

a   his influences
b   his plans
c   his private life
d   his work

3 Read the profile again. Underline the information that is factual and circle the opinions. Then find two direct quotes from Luhrmann.

4 Which of these adjectives describe the profile? Explain your choice(s).

balanced	biased	informative
objective	personal	subjective

Baz Luhrmann is a director whose movies include *Strictly Ballroom*, *Romeo+Juliet*, *Moulin Rouge!*, and *Australia*. I have seen every one of his movies and in my opinion, his work just gets better and better. He says that "putting on a show" has always come naturally to him and that Bollywood is his biggest influence. Although he is best known as a film director, Luhrmann has also directed opera. As a result, his movies are usually vibrant, energetic, and spectacular. They have had box office success despite being unusual: in *Romeo+Juliet*, the actors speak in verse, and in *Moulin Rouge!*, they sing their lines. On the other hand, the epic *Australia* didn't go over so well with the critics. Nevertheless, as an ordinary movie fan, I thought it was absolutely fantastic. Luhrmann says the high point of his career has been "achieving so many of the dreams I had as a kid— from going to the Oscars to getting a letter from Marlon Brando." To me, his films have the power of dreams. They take you into thrilling, unforgettable worlds.

5 Writing skill linking ideas (1)

a Look at the table. Which group of words can replace each highlighted word in the profile? Write the words from the profile in the table.

in spite of	even though while	in contrast but however	because of this for that reason so therefore

b Look at the words in bold in the sentences. With which word does the verb form change? When do we use a comma?

1   **Although he is** best-known as a film director, Luhrmann has also directed opera.
2   **Despite being** best known as a film director, Luhrmann has also directed opera.
3   He is best known as a film director. **However**, Luhrmann has also directed opera.

c Rewrite the sentences using the words in parentheses. Make any necessary changes to verbs and punctuation.

1   They have had box office success despite being unusual movies. (even though)
2   I enjoyed *Romeo+Juliet* in spite of not understanding all the dialogue. (but)
3   While I love epic movies, I didn't enjoy this one. (Nevertheless)
4   Although they praised Luhrmann's earlier movies, the critics did not like *Australia*. (In spite of)
5   I've seen all of the movies, but I haven't seen any of the operas. (however)
6   His last movie was absolutely superb. Because of this, I'm looking forward to seeing the next one. (so)

6 Write a profile of an artist whose work you know and enjoy. Make notes under each heading, then write about 150 words. Use a variety of adjectives and linking words.

- Basic biographical information
- Facts (life, work)
- Opinions (mine, others')

7 Use these questions to check your profile.

- Have you used linking words correctly?
- Have you expressed clearly why you like this person's work?

8 Read some of your classmates' profiles and discuss:

- What do you learn about the person from reading the profile?
- Do you agree with the opinions expressed in the profile?

"You hit this point where you're just completely free."

Before you watch

1 Work in groups. Look at the photo and discuss the questions.

1 What is the man in the photo doing?
2 How do you think he feels?
3 What do you think the caption means?

2 Which of these things do you think you will see in this video?

audience	dance	drum		drummer	drumstick
guitar	piano	rock group	theater		

While you watch

3 Check your answers from Exercise 2.

4 Answer the questions.

1 What is taiko?

2 Where does it come from?

3 What has been added recently to traditional taiko?

4 What three things does taiko bring together?

5 What effect do pain and fatigue have on some taiko drummers?

5 Make notes about the history of taiko.

2,000 years ago	
The early 1900s	
The mid-1900s	
1968	
Now	

6 Complete the information about Grand Master Seiichi Tanaka and taiko. Then watch the video again and check your answers.

Seiichi Tanaka traveled by ¹_____ from Japan to ²_____ in the late 60s. When he arrived, he started playing ³_____ with other people. In the following years, he taught people how to play taiko. Taiko drumming soon became popular. In the 1960s there were only a dozen or so taiko groups, but now there are over ⁴_____ in the United States and ⁵_____ . Master Tanaka believes that energy from nature flows through the ⁶_____ of the drummer to the ⁷_____ and into the drum.

After you watch

7 Roleplay **finding out about taiko drumming**

Work in pairs.

Student A: You want to join a taiko drum group. Use the ideas below to prepare questions to ask a taiko master.

Student B: You are a master in taiko drumming. Use the ideas below to prepare what you are going to tell someone who wants to join a taiko drum group.

- where it comes from
- what you have to wear
- how fit you have to be
- what you need to buy
- how long it takes to learn

Act out the conversation. Then change roles and act out the conversation again.

8 Work in groups. Discuss the questions.

1 Have you ever played a musical instrument? Which instrument? When?
2 Are there any traditional instruments in your country? What are they?
3 Do you think it is important to maintain traditional forms of music and dance?

---

audience (n) /'ɔdiəns/ a group of people who watch or listen to something
beat (n) /bit/ rhythm
beat (v) /bit/ hit again and again
boundary (n) /'baʊndri/ limit
community (n) /kə'myuniti/ a group of people who live in an area
drain (v) /dreɪn/ take away from
bring together (v) /'brɪŋ tə'geðər/ join
drum (n) /drʌm/ a musical instrument that you hit with a stick
drum (v) /drʌm/ play a drum

drummer (n) /'drʌmər/ a person who plays a drum
drumstick (n) /'drʌm,stɪk/ the stick a drummer uses to hit the drum
essence (n) /'esəns/ the most important aspect of something
fear (v) /fɪər/ be afraid of
performance (n) /pər'fɔrməns/ the act of playing music for other people
pioneer (n) /ˌpaɪə'nɪər/ one of the first people to do something
unity (n) /'yunəti/ the feeling of being together
warrior (n) /'wɔriər/ a soldier

UNIT 2 REVIEW

Grammar

1 Work in pairs. Look at the photo and discuss the questions.

1 Are the people spectators or performers?
2 What time of year do you think it is?
3 Where do you think this festival is?

I've lived in Japan [1] _____ three months now and I'm really enjoying it. I [2] _____ learned some Japanese, including the word *matsuri*, which means "festival." One of my favorite pastimes is [3] _____ to matsuri. I've [4] _____ returned from the Nango summer jazz festival. It was great [5] _____ sit in the sunshine and listen to wonderful music! Next is the Tenjin matsuri here in Osaka. It has [6] _____ part of Osaka's summer events [7] _____ about a thousand years, and some performances have hardly changed [8] _____ then—the traditional kagura music, for example. There's also a puppet theater, and we're hoping [9] _____ join the big procession of boats on the river.

2 Read the blog and check your ideas from Exercise 1.

3 Complete the blog with these missing words. You can use some of the words more than once.

been	for	going	have	just	since	to
yet						

4 Tell your partner about a festival you have been to or would like to go to.

I CAN	
talk about things that have happened in a time period up to or including the present	☐
use verb patterns correctly	☐

Vocabulary

5 Work in pairs. Choose the two people who are usually involved in these performances. Then choose four types of performers and tell your partner about people you have heard about.

1 FILM: actor, director, magician
2 CONCERT: clown, conductor, musician
3 BALLET: choreographer, comedian, dancer
4 MUSICAL: photographer, singer, dancer

6 Work in groups. In two minutes, write the names of as many popular art events (movies, plays, exhibitions, performances) as you can. Then discuss the ones you have all heard of using the words in the box. You can't use more than two words to describe one event, but you must continue until everyone has used all the words at least once.

disappointing	depressing	superb	boring
entertaining	fascinating	terrible	dull
unforgettable	spectacular	thrilling	terrific

7 Work in pairs. Describe what kind of music makes you do the following.

cry	feel happy	feel sad	laugh	smile

I CAN	
talk about performers and performances	☐
describe different types of music	☐
give my opinion about art events	☐

Real life

8 Work in pairs. Choose the correct option in the questions. Then take the roles of A and B and act out the conversation, giving answers to the questions and adding more information.

1 A: Do you feel like *to go / going* out tonight?
2 A: Would you like *to see / seeing* a movie?
3 A: *Do you / Would you* like the sound of that?
4 B: Who's *in / on* it?
5 B: Who's it *by / to*?
6 B: What's it *about / of*?

I CAN	
ask for and give information about arts events	☐

Speaking

9 Work in groups. The director Baz Luhrmann says that in his career he has achieved many of the dreams he had as a kid. Which childhood dreams have you already achieved? Which ones have you not achieved yet? Tell your group.

Unit 3 Water

Women in Kenya spend up to five hours a day getting water.
Photograph by Lynn Johnson

FEATURES

1 Work as a class. Look at the photo and answer the questions.

1 Where do you think the women are going?
2 How often do you think they make this trip?
3 What do they do with the water they collect?

2 Work in pairs. Complete the sentences with five of these numbers. Then check your answers with your instructor.

⅕	⅔	3	17	10	46	70	200

1 About _____ percent of the Earth's surface is covered in water.
2 Only _____ percent of the Earth's water is fresh water.
3 Around _____ percent of people don't have running water in their homes.
4 A person in the developing world uses about _____ liters of water each day.
5 In Europe, the average is _____ liters a day.

3 Work in groups. Discuss the questions.

1 Do you know how much water you use every day?
2 Do you try to save water at home? How? Why?

3a Behind the photo

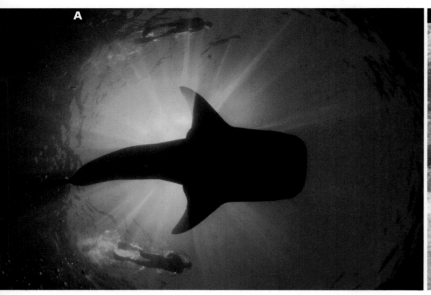

Vocabulary water and recreation

1 Work in pairs.

Student A: Describe what's happening in one of the photos (A–C). Use words from the boxes.

Student B: Which photo is Student A describing?

Then change roles and repeat.

Activities			
diving	fishing	jet-skiing	kayaking
rafting	rowing	sailing	snorkeling
surfing	swimming	water-skiing	windsurfing

Places				
lake	marina	ocean	pool	reservoir
river	sea	stream	waterfall	

2 Look at the words in Exercise 1 again. Which do you think are the best places to do the activities?

3 Do you do any of the activities in Exercise 1? Tell your partner.

> *I go fishing about once a month with my brother.*

Listening

4 🎵 **9** Listen to the people in two of the photos talking about their photo. Are the sentences true (T) or false (F)?

1 The girl was rafting down the Zambezi.
2 The raft was approaching some rapids.
3 She saw a hippo near the river bank.
4 The boy learned to dive because he was bored.
5 He went diving in a dangerous cenote.
6 He wasn't concentrating on what he was doing.

5 🎵 **10** What do you think happened next? Choose one of these options (a–c). Then listen to the ending of the story and check your ideas.

1 a The hippo came after them and attacked the raft.
  b A crocodile jumped into the river close to the raft.
  c The raft capsized and they all swam to the river bank.
2 a His air ran out and he had to go to the surface.
  b His mother panicked when she saw a sea snake.
  c He almost got lost in a labyrinth of tunnels.

> ▶ **WORDBUILDING adverbs**
> Most adverbs are formed by adding *-ly* to adjectives. Some adverbs and adjectives are the same.
> *quick* (adjective) → *quickly* (adverb)
> *fast* (adjective) = *fast* (adverb)

C

Grammar simple past and past continuous

6 Read these sentences. Underline the simple past verbs and circle the past continuous verbs.

1 We were going around a small island.   *PC*
2 It jumped into the water.   *SP*
3 The sun was shining in through an opening in the roof.   *PC*
4 My mom realized pretty quickly that I was missing and she came after me.   *SP*

7 Match the sentences (1–4) in Exercise 6 with their meanings (a–d).

a   an unfinished activity
b   a description
c   a finished action
d   a sequence of actions in a story

8 Underline the key event in these questions about the rafting story in Exercise 4. Then match the questions (1–2) with the answers (a–b).

1   What were they doing when they saw the hippo?
2   What did they do when they saw the hippo?

a   They tried to get away.
b   They were coming down the river.

9 Choose the correct option.

1   Questions in the *simple past / past continuous* refer to activities before the key event.
2   Questions in the *simple past / past continuous* refer to activities after the key event.

▶ SIMPLE PAST and PAST CONTINUOUS

Simple past
I noticed a big hippo near the river bank.
What did it do?
Past continuous
A crocodile was lying in the sun.
Where was it lying?

For more information and practice, see page 158.

10 Write sentences with the simple past and past continuous. Use *because, when, while,* and *so.*

1   I ___While was taking___ (take) a photo of the hippo / ___when___
    I ___dropped___ (drop) my camera in the water
2   My friend ___fell___ (fall) out of the raft / he ___because___
    ___wasn't___ (not / hold) on ___holding on / didn't hold on___
3   I ___saw___ (see) some strange fish / ___while___
    I ___was diving___ (dive)
when 4   I ___had___ (have) some problems with my
    mask / ___so___ my brother ___helped___ (help) me

11 Complete the paragraph about photo A.

When I [1] ___was working___ (work) in the Maldives,
I [2] ___heard___ (hear) that there were whale sharks in
the area. That's why I [3] ___began___ (begin) snorkeling—
whale sharks are the world's biggest fish! I [4] ___bought___
(buy) a cheap snorkel and [5] ___went___ (go) with
a group of friends. It was a beautiful day. Almost
immediately, a whale shark [6] ___swam___ (swim) past
the boat. It [7] ___moved___ (move) really quickly, but we
[8] ___caught up___ (catch up) with it. We all [9] ___got___
(get) into the water and [10] ___spent___ (spend) about
two minutes with the shark. Afterwards, I [11] ___felt___
(feel) absolutely amazing! It was one of the most fantastic
adventures of my life. ⑦ *it was moving*

Speaking

12 Work in pairs.

Student A: Think about the first time you tried a new skill, or did a hobby or sports activity. Answer your partner's questions without saying what the activity was.

Student B: Ask ten questions and try to find out your partner's activity.

Where were you?

On a boat.

Were you on a lake?

No, the ocean.

Did you have any special equipment?

3b Return to the *Titanic*

Reading

1 Read the interview with the man who discovered the wreck of the *Titanic*. Write the number of the paragraph (1–3) next to the question. There are two extra questions.

a Did you know you were looking at *Titanic* when you saw the first pieces of debris?
b How did the discovery of *Titanic* in 1985 come about?
c How long did it take to locate *Titanic*?
d Tell me about the experience of seeing *Titanic* again in 2004.
e What did you find out about how *Titanic* sank?

2 Read the interview again. Answer the questions.

1 What was the secret mission that Ballard was involved with?
2 How did Ballard and his team feel when they located the *Titanic*?
3 How did Ballard feel when he returned to the wreck in 2004?

3 Do you think the remains of the *Titanic* should be left on the sea bed or should they be put in a museum? Tell your partner.

RETURN *to the* TITANIC

On April 15, 1912, the largest passenger steamship ever built, appropriately named the *Titanic*, sank in the North Atlantic Ocean after hitting an iceberg. The *Titanic* had left Southampton, England, five days earlier and was on her maiden (first) voyage.

In 1985, National Geographic Explorer-in-Residence Dr. Robert Ballard located the wreck of the *Titanic*. He went back to the *Titanic* nineteen years later to see how it had changed.

It was the height of the Cold War and in fact I was on a secret mission when we found the *Titanic*. The US Navy had agreed to finance the development of our underwater video technology. In return, we had agreed to use the technology to find two US nuclear submarines that had disappeared in the 1960s.

Not at first, because many ships had sunk in that area. When we realized it was the *Titanic*, we jumped for joy. Then we realized we were celebrating at a place where people had died. We actually stopped our work and held a memorial service at that point.

3 I saw champagne bottles, intact, with the corks still in. The box holding the bottles had disappeared long ago. Suddenly, my eye was drawn to a woman's shoe. Nearby I saw a pair of smaller shoes that had perhaps belonged to a child. I felt that the people who had died here in 1912 were speaking to me again. But I knew that a private salvage company had legally removed thousands of objects from the site. A Russian submarine had taken Hollywood filmmaker James Cameron to the wreck. A New York couple had even gotten married on the *Titanic*'s bow. It was exactly what I didn't want to happen. I'd asked people to treat the *Titanic*'s remains with dignity. Instead, they'd turned her into a freak show. The story of the *Titanic* is not about the ship, it's about the people.

See the whole story on the National Geographic Channel.
Titanic: The Final Secret

bow (n) /baʊ/ the front of a ship or boat
freak show (n) /'frik ˌʃoʊ/ something unusual that people watch for entertainment (often used negatively)
salvage (n) /'sælvɪdʒ/ things recovered from places that have been destroyed in accidents (shipwrecks, fires)

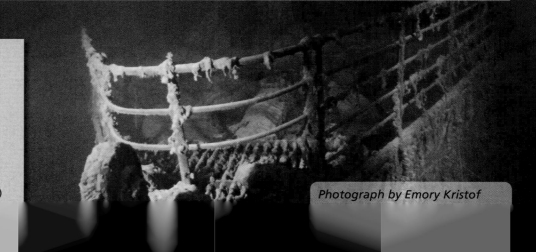

Photograph by Emory Kristof

Grammar past perfect

4 Put each group of events (a–c) in the order they actually took place. Which of these verbs are in the past perfect in the interview? Why?

1. a Ballard found *Titanic*.
   b The US Navy agreed to finance the video technology.
   c Ballard agreed to look for two submarines.
2. a Ballard held a memorial service.
   b Many people died.
   c Ballard celebrated the discovery.
3. a A Russian submarine took James Cameron to the wreck.
   b Ballard noticed a shoe.
   c The box for champagne bottles disappeared.

5 Read these sentences from the interview. Underline what happened first.

1. He went back to the *Titanic* nineteen years later to see how it had changed.
2. Then we realized we were celebrating at a place where people had died.
3. Nearby I saw a pair of smaller shoes that had perhaps belonged to a child.

6 Choose the correct option.

1. We use the past perfect to show that an event took place *before / after* other events we have related.
2. When we relate past events in the same order they actually happened, we *have to / don't have to* use the past perfect.

> ▶ **PAST PERFECT**
>
> statements: subject + *had (not)* + past participle
> questions: *had* + subject + past participle?
>
> For more information and practice, see page 160.

7 Choose the correct options.

1. When the *Titanic* hit the iceberg, it *was / had been* at sea for four days.
2. When it hit the iceberg, it *sank / had sunk*.
3. By the time they sounded the ship's alarm, it *was / had been* too late.
4. By the time Ballard found the wreck, many items *disappeared / had disappeared*.
5. They developed video technology because other techniques *didn't locate / hadn't located* the wreck.
6. James Cameron made his movie because he *visited / had visited* the wreck.

8 Use the past perfect to answer the questions with your own ideas. Then work in pairs and compare your answers.

1. Why did the *Titanic* collide with an iceberg?
2. Why did so many people die when the ship sank?
3. Why was Dr. Robert Ballard upset in 2004?
4. Why do you think a couple got married at the wreck site?
5. Why do you think James Cameron visited the wreck?

9 Complete the paragraph with the simple past or past perfect form of the verbs.

Captain Henry Morgan [1] _____ (be) one of the most notorious pirates of the 17th century. In 2010, archaeologists [2] _____ (begin) to lift cannons from a ship they [3] _____ (discover) two years earlier, near the coast of Panama. The archaeologists [4] _____ (feel) confident that the ship was Morgan's main ship, *Satisfaction*. This ship and several others [5] _____ (sink) in 1671 when they [6] _____ (hit) rocks. At this time, Morgan [7] _____ (already make) a fortune from his pirate attacks. Three years later he [8] _____ (retire) from pirate activities to become the governor of Jamaica.

Speaking

10 Work in two pairs within a group of four. Read these puzzles.

Pair A: Turn to page 153 and follow the instructions.

Pair B: Turn to page 154 and follow the instructions.

A A ship came across a yacht in the middle of the ocean. There were no other ships or boats in the area. The bodies of several people were floating in the water nearby. What had happened?

B A man was in the middle of the sea in very deep water. He couldn't swim and he wasn't wearing a life jacket. He had been in the water for hours when he finally made it to shore. Why didn't he drown?

3c Love and death in the sea

Reading

1 Work in pairs. Discuss these questions.

1 Do you enjoy swimming?
2 Where do you usually go?
3 Are there any places you would not go swimming? Why not?

2 Enric Sala is a marine ecologist. Read his article on page 39 and answer the questions.

1 What happened to Enric Sala and why?
2 How has the experience changed him?

3 Find these expressions in the article. What do they mean? Choose the correct option.

1 a couple of times
   on *several / two* occasions
2 My guts jump to my throat.
   I feel *afraid / angry*.
3 I decided to call it a day.
   I decided to *stop / try again tomorrow*.
4 I was having a hard time.
   It was difficult for me. / It took a long time.
5 I decided to let myself go.
   I decided to *stop swimming / try again*.
6 I scrambled onto the beach.
   I moved *quickly / slowly*.

4 Discuss the questions with your partner.

1 Sala talks about three decisions he made. What were they and what were the consequences of each one?
2 Sala describes how he feels about the sea. Do you think what he says is unusual? Why?
3 Read the last sentence. What do you think Sala means?
4 Do you think the title of the article is a good one? Why?

Critical thinking **reading between the lines**

5 Do you think these statements are true (T) or false (F)? Why?

1 The Costa Brava is dangerous for swimmers.
2 Enric Sala likes to take risks.
3 He was lucky to escape with his life.
4 He has recovered from the experience now.
5 He respects the sea more than he did before.

Word focus *get*

6 Look at the verbs in bold in these sentences. Find expressions with *get* in the article that match the verbs. Then rewrite the sentences with *get*.

1 I **entered** the pool.
2 The weather **didn't improve**.
3 I couldn't **reach** the shore.
4 I wasn't **moving towards** the land.
5 We **receive** so much from nature.
6 I'd **escaped from** that dangerous situation.

7 Write six other sentences about your own experiences using the expressions with *get* from the article.

Speaking

8 Think of a story about an unforgettable experience you have read about or had. Use the points to plan your story.

- the place / situation
- the people involved
- the weather / any other relevant conditions
- what happened
- why it happened
- how it happened
- what happened next

9 Use your notes to practice telling the story. Then work in small groups and tell your story.

> This happened a few years ago. I was coming home from work when I saw an old friend.

Love & death
and death in the sea

The sea has almost killed me a couple of times. It wasn't her fault; it was mine, for not respecting her. I still remember the last time, a stormy day off the Costa Brava of Spain, in early summer 2008. Every time I think about it, my heart races and my guts jump to my throat.

The cove where I used to swim every day was hit by a storm with strong eastern winds. The turquoise, transparent waters quickly transformed into a dirty soup of sand and cold gray water. Unfriendly waves were breaking in chaotic patterns. But beyond the surf zone, the sea seemed swimmable. In a moment of Catalan bravado, I put on my swimsuit, mask, and fins, and got into the water. It was crazy, but I did it. I swallowed mouthfuls of sand and salt while I was trying to break through the surf zone. Unpleasantly fighting, I swam— I still don't know why—for twenty minutes. The storm got worse and I decided to call it a day. I turned to swim back. Then I realized I couldn't get to the beach.

Waves were breaking all around me. I tried to bodysurf one wave to the shore, but it collapsed suddenly and took me down under the water. When I surfaced to take a breath, I turned around and a second wave hit me just as hard, taking me down again. I hit the sandy bottom. I pushed myself up, but once again, waves were coming and I couldn't rest or breathe. I was caught in the surf zone, with waves pushing me out and a current pulling me in. I wasn't getting any closer to the beach.

The sea is our mother, sister, and home, and as such I love her. We get so much from the sea: life, oxygen, food. She regulates the climate and she makes ours a wonderful life. We should thank the sea, the ocean, every day. Without the ocean and all the life in her, our planet would be much poorer. But on this day, I was having a hard time feeling grateful.

After a few more attempts, I decided to let go and give up the fight. I took a deep breath. The next wave took me down and forward. I hit the bottom with my back. I rolled over, hit my head, and after what seemed the longest minute of my life, I found myself lying in a foot of water. I scrambled onto the beach. I'd gotten out, but my whole body was sore, as if a gang of boxers had punched me viciously. I sat on the beach, breathless, watching the sea and feeling lucky to be alive. I walked home slowly, ears down like a beaten dog.

Some days the sea wants us and some days she doesn't. Since that day, I have not been to the sea when she does not want me. I have learned my lesson. I now thank the sea every day the surface is calm, the waters are clear, and diving is easy. And I ask for forgiveness every time I dive and see no fish.

---

bravado (n) /brəˈvɑdoʊ/ false bravery
cove (n) /koʊv/ a small bay on the coast
gang (n) /gæŋ/ a group of people (usually has a negative meaning)
grateful (adj) /ˈgreɪtfəl/ thankful and appreciative
guts (n) /gʌts/ stomach and intestines

3d No way!

Real life telling stories

1 Work in groups. Which of these statements (a–e) are true for you? Tell your group.

a When I'm in a group, I listen more than I talk.
b I'm always telling funny stories about things that happen to me.
c I like jokes, but I can never remember the punch line.
d I'm hopeless at telling stories, but I'm a good listener.
e People say I exaggerate, but they always laugh at my stories.

2 Look at the photo. Which group of words (A or B) do you think are from the story of the photo? Working in pairs, compare your ideas and explain your reasons.

A looking after it	**B** our house was like a zoo
food and water	jump in the air
empty cage	above the kitchen sink
searched	a lid on a tank
everywhere	there was some water
taking a bath	in it

3 🎵 **11** Listen to two stories. Which one matches the photo? What would a photo of the other story show?

4 🎵 **11** Look at the expressions for telling stories. Then listen to the story again and mark the expressions the speakers use.

> ### ▶ TELLING STORIES
>
> **Beginning a story**
> Did I ever tell you about... ?
> I remember once,...
> A couple of years ago,...
> You'll never believe what happened once...
>
> **Saying when things happened**
> after we saw...
> after a few days
> a couple of weeks later
> one day
> all of a sudden
> suddenly
> immediately
> then
> the next thing was
> while I was...
> during the night

5 Only one of the stories is true. Which one do you think it is?

6 Pronunciation *was* and *were*

a 🎵 **12** Listen to the sentences from the stories in Exercise 3. Notice the sound /ə/ in *was* and *were*.

b 🎵 **12** Listen again and then repeat these sentences. Pay attention to how you say *was* and *were*.

1 Especially when someone was doing the dishes.
2 They were lying in the sink!
3 We were looking after this friend's parrot.
4 I was going around the house calling "Polly!"

7 Working in pairs, choose one of the stories from Exercise 3 and each take a role. Use the audioscript on page 174 and practice the conversation. Change roles and repeat with the other story.

8 Work in pairs.

Student A: Tell your partner about something that happened to you or to someone you know. At least one part of the story should be untrue. Use the expressions for telling stories to help you.

Student B: Try to guess which part of your partner's story is untrue.

> *Did I ever tell you about the time my uncle went fishing?*

> *No, you didn't.*

3e What a weekend!

Writing a blog post

1 Do you keep a blog or know someone who does? What kind of things do people write about in personal blogs? And in professional blogs?

2 Read the blog post and answer the questions.

1 What is the topic of this blog post?
2 What do you think *beach stuff* refers to?
3 Who do you think Ellie, Louis, and Oscar are?

3 Put the main events of the story (a–g) in the correct order.

a Ellie, Louis, and Oscar **ran** to the water.
b The sun **started to shine**.
c There was a storm.
d A ship lost a cargo of sneakers.
e They **got** into the car.
f They **picked up** things to take to the beach.
g They **went** to the beach.

4 Writing skill interesting language

a Compare the post with the sentences in Exercise 3. Which verbs does James use instead of the verbs in bold in Exercise 3? Why?

b Circle the verbs and adjectives James uses instead of these words.

raining	full of people	looking
arrived	holding	

c Read the sentences. Which words do you think are missing? Then complete the sentences with the words in the box.

1 The kids _____ along the street.
2 I felt _____ after my walk.
3 The weather was _____ hot.
4 We _____ up the river bank with difficulty.
5 I _____ along the beach in no hurry.
6 At the end of the game, we _____ on the sand.

boiling	collapsed	exhausted
raced	scrambled	wandered

5 Think about a recent weekend or one when something unusual happened. Make notes of the main events in your weekend. Then add notes with background information.

The calm after the storm

It was pouring rain all weekend, so we spent almost the whole time indoors trying to entertain the kids. Then, unexpectedly, the sun came out late on Sunday afternoon. We grabbed our beach stuff, jumped into the car, and headed down to the bay. When we got there, we realized that everyone had had the same idea! The beach was packed. But everyone was staring out to sea and picking stuff up off the sand. Ellie, Louis, and Oscar rushed down to the water's edge, full of excitement. It turned out that a ship had lost its cargo in Saturday's storm. Five containers of Nike sneakers had washed up on the beach! Everyone was clutching odd shoes, looking for the other one to make a pair! What a strange weekend!

Written by James   Feb 28, 11:14PM

See older posts

6 Write a first draft of a blog post about your weekend. Then look at the vocabulary you have used. Make any changes to make your post as interesting as you can. Use these questions to check it.

- Have you used different past tenses correctly?
- Have you used interesting vocabulary?

7 Work in pairs. Exchange posts. Has your partner written an interesting post?

3f One village makes a difference

The Yamuna River is the city's main source of drinking water.

Before you watch

1 Work in groups. Look at the photo of the Yamuna River in northern India and discuss the questions.

1 Why do you think the river looks like this?
2 What problems do you think this creates for the people of New Delhi?
3 Where do you think people who live far from this river get their water from?

2 The video shows people in northern India using water for a variety of things. Write down five things you think you will see.

While you watch

3 Watch the video and check your ideas from Exercise 2.

4 Watch the first part of the video (to 02:21). Are these sentences true (T) or false (F)?

1 Fifty million gallons of waste are thrown into the Yamuna River every day.
2 Fourteen million people in and around Delhi get their water from water tankers.
3 There is never enough water for everyone.
4 The people of New Delhi need about one million gallons of water a day.
5 The residents of the city are surviving on a quarter of the water they need.
6 Rich people have their own supply of water.
7 The monsoon season replaces all the water used during the year.
8 Everyone agrees that new dams are the only solution to the water shortage.

5 Watch the second part of the video (02:23 to the end). Put the stages of making traditional dams and the results in the correct order.

a the level of water under the ground rises
b put down a layer of porous stone, earth, and clay
c create wells to irrigate farms
d make small pits or holes near the dams
e make small earthen dams of stone and rock

6 Complete these sentences with words from the glossary. Then watch the video again and check your answers.

1 The heavy _____ that fills the sky is so unclean that it's difficult to see the city.
2 When villagers reach a _____ , they often have to drink next to their animals.
3 India's dams have contributed to the water shortage by drying up _____ and wells.
4 We're building water _____ and dams to save rainwater.
5 The _____ methods of Alwar aren't practical for New Delhi.

After you watch

7 Roleplay **talking about a development project.**

Work in pairs.

Student A: You are Rajendra Singh. Read the instructions below and make notes.

• You are going to meet with an official from the United Nations to discuss a project.
• Welcome your visitor, explain your project, and answer the visitor's questions.

Student B: You are a United Nations official. Read the instructions below.

• You are going to visit a traditional dam project in India.
• Make a list of questions to ask Rajendra Singh, the project organizer.
• When you are ready, say hello, ask Mr. Singh to explain the project, and ask him your questions.

8 Work in pairs. Discuss these questions.

1 Where do cities in your country get their water?
2 Have there ever been any water shortages where you live? What effect did they have?
3 What can we do to protect Earth's water for future generations?

---

available (adj) /əˈveɪləbəl/ ready for use
clay (n) /kleɪ/ thick, sticky earth
dam (n) /dæm/ a wall built across a river or stream
earthen (adj) /ˈɜrθən/ made of earth
industrial waste (n) /ɪnˈdʌstriəl ˈweɪst/ chemical substances that factories throw away
irrigate (v) /ˈɪrɪˌɡeɪt/ water plants or fields
lifeless (adj) /ˈlaɪflɪs/ dead
monsoon (n) /mɑnˈsun/ a season of heavy tropical rain
porous (adj) /ˈpɔrəs/ allowing water to pass through
prosperous (adj) /ˈprɑspərəs/ wealthy
replace (v) /rɪˈpleɪs/ put back

reservoir (n) /ˈrezərˌvwɑr/ an artificial lake
rise (v) /raɪz/ go higher
river bed (n) /ˈrɪvər ˌbed/ the bottom of a river
shortage (n) /ˈʃɔrtɪdʒ/ when there is not enough of something
shower (n) /ˈʃaʊər/ a short period of rain
small-scale (adj) /ˈsmɔl ˈskeɪl/ not very big
smog (n) /smɑɡ/ a kind of fog caused by pollution
source (n) /ˈsɔrs/ the place something comes from
store (v) /ˈstɔr/ save for later use
well (n) /wel/ a deep round hole in the ground that people make to get water

UNIT 3 REVIEW

Grammar

1 Work in pairs. Look at the photo. Have you ever done anything like this? Would you like to?

I [1] *learned* to surf a few years ago when I [2] *was* in my teens. My dad [3] *paid* for lessons, as a present, because I [4] *just passed* some important exams. It [5] *was* a sunny weekend in June and the whole first day [6] *went by* and I [7] *didn't manage* one successful ride. All my friends [8] *watched* and of course I [9] *wanted* to impress them. I eventually [10] *paddled out* for my last attempt of the day when the sun [11] *set* over the bay. I [12] *scrambled* onto the board and for the first time I [13] *didn't fall off* right away. I [14] *just got up* on the board when someone almost [15] *crashed* right into me! But I [16] *stayed* on!

2 With your partner, change the verbs in the story to the past continuous or past perfect where appropriate. Do you think the photo illustrates this story? Why?

I CAN	
talk about a sequence of events in the past (simple past, past perfect)	☐
describe the background to past events (past continuous)	☐

Vocabulary

3 Rewrite the words with the missing vowels to give names for places with water. Race your partner to see who can finish first. How many examples of each place can you name?

Example:
lake – Lake Nasser

lk	pl	s
mrn	rsrvr	strm
cn	rvr	wtrfll

4 Work on your own. Choose the two activities you think best match each category (1–4). Then work in pairs to discuss your reasons.

1 people find this relaxing
2 people do this to get a thrill
3 it's best to do this with other people
4 people do this on weekends

diving	fishing	jet-skiing	kayaking
rafting	rowing	sailing	snorkeling
surfing	swimming	water-skiing	windsurfing

5 Work in pairs. Discuss the questions.

1 How many times did you use water yesterday? What did you use it for?
2 Do you think you waste water? Why?
3 Why is it important not to waste water?

I CAN	
talk about water sports	☐
talk about water use	☐

Real life

6 Work in groups. Tell a story starting with this sentence. Take turns adding a sentence to the story, using one of these expressions.

Did I ever tell you about the time my cat ate my homework?

a couple of… later	one day
after a few…	suddenly
all of a sudden	the next thing was
during the…	then
immediately	while I was…

7 Use one of these sentences to tell another story.

I remember once, I was waiting at the bus stop.

A couple of years ago, I went for a job interview.

You'll never believe what happened once when I was taking an exam.

I CAN	
tell a story	☐
say when things happened in a sequence of events	☐

Speaking

8 Work in groups. A person was about to start a challenging new job when a friend commented "You'll either sink or swim." What do you think the expression means? Talk about times in the past when you have faced a challenge. How did you feel? What happened in the end?

Unit 4 Opportunities

Schoolchildren

FEATURES

1 Work in pairs. Look at the photo. How old do you think the children are? What do you think they study in school? Do you think they like school?

2 Did you want to do any of these jobs when you were a child?

athlete	ballerina	firefighter	pilot
movie star	police officer	rock star	scientist
train conductor	vet		

3 Which words describe the jobs in Exercise 2?

badly paid	boring	dangerous	demanding
dirty	exciting	glamorous	responsible
rewarding	routine	satisfying	secure
stressful	well-paid		

4 Work in pairs. Answer the questions about yourself.

a What job have you always wanted to do?
b Which job do you do now or plan to do?
c How would you describe your dream job?

4a Fast lane to the future

Reading

1 Work in pairs. Look at the title of the article, the photo, and the map. What do you think the article is about?

2 Read the article and check your ideas from Exercise 1.

3 Complete the table.

Name	Job	Employer
Meena Shekaran	1	an importer
Tamil Selvan	2	3 ....
Kashinath Manna	4	self-employed
Morten Andersen	5	6 ....

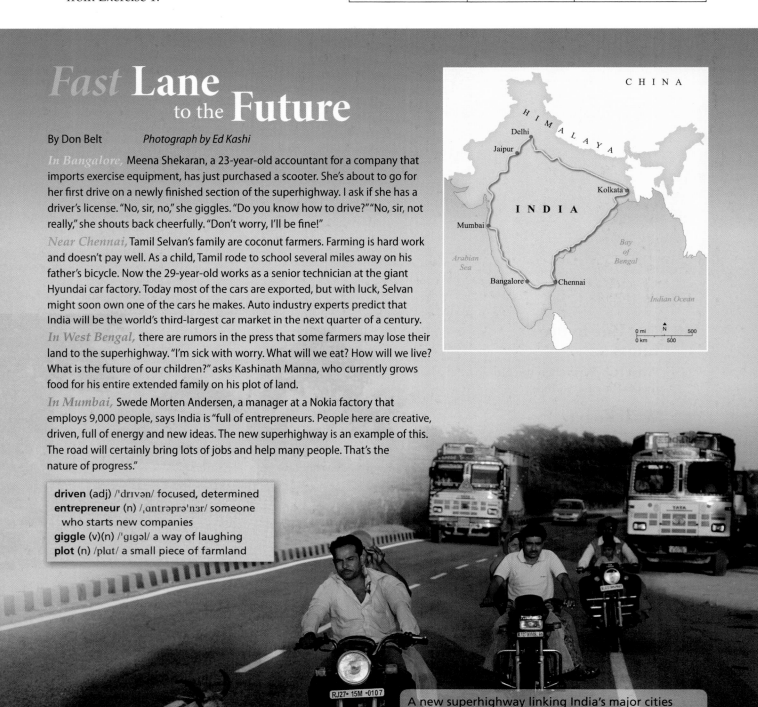

Fast **Lane** to the **Future**

By Don Belt   *Photograph by Ed Kashi*

In Bangalore, Meena Shekaran, a 23-year-old accountant for a company that imports exercise equipment, has just purchased a scooter. She's about to go for her first drive on a newly finished section of the superhighway. I ask if she has a driver's license. "No, sir, no," she giggles. "Do you know how to drive?" "No, sir, not really," she shouts back cheerfully. "Don't worry, I'll be fine!"

Near Chennai, Tamil Selvan's family are coconut farmers. Farming is hard work and doesn't pay well. As a child, Tamil rode to school several miles away on his father's bicycle. Now the 29-year-old works as a senior technician at the giant Hyundai car factory. Today most of the cars are exported, but with luck, Selvan might soon own one of the cars he makes. Auto industry experts predict that India will be the world's third-largest car market in the next quarter of a century.

In West Bengal, there are rumors in the press that some farmers may lose their land to the superhighway. "I'm sick with worry. What will we eat? How will we live? What is the future of our children?" asks Kashinath Manna, who currently grows food for his entire extended family on his plot of land.

In Mumbai, Swede Morten Andersen, a manager at a Nokia factory that employs 9,000 people, says India is "full of entrepreneurs. People here are creative, driven, full of energy and new ideas. The new superhighway is an example of this. The road will certainly bring lots of jobs and help many people. That's the nature of progress."

> **driven** (adj) /ˈdrɪvən/ focused, determined
> **entrepreneur** (n) /ˌɑntrəprəˈnɜr/ someone who starts new companies
> **giggle** (v)(n) /ˈgɪgəl/ a way of laughing
> **plot** (n) /plɑt/ a small piece of farmland

A new superhighway linking India's major cities is throwing together the old and the new India.

4 Read the article again and complete the sentences.

1 .... believes that the road represents progress in India.
2 .... has bought a new vehicle to drive on the road.
3 .... is worried about the future.
4 .... makes cars that might end up on the road.

5 Do you think the new road is a good thing or a bad thing? Why?

Grammar predictions

	PREDICTIONS WITH *WILL*	
The future	*will (not)* *may (not)* *might (not)* *could* *will certainly / definitely / probably* *certainly / definitely / probably won't*	*be difficult.*

For more information and practice, see page 160.

6 Look at the grammar box. Which verb forms from the box are in the article? Underline them in the article.

7 Look at the sentences with the underlined verb forms in the article. Answer the questions for each sentence.

1 Who makes the prediction?
2 Is the person 100 percent sure of his/her prediction?

8 Cross out the option that is not logical, as in the example.

1 Meena has bought a scooter. She *might / will / won't* learn to drive soon.
2 The road links the major cities. It *could / may not / will* affect many people.
3 Ravi isn't very good at his job. He *might / might not / will* get a promotion.
4 Hyundai is building a new factory. They *could / might not / will* need more workers.
5 We haven't seen the plans for the road. It *may / might not / will* go near our house.
6 I get bored at work. I *may / may not / might* look for a new job.

9 Look at the sentences in Exercise 8 again. What is the difference between the correct options in each case?

10 Write predictions, as in the example, using one of the options. Then work as a class and compare your sentences.

1 Meena / not crash (probably / certainly)
Meena probably won't crash on her first drive.
2 Tamil Selvan / buy a car (definitely / probably)
3 Kashinath Manna's life / not change (definitely / might)
4 the Nokia factory / expand (certainly / probably)
5 job opportunities / increase (definitely / might)
6 traveling around / be easier (certainly / probably)
7 people's standard of living / improve (certainly / might)

Vocabulary *job* and *work*

11 Look at the examples from the article (a–c). Then complete the sentences (1–8) with the correct form of *job* or *work*.

a Farming is hard work and doesn't pay well.
b …the 29-year-old works as a senior technician…
c …the road will bring lots of jobs…

1 Where do you .... ?
2 Do you have an interesting .... ?
3 Do you usually have a lot of .... ?
4 Is your company good to .... for?
5 Want to go out later? I get off .... at 5.
6 Don't use that phone. It doesn't ....
7 I'll be home late tonight. There are a few .... to finish here.
8 "Is your dad around?" "No, he's at ...."

12 Work in pairs. Take turns asking and answering questions 1–4 from Exercise 11.

Speaking

13 Work in pairs. Discuss and agree on six predictions about your own country or town. Talk about these issues or use your own ideas.

- economy
- environment
- jobs
- local politics
- prices
- roads

> I think the new shopping center will definitely make my life easier.

> You're probably right, but how will it affect the small stores around here?

4b What's next?

Devi
Wayne

Elisabeth

Sahera with her friends

Listening

1 Work in pairs. Have you made any important decisions recently? Tell your partner about one of them.

> *I've decided to change careers. I don't want to work in an office.*

2 🔊 **13** Listen to part of a radio program about International Women's Day. Choose the correct option for the three women featured in the program.

1 Devi *works / studies.*
2 Devi wants to be *a boss / a nurse.*
3 Elisabeth *has a job / doesn't have a job.*
4 Elisabeth intends to *leave work / retire.*
5 Sahera has just *started college / graduated from college.*
6 Sahera plans to *stay in Kabul / leave Kabul.*

3 🔊 **13** Listen again and correct the factual mistakes.

1 Devi isn't going to stay at home forever.
2 Devi is taking a test tomorrow.
3 Elisabeth is going to start a new job.
4 Elisabeth is meeting her new boss on Wednesday.
5 Sahera's friend is going to work in the United States.
6 Sahera's friend is leaving Kabul next month.

4 Which of the women has decided what she is going to do? Who doesn't know yet?

Grammar **future forms**

5 Look at the audioscript on page 175. Find the following.

1 something Devi has already decided to do
2 something Devi has arranged to do
3 something Devi decides to do as she is speaking

6 Read what Elisabeth and Sahera say in the audioscript. Underline more sentences like those in Exercise 5.

7 Look at the grammar box. Match the verb forms (1–3) with their uses (a–c).

a   a plan or intention decided before the moment of speaking
b   a decision made at the moment of speaking
c   an arrangement to do something at a specified (or understood) time in the future

8 Choose the correct option.

I left school last month. **¹** *I'll take / I'm taking* the summer off, but on September 3 **²** *I'll start / I'm starting* as an apprentice in a garage. **³** *I'll take / I'm going to take* an evening course too. That starts in October. I'm not sure how **⁴** *I'm managing / I'm going to manage*! I'm lucky—some of my friends don't know what **⁵** *they are doing / they are going to do*. My mom thinks **⁶** *I'm being / I'm going to be* a great mechanic. Maybe **⁷** *I'll have / I'm going to have* my own garage one day.

9 Complete the responses with the most logical future form. Then work in pairs. Compare and discuss your answers.

1   A: Do you have any plans for when you leave college?
    B: Yes, I _____ (take) a year off.

2   A: I can't decide what to do.
    B: It's OK, I _____ (help) you.

3   A: Is it true that Samira is leaving?
    B: Yeah, she _____ (get) married next month.

4   A: Did you enroll in evening classes?
    B: Yes, _____ (go) to my first class tonight.

5   A: I can't get this can open!
    B: Here, give it to me. I _____ (open) it.

Vocabulary education

10 How do these events affect one another? Complete the timelines with these expressions. More than one answer is possible.

take a (training) course	get bad grades
fail an exam/a test	pass/retake an exam/ a test
get a degree in…	stay in school

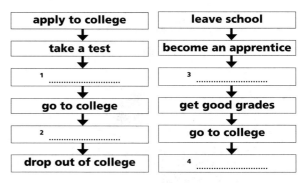

apply to college
↓
take a test
↓
1 ....
↓
go to college
↓
2 ....
↓
drop out of college

leave school
↓
become an apprentice
↓
3 ....
↓
get good grades
↓
go to college
↓
4 ....

11 Work in pairs. Discuss these questions.

1   How similar or different are the events in Exercise 10 to your own experience?
2   What kinds of factors influence these decisions?
3   What plans do people you know have?

12 What will your own educational path be like in the next two years? Write your own timeline. Then get together with a partner and explain your plans.

Speaking

13 Work in pairs. You need to meet several times for a project for your English class. Find dates when you can get together.

What are you up to next week? Maybe we can get together early in the week.

OK. Do you have any plans for Monday?

4c A better life?

Reading

1 Work in groups. What kind of things happen in an economic boom and in an economic crisis? Give examples.

> *In an economic boom, there is more work.*

> *Yes, and people can buy more luxury goods.*

2 Read the article on page 51 quickly. Which paragraphs talk about these topics?

a training and education
b China and the world
c the movement of people
d new towns

3 Read the first paragraph of the article. Put these things (a–f) in the order they appear in a new town in China.

a basic stalls
b cellphone companies
c clothing stores
d construction work *1*
e entrepreneurs
f female factory workers

4 Read the rest of the article. Are the sentences true (T) or false (F)?

1 Most of the population is young.
2 About ten million people a year migrate to the cities.
3 Few school drop-outs in China are interested in higher education.
4 It's difficult to find training courses in factory towns.
5 So far China has focused on making products for foreign markets.

5 Work in pairs. What do these sentences from the last paragraph mean?

> Nobody in the developed world should criticize China without taking a look in the mirror.
>
> There's nothing foreign about the materialistic dreams of the average Chinese worker.

Critical thinking arguments

6 The title of the article is *A better life?* Read these sentences from the text. Decide if what they describe is positive (P), negative (N), or both (B).

1 Most people in China have seen their standard of living go up in recent years.
2 Social scientists predict that the urban population will be 60 percent by 2030.
3 Clearly there are environmental costs from China's rapid growth.

7 Which of these statements (a–c) describes the author's opinion of China?

a The changes described will probably be better.
b The changes described will probably be bad.
c The changes could be good or bad.

8 Work as a class. What things do you think make "a better life"?

Vocabulary and speaking pay and benefits

9 Work in pairs. Read each sentence and think of a profession it describes.

> *Doctors work long hours!*

1 They work **long hours**.
2 They get a lot of **paid vacation**.
3 They get regular **pay raises**.
4 Their **salary** is excellent.
5 They can choose to work **flex time hours** if they need to.
6 There are lots of opportunities for **promotion**.
7 They often have to work **overtime**.
8 They get a generous **retirement package.**

10 Put the words in bold in Exercise 9 into three groups: *money* (M), *hours* (H), and *benefits* (B). Then add these words to the groups.

bonuses	free language classes
clocking in and out	health insurance
company car	part-time hours
discounts on company products	hourly wage

11 Tell your partner about your ideal job. Talk about pay, conditions, and responsibilities. What's the most important aspect of the job for you?

> *Well, my ideal job is working outdoors.*

A better life?

In Shenzhen, factory workers pose for a portrait at the morning shift change.

China's expectations are rising, with no end in sight. What's next?
By Peter Hessler
Photographs by Fritz Hoffmann

The beginning of a Chinese factory town is always the same: in the beginning, nearly everybody is a construction worker. The growing economy means that everything moves fast and new industrial districts rise in several stages. Those early laborers are men who have migrated from a rural village. Immediately they are joined by small entrepreneurs. These pioneers sell meat, fruit, and vegetables from stalls, and later, when the first real stores appear, they stock construction materials. After that, cellphone companies arrive, selling prepaid phonecards to migrants. (One popular product is called the Homesick Card.) When the factories start production, you start to see women. Young women have a reputation for being hard-working. After the arrival of the women, the clothing stores appear. An American poet once described an industrial town in the US as "springing up, like the enchanted palaces of the Arabian tales, as it were in a single night." Today it's the factory towns of China that seem to belong to another world. The human energy is amazing: the courageous entrepreneurs, the quick-moving builders, the young migrants. A combination of past problems and present-day opportunities has created an extremely motivated population. Most people in China have seen their standard of living go up in recent years.

The size of the population is both a strength and a challenge to China. Of its 1.3 billion people, 72 percent are between the ages of 16 and 64. The movement of people from the country-side to the cities has transformed China into the world's factory floor. In 1978, there were only 172 million urban residents. Now there are 577 million. Social scientists predict that the urban population will be 60 percent of the total population by 2030. Each year about ten million rural Chinese move to the cities, so the factories have a constant labor supply.

Chinese schools have been very successful. The literacy rate is over 90 percent. The next step is to develop higher education. Many people are looking for better training. In a Chinese factory town, there are many private classes: English, typing, technical. In Zhejiang, I met Luo Shouyun, who had spent a quarter of his wages on training. Now he is a master machinist, with a salary that makes him "middle class." Another young man had learned Arabic in order to translate for Middle Eastern buyers.

Clearly there are environmental costs from China's rapid growth. Collaboration between China and other countries will be crucial in managing environmental problems. Nobody in the developed world should criticize China without taking a look in the mirror. The nation has become successful by making products for overseas consumers. There's nothing foreign about the materialistic dreams of the average Chinese worker.

Individual portraits in Beijing on Chinese National Day

literacy rate (n) /ˈlɪtərəsi ˌreɪt/ the number of people who can read and write
materialistic (adj) /məˌtɪəriəˈlɪstɪk/ interested in possessions and consumer goods
migrant (n) /ˈmaɪɡrənt/ someone who moves around, often for work
overseas (adj) /ˈoʊvərˈsiz/ foreign, from another country

4d Would you mind…?

Vocabulary job requirements

1 Read the job ad and find the following.

1 responsibilities
2 deadline for applications
3 skills and qualifications required
4 personal qualities required

2 Which of these qualities would be useful for the job in the ad?

conscientious	creative	energetic
hard-working	methodical	self-confident

3 Work in pairs. Choose three jobs you know something about. What are the most important requirements for those jobs? Compare your ideas.

Real life making and responding to requests

4 🎵 14 Listen to two friends talk about the ad. Answer the questions.

1 Does he meet all the requirements?
2 Is his resume ready?
3 What will he need for the interview?

5 🎵 14 Look at the expressions for making and responding to requests. Listen to the conversation again and mark the expressions you hear.

> ▶ MAKING AND RESPONDING TO REQUESTS
>
> **Making requests**
> Is it all right if I give you as my reference?
> Would it be OK to borrow your suit?
> Is it OK to take your car?
> Would it be all right if I used your phone?
>
> Would you mind checking my application form?
> Do you mind helping me with my resume?
>
> Could you give me a ride to the interview?
> Can you have a look at my cover letter?
> Will you be able to do it today?
>
> **Responding to requests**
> Of course (not).   Yes, I will.
> I'm not sure about that.   Sure, no problem.

6 Would you like to do a job like the one in the ad? Why?

7 Pronunciation **weak and strong auxiliary verbs**

a 🎵 15 Listen to this exchange and repeat it. Notice how the auxiliary verb *will* is not stressed in the full question and is stressed in the response.

A: Will you be able to do it today?
B: Yes, I will.

b Match the questions (1–6) with the responses (a–f). Check your answers with your instructor, then practice the exchanges in pairs.

1 Are you going to apply for the job?
2 Will he help you with your resume?
3 Are they still advertising that job?
4 Does she meet our requirements?
5 Will it be an all-day interview?
6 Is it OK to call your cell?

a I don't think she does.
b I think it might.
c No, they aren't.
d Of course he will.
e Yes, I think I will.
f Yes, of course it is.

8 Work in pairs. You are going to act out 90-second conversations in different situations. Turn to page 155.

4e I am enclosing my resume

Writing a cover letter

1 Work in pairs. Have you ever applied for a job in these ways? Tell your partner.

> a resume   a phone call
> a letter   an application form
> a personal contact

2 Read the cover letter. Mark the information it includes. What (if anything) can you omit if you send an email?

> a reference to your resume
> the date
> the name and address of the person you
>   are writing to
> the reason for your letter
> your address
> your interest in the position
> your phone number
> your education, experience, and skills

3 Compare the letter to the style you use in your country. Answer the questions.

    1   Is the layout different? How?
    2   Does it include the same information?
    3   Is the information in the main part of the letter sequenced in the same way?

4 **Writing skill** **formal style**

a A formal letter in English uses these conventions. Underline examples of each one in the letter.

    • concise sentences
    • formal phrases to begin sentences
    • no contractions
    • standard opening and closing phrases

b Rewrite the sentences in a more formal style.

    1   I'm finishing my degree soon.
    2   Give me a call.
    3   I was looking through the paper and I saw your ad, and I thought it looked really interesting.
    4   My phone number is on my resume, which I've also sent you.
    5   I'll be free in August.

---

14 Washington Street
Brighton, MA 02135
June 7, 2014

NHN TV
1200 Commonwealth Ave.
Boston, MA 02101

Dear Sir or Madam,

I am writing in reply to your advertisement in the Daily Herald for the post of Research Assistant. I will graduate in Digital Media this month from Boston University. I have experience in video production and post-production, having worked part-time in the university television station for the last year.

I consider myself to be hard-working and organized in my work. As part of my job, I was responsible for planning schedules and archiving past programs.

I am available for an interview at any time and can start work after July. I am willing to relocate if necessary.

I am enclosing my resume that gives full details of my education, work experience, and skills as well as my contact details.

I look forward to hearing from you.

Yours sincerely,

Mani Banerjee

---

5 Write a cover letter to go with a job application. Follow the layout and style of the letter above.

6 Exchange letters with your partner. Use these questions to check your partner's letter.

    • Is it clear how to contact this person?
    • Is the style appropriate?
    • Does the person sound like a good candidate?

7 On the basis of the letter your partner has written, would you give him/her an interview? Explain your reasons.

Confucianism in China

China is one of the largest and oldest countries in the world.

Before you watch

1 Work in groups. Look at the photos. Write down everything you know about China and about Confucius. You have three minutes. Then compare what you have written with other groups.

2 You are going to watch a video about China. Write down one image that you think:

1 you will definitely see.
2 you might see.
3 you definitely won't see.

While you watch

3 Check your answers from Exercises 1 and 2.

4 Watch the first part of the video (to 01:59). Choose the correct option to complete the sentences about the early history of China.

1 Confucius lived from:
   a 551 to 479 BCE.   b 500 to 600 BCE.

2 Around 500 BCE, central China was governed by the _____ dynasty.
   a Han   b Zhou

3 The rulers were:
   a weak.   b very unhappy.

4 Local warlords:
   a fought for land and power.
   b fought for justice in the country.

5 Confucius traveled across China to convince people:
   a to fight against the warlords.
   b that his ideas could restore order.

6 Three hundred years after Confucius died, the Han dynasty:
   a adopted his philosophy.
   b banned his teachings.

5 Watch the second part of the video (02:02 to the end). Number the sayings in the order you hear them.

a Virtue is the root; wealth is the result.
b Is it not pleasant to learn with a constant perseverance and application?
c A youth should be respectful of his elders.

6 Watch the video again and complete the sentences with words from the glossary.

1 Millions of Chinese people _____ a rich history that has lasted for thousands of years.
2 The country of China was _____ up in a dark period of war and unhappiness.
3 Traditionally, sons _____ the family name and support their parents.
4 Throughout the history of China, an education has been an opportunity to _____ in the world.
5 Because Confucianism is often associated with China's past, many people aren't _____ of its influence on present-day society. .

After you watch

7 Roleplay **talking about a country's culture**

Work in pairs.

Student A: You are Chinese. Make notes about the three aspects of culture below, then explain to your partner how Chinese culture is different from his/hers.

Student B: Your partner is Chinese and studying abroad. Write questions to ask about how the three aspects below are different from the culture in your country.

• respect • learning • virtue and wealth

Act out the conversation, then change roles.

8 Work in groups and discuss these questions.

1 Do you agree with what Confucius says about youth, education, and wealth? Why?
2 Do you think Confucius's philosophy has anything to offer your country? What in particular?

---

attain (v) /əˈteɪn/ get
be aware of (v) /ˈbi əˈweər əv/ know about
be caught up in (v) /ˈbi kɔt ˈʌp ɪn/ be in the middle of
carry on (v) /ˈkæri ˈɑn/ continue
conduct (n) /ˈkɑndʌkt/ a way of behaving
convince (v) /kənˈvɪns/ make someone believe something
dutiful (adj) /ˈdutɪfəl/ doing what you are supposed to do
dynasty (n) /ˈdaɪnəsti/ a family that rules a country for several generations
ethical (adj) /ˈeθɪkəl/ relating to what is right and wrong
foundation (n) /faʊnˈdeɪʃən/ base
govern (v) /ˈgʌvərn/ administer a country
harmony (n) /ˈhɑrməni/ a state when people live together without problems
in decline (adv) /ˈɪn dɪˈklaɪn/ becoming weaker, poorer

joy (n) /dʒɔɪ/ happiness
move up (v) /ˈmuv ˈʌp/ progress
perseverance (n) /ˌpərsəˈvɪərəns/ the capacity to keep going in difficult conditions
prosper (v) /ˈprɑspər/ be successful
respectful (adj) /rɪˈspektfəl/ polite and obedient
restore (v) /rɪˈstɔr/ bring back
root (n) /rut/ base
ruler (n) /ˈrulər/ the head of a country
share (v) /ʃeər/ have something in common
subject (n) /ˈsʌbdʒəkt/ a person who lives in a country that has a ruler
virtue (n) /ˈvɜrtʃu/ behaving in a moral way
warlord (n) /ˈwɔrˌlɔrd/ the leader of a private army
wealth (n) /welθ/ a large amount of money

UNIT 4 REVIEW

Grammar

1 Work in pairs. Look at the photo of student chefs in China cooking vegetables. What do you think they are thinking about?

2 Complete the comments with one word. Which do you think were made by the Chinese student chefs in the photo?

1 "I'm sure nobody _____ be able to eat this!"
2 "I think I _____ change jobs soon."
3 "I _____ having a drink on my next break."
4 "This _____ definitely impress the diners."
5 "I' _____ be the best chef in the country."
6 "My parents are going _____ be proud of me."
7 "This may _____ turn out as I expected."
8 "Wow, my hat is _____ to catch fire."
9 "My friends _____ believe me when I tell them about my day."
10 "I'm _____ take-out for dinner tonight."

3 Work in pairs. Imagine you are the students in the photo. Ask each other about your plans for when the course ends.

I CAN	
make predictions about future events (*will*)	
show different degrees of certainty about predictions (*may, might, could*)	
ask and answer questions about future plans and arrangements (*going to*, present continuous)	

Vocabulary

4 Work in pairs. You each get ten seconds to choose a word and name a job that the word describes. Take turns naming jobs with that word and keep going until one person has no more ideas. The other person then gets one point. Repeat with another word. The person with the most points at the end wins.

badly paid	dangerous	glamorous	indoors
manual	outdoors	rewarding	routine

5 Work in pairs. For each of these jobs, discuss what qualities and qualifications you need and what the pay and conditions are like. Then say which job would be best for your partner and give reasons.

accountant	chef	firefighter	pilot	vet

6 Work in groups. Do you agree or disagree with these statements? Why?

1 Everyone should go to college.
2 Failing a test can be a good experience.
3 Dropping out of school is not the end of the world.
4 We never stop learning.

I CAN	
describe different jobs, job requirements, and conditions	
talk about stages in education	

Real life

7 Work in pairs. Match the sentence parts and make requests. Then act out a conversation that includes the requests and appropriate replies.

1 Could you
2 Is it all right if I
3 Would you mind
4 Would it be all right if I

a borrow your phone?
b help me with this application?
c lending me some money?
d took off my jacket?

8 With your partner, act out similar conversations for two of these situations.

> a problem at work
> a meeting with a new boss
> your first day at college

I CAN	
make and respond to requests	

Speaking

9 Work in groups. Each person needs four pieces of paper. Write predictions for these four topics on the pieces of paper. Write two negative and two positive predictions. Put all the pieces of paper together and select them one by one at random. Discuss the probability of the predictions coming true and try to guess who made each one.

entertainment	music	shopping	sports

Tourists take photos of an emperor penguin on the frozen Amundsen Sea in Antarctica.

FEATURES

1 Work in pairs. Look at the photo. Discuss the questions with your partner.

1 What kind of vacation do you think this is? Why?
2 Do you think the people take this kind of trip often? Why?
3 Would you like to take a trip like this?

2 Work in pairs. Which of these travel experiences have you had? Give each other travel tips about them.

being on planes	planning
short business trips	a round-the-world trip
day trips	taking local buses and trains
delays	traveling for work for a week or more
lost luggage	weekends away

3 Which countries or cities have you been to? Find people in your class who have had similar experiences.

Have you been to Russia?

Yes! Have you seen the Kremlin in Moscow?

5a Walking for wildlife

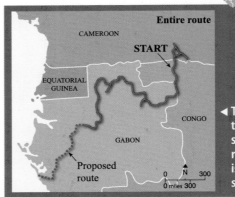

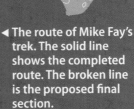

A F R I C A

AREA ENLARGED

Listening and reading

1 🔊 16 Look at the map showing the conservationist Mike Fay's trek through central Africa. Choose the options you think are correct. Then listen to part of a radio program and check.

1 The trek covers *almost 2,000 miles / over 3,000 miles*.
2 The route goes through *Kenya / Gabon*.
3 Fay and his companions are *on a walking vacation / working on a project*.
4 The best way to travel in this area is *on foot and by boat / by motorbike and jeep*.
5 It will take *five months / fifteen months* to complete the trek.

2 Read the profile of Mike Fay. Write the number of the paragraph (1–5) next to the heading.

a Has he had any dangerous experiences?
b What has he done?
c What luggage does he usually take?
d Who is he?
e Why does he do it?

Entire route
CAMEROON
START
EQUATORIAL GUINEA
CONGO
GABON
Proposed route
N
0 300
0 miles 300

◄ The route of Mike Fay's trek. The solid line shows the completed route. The broken line is the proposed final section.

3 Are the sentences true (T) or false (F)? Test your memory. Then read the profile again and check.

1 He's done conservation work in Africa but not in America.
2 He's slept in 50 different beds in the last ten years.
3 An elephant nearly killed him once.
4 He wore his last pair of sandals for 1,200 miles.
5 He has succeeded in his aims with his work.

4 Work in pairs. Compare Fay's style of traveling with your own. What appeals—or doesn't appeal—to you? Tell your partner.

Walking for wildlife

NATIONAL GEOGRAPHIC PROFILE: MIKE FAY

1 He's a biologist with the Wildlife Conservation Society (WCS). He's lived in central Africa for six years.

2 Fay has worked on several major conservation projects in Africa and America. He's counted all the elephants in the central African country of Chad—twice! He's walked over 1,800 miles across North America. He spends so much time outdoors that he hasn't slept in a bed more than 50 times in the last ten years!

3 A few years ago, he survived a plane crash! And on one trip, he came face to face with a very angry elephant that attacked him. Amazingly, his injuries weren't life-threatening. Less dramatically, but just as seriously, he's had malaria in Africa many times and once he almost died.

4 Fay travels light—he usually just takes a T-shirt, a pair of shorts, and his favorite footwear, sandals. His most recent pair of sandals lasted 1,200 miles before they fell apart! The few items he never travels without include his penknife, a lighter, and a sleeping mat.

5 Fay wants to show people how beautiful and precious the planet is so they will take care of it. And he succeeds. His work has drawn attention to conservation issues and made people act. After he started work on the elephant project in Chad, the number of elephant deaths fell significantly. And in Gabon, the government has created thirteen new national parks covering 10,000 square miles of forest.

trek (n) /trek/ a long, difficult journey, usually on foot

Grammar present perfect and simple past

5 Look at the example. Then read the sentences and choose the correct option.

He's had malaria in Africa many times and once he almost died.

1 We use the *present perfect / simple past* when we don't say exactly when something happened.
2 We use the *present perfect / simple past* when we say—or it is clear from the context—when something happened.

6 Underline the present perfect verbs and circle the simple past verbs in the profile. Which ones have different simple past and past participle forms?

> ▶ **PRESENT PERFECT and SIMPLE PAST**
>
> Present perfect: *He's lived in central Africa for years.*
> Simple past: *A few years ago, he survived a plane crash.*
> Regular verbs: *live, lived, lived*
> Irregular verbs: *have, had, had; come, came, come*
>
> For more information and practice, see page 161.

7 Look at the grammar box. Complete the additional information about Mike Fay with the present perfect and simple past form of the verbs. Then check your answers with your instructor.

> In addition to walking, Fay and his team ¹ _____ (also / fly) over large parts of Africa. Besides his work in Africa, Fay ² _____ (do) extensive conservation work in North America. He ³ _____ (once / spend) 11 months walking the Pacific coast, surveying giant redwood trees. Since he ⁴ _____ (not have) access to electricity for most of that journey, he ⁵ _____ (fill) 24 notebooks with data. He estimates that he ⁶ _____ (use) up hundreds of notebooks over the years.

Pronunciation *has, have*

8 🔊 **17** Listen to these sentences and repeat. Notice the pronunciation of *has* /həz/ and *have* /həv/.

1 The WCS has financed the work.
2 The trip has taken longer than expected.
3 The team members have worked hard.
4 The results have surprised us.
5 The project has been a great success.
6 The government has helped the project.

9 Find these time expressions in the profile. Complete the table with the expressions.

> for   in the last ten years   a few years ago   once

Present perfect	Simple past
already	in 2009
since	last summer
so far	yesterday
this month	_____
_____	_____
_____	

> ▶ **FOR**
>
> We use *for* + period of time with both the present perfect and the simple past.
>
> For more information, see page 162.

10 Complete the sentences so that they are true about you. Then work in pairs and compare your sentences.

1 I've improved my English a lot in the last _____ .
2 I've lived in _____ for _____ .
3 I've _____ many times.
4 I've already _____ this month.
5 I had a great vacation _____ ago.
6 I once worked in a _____ for _____ .
7 I _____ at lunchtime.
8 After I left school, I _____ .

Speaking

11 Have you had any unusual travel experiences? Make as many true or false sentences as you can with these verbs. Then work in pairs and talk about your experiences. Can your partner identify the false sentences? Ask follow-up questions as necessary.

> catch   climb   do   fly   go   have
> make   meet   run   sail   see   sing
> sleep   swim   take   walk

> *I've flown in a helicopter many times.*

> *Really? I've never done that. Where did you fly to?*

> *I've seen elephants in the wild.*

> *Wow! Did you take any photos?*

5b A good vacation

Vocabulary and reading vacation destinations

A   B   C   D

1 Which of these words describe the photos (A–D)?

busy street	remote village
crowded market	safe resort
exotic scenery	tropical beach
peaceful setting	unspoiled coastline
relaxing surroundings	vibrant city

2 Work in pairs. Match the features in Exercise 1 with the vacation destinations shown on the map.

3 Read about vacationers. Complete the table with the kinds of vacations for each place.

4 Have you been on any of these kinds of vacations? What is popular in your country?

GEOGRAPHY

Once, a typical vacation was a week at the beach or a lake—near home or somewhere with more reliable weather. But recently, vacationers have been looking for a different vacation experience. Perhaps inspired by wildlife documentaries on television, tourists have been flocking to places like Kenya and South Africa for safaris and bush camps. Interest in China has been growing too. Large numbers of tourists have visited China on cultural tours since the 2008 Olympic Games. Meanwhile, travel companies have been promoting the traditional vacation package with a new twist to attract more customers: spa vacations in Spain and luxury historical tours in Egypt.

One of the most notable changes is that the older generation of vacationers has been traveling like never before. The number of vacationers over 60 has been growing. Cruise destinations in the Caribbean or even to Antarctica are no longer just for young adventurers.

flocking: together in large numbers

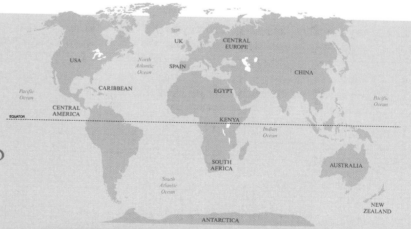

TRAVEL DESTINATIONS AND ACTIVITIES	
Caribbean and Antarctica	1 *Cruises*
Kenya and South Africa	2 *Safaris*, 3 *bush camps*
Spain and Egypt	vacation packages
China	4 *cultural tours*
US, Australia, and New Zealand	independent travelers, backpackers

Grammar present perfect continuous and present perfect

5 Look at the example. Underline four other present perfect continuous sentences in the text.

But recently, vacationers have been looking for a different vacation experience.

6 Answer the questions.

1 Which verbs are used to make the present perfect continuous? *have/has/been + ing*
2 Do the main verbs describe states or actions? *actions*
3 Do the sentences refer to activities that have finished or that are continuing, or both? *Continuing*

> ▶ **PRESENT PERFECT CONTINUOUS**
>
> subject + *have/has (not) been* + *-ing*
>
> *have/has* + subject + *been* + *-ing*?
>
> For more information and practice, see page 162.

7 Compare the present perfect with the present perfect continuous tenses.

1 Which tense emphasizes a completed action?
2 Which tense emphasizes the duration of an activity?
3 Which tense expresses the result of an activity?

8 Match the activities (1–6) with the results (a–f). Then write sentences as in the example.

Example:
1 *We've been tracking elephants today—we've taken some amazing photos.*

1 track elephants a finish my book
2 lie by the pool b not find one
3 look for a cheap deal c see dozens of churches
4 tour European cities d spend a fortune
5 follow the coastal path e take amazing photos
6 visit local markets f walk ten miles

Listening

9 💿 **18** Listen to three conversations that Matt has during his vacation. Choose the correct name.

1 *Matt / Li* has been coming here for four years.
2 *Matt / Li* thinks the nightlife is awesome.
3 *Matt / Li* thinks good weather is what you need on vacation.
4 *Matt / Rosa* recommends the food at the SeaView.
5 *Matt / Rosa* wants a relaxing break this year.
6 *Matt / Ping* has good memories of his vacations.
7 *Matt / Ping* has been sky-diving for a long time.
8 *Matt / Ping* spends his vacations with friends.

10 💿 **18** Listen again and complete Matt's questions.

1 How long _____ here?
About six years.
2 How long _____ here?
We just got in yesterday.
3 So, how long _____ sky-diving?
For quite a few years now.
4 How long _____ you?
It took a while!

Grammar How long... ?

> ▶ **HOW LONG... ?**
>
> We use *How long... ?* with the present perfect, present perfect continuous, and simple past to ask about the duration of an activity. Verbs like *be, have, know,* and *like* are not usually used in the continuous form.
>
> For more information and practice, see page 162.

11 Look at the exchanges in Exercise 10. Which tense is used in the questions—and why?

12 Write questions with *How long... ?* for these sentences. Then work in pairs and continue the conversations.

1 I went to Thailand last year.
2 I'm waiting for the bus to the beach.
3 We're backpacking around India.
4 I'm doing a diving course.
5 We've finally made it home!

Speaking

13 What do you think makes a good vacation? Look at the list and add three ideas of your own.

- getting there: journey time, transportation, _____
- at your destination: things to do, nightlife, beaches, weather, food, friends, _____
- afterwards: good memories, _____

14 Work in pairs. Decide which five things are the most important for a good vacation. Explain your choices with examples from your own vacation experiences.

15 Work with another pair. Compare your ideas. Try to agree on the three most important things. Tell the class.

> *We all agree that good weather is important.*

5c The real cost of travel

Reading

1 What kind of tourism is there in your country or region? List some of the advantages and disadvantages of tourism.

2 Look at the photos in the article on page 63. What aspects of tourism do you think each one shows?

3 Read the article quickly and choose the best option (a–c).

a It describes how tourists have been getting involved in conservation activities.
b It compares harmful and beneficial effects of tourism.
c It looks at the negative impact of tourism.

4 Read the article again and complete the table.

Place	Type of tourism / activity	Effect
Patagonia	1	waste affects 2 ....
Everest	climbing expeditions	the mountain is covered in 3 ....
the Mediterranean	beach resorts	4 .... is out of control
Europe	5	a big impact on 6 ....

5 Answer the questions with information from the article.

1 Why are cruises bad for the environment?
2 Expeditions normally climb Everest to reach the top. What other expeditions does the article mention?
3 Why, aside from the cost, are low-cost flights so popular?
4 Does the article suggest better ways to travel? How?

Vocabulary conservation

6 Find these words in the article. Then complete the sentences. In one sentence, more than one word is possible.

population	habitats	impact	trash
waste	pollute	greener	

1 Human activity has a big .... on wildlife.
2 On average, each person in the US produces about 1,600 pounds of .... each year.
3 The world .... has doubled since 1960.
4 We need to protect different natural ....
5 Recycling is .... than throwing things away.
6 When we fly, we .... the environment.

Critical thinking close reading

7 Mark these statements true (T), false (F), or not enough information (N) based on the article.

1 Mass tourism has grown steadily and has now reached its peak.
2 Cruises have had a negative effect on penguins and other animals.
3 Non-industrial countries accept the negative effects of tourism.
4 Economic problems mean that construction on the Mediterranean coast has stopped.
5 There are less damaging ways of seeing the world than air travel.

8 Discuss the last sentence of the article as a class.

Speaking

9 Work in pairs. Look at these activities and decide their position on the green scale.

buying out-of-season food flown in from distant destinations
flying to vacation destinations
recycling household waste
saving water
turning off lights and appliances
traveling (by bike, car, public transportation)
upgrading cell phones, computers, and TVs frequently
using eco-friendly cleaning products

10 How easy is it for you to switch to greener activities? Tell your partner about your experiences with the activities in Exercise 9.

11 Work in groups. Compare your green activities and their results. Is your group "light green" or "dark green"?

This year I've been using a composter. I've reduced my weekly trash to one small bag!

THE REAL COST OF TRAVEL

Mass tourism is a relatively recent phenomenon. The tourism industry took off in the middle of the last century and it's been growing ever since. In the last ten years especially, more and more people have been traveling to places we had previously only read about or seen on television. But what kind of impact does tourism have on the planet?

A VOYAGE TO THE END OF THE EARTH?

A large cruise ship can carry as many as 6,000 passengers and there are upwards of 50 such ships currently sailing the seas. Cruise ships dump about 90,000 tons of waste into the oceans every year. Any harmful effects of this are made even worse by the fact that cruises tend to visit the same places over and over again, thus concentrating the waste in specific places. In Patagonia, this is now having a visible effect on wildlife. The population of animals such as these Magellanic penguins has been in decline for some years now, and things show little sign of changing.

TRASH ON TOP OF THE WORLD

From remote ocean habitats to the world's highest mountain, our trash is everywhere. Despite the fact that far fewer people go climbing or trekking in the Himalayas than on a cruise, their impact is still felt. Tourism is vital to the economy of Nepal, as it is to many non-industrial countries. But for decades, climbers have been abandoning their unwanted equipment on Everest. For the last few years, clean-up teams of local and international climbers have been organizing expeditions just to pick up the waste. One group has brought over eight tons of waste down from the mountain! But their actions don't stop there. The Japanese teams, for example, have also been educating other climbers back home in Japan about being more responsible on the mountain.

WHEN MORE IS NOT BETTER

Tourism of a different kind is causing problems in Europe. Construction on the Mediterranean coast has been spiraling out of control for years. Beach resorts form an almost unbroken line from Gibraltar to Greece, and natural habitats have disappeared under miles of concrete. And so we pollute the sea, the land, and the air. Low-cost air travel is booming, in spite of (or perhaps helped by) economic problems. For many Europeans, low-cost flights allow them to take several short vacations a year. Yet curiously, short flights actually have a much bigger effect on climate change than long-haul flights. So, are there less damaging ways of seeing the world? Traveling by train, for example, is a much greener way of getting around. And many places have been experimenting with low-impact tourism such as ecotourism. It's time to ask ourselves some difficult questions. Have we been destroying the very places we're escaping to?

> **damaging** (adj) /ˈdæmɪdʒɪŋ/ destructive
> **in decline** (adv) /ˈɪn dɪˈklaɪn/ falling in numbers or quality
> **downside** (n) /ˈdaʊnˌsaɪd/ the negative aspect
> **upwards of** (adv) /ˈʌpwərdz əv/ more than

5d Is something wrong?

Vocabulary travel problems

1 Work in pairs. Have you ever had any travel problems involving these things? Tell your partner. Can a tour guide help you with any of them?

baggage allowances	hotel rooms
boarding passes	infectious diseases
car rental	jetlag
customs	motion sickness
flight delays	passport control
food poisoning	travel documents

> ▶ **WORDBUILDING compound nouns (noun + noun)**
>
> We can use two nouns together to mean one thing.
> *baggage allowances*   *boarding passes*

Real life dealing with problems

2 🔊 **19** Listen to two conversations between a tour guide and tourists. Write the number of the conversation (1–2) next to the problem they talk about. You will only use two options.

a The person has missed his/her flight home.
b The luggage hasn't arrived.
c The flight has been delayed.
d The person has lost his/her plane tickets.
e Someone is ill.

3 🔊 **19** Mark each expression for dealing with problems G (guide) or T (tourist) depending on who said it. Then listen again and check.

> ▶ **DEALING WITH PROBLEMS**
>
> I wonder if you could help us?
> Is anything wrong?
> Can I help?
>
> Our luggage hasn't arrived.
> Which flight were you on?
> How did that happen?
> Do you know where our bags have gone to?
> When's the next flight?
> It's about my wife.
> The hotel hasn't provided mosquito nets.
> How long has she been feeling like this?
> Is there anything you can do?
>
> I'm afraid the luggage has gone to Shanghai.
> Don't worry, we'll arrange everything.
> I'll ask the hotel to call a doctor.

4 Work as a class. Are the problems solved? How?

5 Pronunciation **strong and weak forms**

a 🔊 **20** Look at the position of *to* in these sentences. Listen to the sentences. In which sentence is *to* strong—and in which one is it weak?

1 Do you know which airport our bags have gone to?
2 Yes, I'm afraid the luggage has gone to Shanghai.

b 🔊 **21** Listen and repeat these questions. Use strong or weak forms of *at, from,* and *for.* Then work in pairs. Ask the questions and give your own answers.

1 Which hotel are you staying at?
2 Are you staying at the Ocean Hotel?
3 Where have you traveled from?
4 Why haven't we heard from the airline?
5 What have we been waiting for?
6 Are you waiting for the manager?

6 Work in pairs. Choose one of the conversations from Exercise 2. Take a role each. Look at the audioscript on page 176 and each take a role. Practice the conversation.

7 Take the roles of a tourist and a tour guide. Choose from the problems in Exercise 2 and act out two conversations. Use the expressions for dealing with problems to help you.

5e Hello from Sydney!

Writing a postcard

Hi!

Greetings from Down Under! Finally made it to Sydney after 18-hour delay in Bangkok!!! Weather here glorious, beaches out of this world, and the people are fantastic. So far have: been surfing (fell off every time!), seen the Opera House (wow!), been on a boat trip around the bay. No kangaroos or koalas yet bc haven't been out of city. Text from my uncle in Brisbane – has found me a job there for the summer!

Lynne

ps new pics up on Flickr®

1 Read the postcard and answer the questions.

  1 Where did Lynne come from and where is she now?
  2 Who do you think the postcard is to, friends or family?
  3 What does Lynne say about the people and places?
  4 What has she been doing?

2 Writing skill informal style

a Read the postcard again. Which of these features of informal style does Lynne use?

  - abbreviations
  - comments in parentheses
  - contractions
  - exclamation marks
  - informal expressions
  - listing items
  - leaving out words

b Look at the example. The words *I* and *an* are missing. Mark their position in the complete sentence.

  Finally made it to Sydney after 18-hour delay in Bangkok!

c Mark the places in the postcard where Lynne has omitted words. What are the words?

d Rewrite the sentences. Omit words where possible.

  1 The weather is sunny and it has been very hot.
  2 I've been touring all the typical places— it's exhausting!
  3 The people here are very kind and they have helped me a lot.
  4 I took some photos of some koalas— they're so cute!
  5 I haven't heard anything from Suri yet.
  6 I'm taking a bus up to Brisbane because flying is too expensive.

3 Choose a place you have visited and make notes about it. Use the questions in Exercise 1 as a guide.

4 Write a postcard of about 100 words describing your trip. Use some of the features of informal style from Exercise 2 and omit unecessary words.

5 Send your postcard to someone in your class. Then read the postcard you have received. Use these questions to check your classmate's postcard.

  - Is everything clearly expressed?
  - Are there any sections you do not understand?

6 Work in pairs. Tell your partner about the postcard you have received.

I got a postcard from Daisuke the other day.

Oh, yeah! How's he doing?

A disappearing world

It's an amazing place!

Before you watch

1 Work in pairs. Look at the title of this video and the photo and discuss the questions.

1 What do you think this video is about?
2 Which parts of the world have rain forests?
3 What do you know about the rain forest and its problems?

2 Write down four animals and birds you think you will see in the video.

While you watch

3 Watch the video and check your answers from Exercises 1 and 2.

4 Put the events in the order you see them in the video.

a looking over treetops
b writing a journal
c filming an elephant
d reaching the sea
e climbing a hill
f crossing rapids
g traveling in a canoe

5 Watch the video again. What does this information refer to?

1 September _____
2 1,200 _____
3 5,800 _____
4 one quarter _____
5 half _____
6 eight _____
7 70 or 80 _____
8 360 _____
9 six hundred _____
10 fifteen _____

6 Complete the sentences with words from the glossary.

1 Their _____ is to make a scientific _____ of a world that could be disappearing from Earth.
2 What I'm trying to do, in a _____ way, is to show the world that we're just about to lose the last little _____ in the African continent.
3 Fay's plan is to _____ and record data on almost every part of the rain forest.
4 Their next _____ is to reach a group of strange hills that are made of stone, and that _____ far above the forest floor.
5 This land of fast water and old forests is in danger because of _____.

After you watch

7 Roleplay an interview with an expedition member

Work in pairs.

Student A: You are a writer for National Geographic. You are going to interview a member of Michael Fay's team. Use the ideas below to prepare questions.

Student B: You have just completed the Congo Basin "Megatransect" with Michael Fay. Use the ideas below to prepare what you are going to say to the interviewer.

- purpose of the expedition
- how you traveled
- what you saw
- the most difficult parts
- the best parts
- dangerous experiences

Act out the interview. Then change roles and repeat the interview.

8 During the video, Dr. Fay says: "If we don't do something now, if we don't do it today, we can forget about it." What does he mean?

9 Work in pairs. Discuss these questions.

1 What do you think Dr. Fay did with the information he collected during his expedition?
2 Apart from logging, what other dangers do places like the Congo Basin face?
3 Are you optimistic or pessimistic about whether we will be able to preserve wild places on our planet?

---

aim (n) /eɪm/ objective
challenge (n) /ˈtʃælɪndʒ/ something that tests a person's abilities
collect (v) /kəˈlekt/ pick up or bring things together
desperate (adj) /ˈdespərɪt/ needing to change a very bad situation
gem (n) /dʒem/ something very valuable
logging (n) /ˈlɑgɪŋ/ cutting down trees on a large scale
overwhelmed (adj) /ˌoʊvərˈwelmd/ feeling very emotional
rapids (n) /ˈræpɪdz/ part of a river where the water flows very fast, usually over and between rocks
record (n) /ˈrekərd/ written information about something
rise (v) /raɪz/ go up
stepping stones (n) /ˈstepɪŋ ˌstoʊnz/ large stones that people walk on to cross a river

UNIT 5 REVIEW

Grammar

1 Work in pairs. Look at the photo. Discuss the questions.

1 Where do wild gorillas live?
2 What are the problems facing gorillas in the wild?
3 Have you heard any news stories about gorillas?

2 Read the article and check your ideas from Exercise 1. Then choose the correct option.

Wild gorillas ¹ *faced / have faced* many challenges in recent years. Commercial hunters ² *left / have been leaving* several young mountain gorillas orphaned, and the Ebola virus ³ *devastated / has devastated* the population of lowland gorillas. Gorilla numbers ⁴ *declined / have declined* at a disturbing rate—down over 50 percent since the 1990s. In 2007, their status ⁵ *changed / has changed* from endangered to critically endangered. Projects such as the *Project Protection des Gorilles* ⁶ *rescued / have rescued* young gorillas and they ⁷ *have encouraged / have been encouraging* them to form new social groups, hoping to give them a second chance in the wild. Meanwhile, to counter the threat of the Ebola virus, Peter Walsh and others ⁸ *have worked / have been working* on a vaccine that will prevent the transmission of the virus among gorillas.

3 Have you ever been to any of these places? Ask your partner questions about their experience.

| a safari park | a wildlife sanctuary | a zoo |

I CAN
talk about recent activities and experiences (present perfect and continuous)
relate events that happened at a specific time in the past (simple past)

Vocabulary

4 Work in pairs. Which is the odd one out in each group? Why?

1 exotic, plane, peaceful, vibrant
2 cruise, peaceful, package, safari
3 fly, food, nightlife, weather
4 litter, trash, ticket, waste
5 journey, ocean, tour, trip

5 Work in groups. Discuss the questions.

1 Where do tourists go in your country?
2 What have you done to help the environment?
3 Where did you go for your last vacation? What did you do there?

I CAN
describe vacation destinations
talk about conservation
talk about vacations

Real life

6 Read these sentences from a conversation between two friends. Put the sentences (a–h) in order (1–8).

a A: What? How did that happen?
b A: Well, let's take another look. Calm down.
c A: Have you looked in all your pockets?
d A: Is anything wrong?   *1*
e B: Yes, I have. And I've checked the suitcase.
f B: I've been worrying so much about everything, and now this!
g B: I think I've lost the boarding passes.
h B: I don't know. I thought they were with my passport, but they aren't there now.

7 Act out similar conversations in pairs.

Conversation 1: Student A is a tourist and Student B is a tour guide. Student A has lost his/her passport.

Conversation 2: Student A is an airline official and Student B is a customer. The flight is canceled.

I CAN
talk about travel problems
ask for and give explanations

Speaking

8 Prepare questions to interview someone about their career. Use the ideas below. Then work in pairs and choose a role on page 155.

How long / be a... ?	Where / travel to?
What / do / recently?	When / go to... ?
Have / unusual experiences?	

9 Work with a new partner. Take turns asking and answering your questions.

> *How long have you been a pilot?*

Unit 6 Wellbeing

Food items from the Overall Nutritional Quality
Index, which assesses the nutritional value of food
Photograph by Mark Thiessen

FEATURES

1 Find these foods in the photo. Which ones do you eat?
How often do you eat them?

avocado	bagel	cheese	cheese snacks	chocolate	
fried egg	pasta	peanuts	popcorn	shrimp	steak

2 Work in pairs. Put the foods in Exercise 1 in the order you
think is the most (1) to the least (11) healthy.

3 Answer the questions.

1 Should supermarkets be required to tell you how nutritious
the food on their shelves is?
2 Should restaurants provide nutritional information on their
menus?
3 Where can you already find this kind of information?

4 Discuss the questions with your partner.

1 Have you heard the saying "You are what you eat"?
Do you have a similar saying in your country?
2 How much attention do you pay to your diet?
3 In what ways can food and diet influence your health?

6a Pizza with a pedigree

Reading

1 Work in pairs. Answer the questions.

1   What are the traditional dishes of your country or region?
2   How often do you eat or make them?
3   How often do you eat or make dishes from other countries? Which dishes?

2 Read the text and answer the questions.

1   Why is Pizza Napoletana in the news?
2   What are some of the other foods in the same group as Pizza Napoletana?
3   Which aspects of "authentic" Pizza Napoletana are regulated?

3 Which food and drink products have protected status in your country?

Grammar modal verbs (1)

> **MODAL VERBS**

Obligation or no obligation	
+ *have to / has to, must*	– *don't/doesn't have to*

Prohibition	
	– *can't*

Permission or no permission/prohibition	
+ *can, is/are allowed to*	– *can't, is/are not allowed to*

Recommendation	
	should (not)

The modal *mustn't* is used less frequently in American English than it is in British English. In American English, *must not* or *can't* are more common. For more information and practice, see page 163.

4 Look at the grammar box.

1   Underline the modal verbs in the news item.
2   The modal verbs *have to* and *must* have the same form in the simple past. What is it?
3   Two of the modal verbs in the news item do not express rules. Which verbs?

F O O D

Pizza with a pedigree

There is pizza—and there is Pizza Napoletana. The two, connoisseurs say, have as much in common as virgin olive oil has with generic cooking oil. Now, authentic Pizza Napoletana has joined the elite group of European-Union-certified food and drink products—like Scottish Farmed Salmon, Spanish Melon from La Mancha, and English Blue Stilton cheese—that have to meet very strict criteria.

Once a product is granted Guaranteed Traditional Specialty status, other similar products are not allowed to use the same name. If your champagne doesn't come from that particular region of France, for example, you can't call it champagne. But be warned: it takes longer to read the EU specifications for "real" Pizza Napoletana than it does to make one. To be labeled "Guaranteed Traditional Speciality," the pizza can't be over 14 inches in diameter and the crust can't be more than three-quarters of an inch thick. The ingredients must include type 00 flour and up to three and a half ounces of San Marzano tomatoes applied in a spiraling motion. And the cheese has to be fresh "Mozzarella di Bufala."

Pizza has a long history in Italy. The word first appeared in a 997 CE manuscript from Gaeta, a southern Italian town. A millennium later, in 1997, political groups in northern Italy tried to boycott pizza because it was a symbol of their rivals in the south. Perhaps they should accept that Pizza Napoletana is here to stay now. Thankfully, you don't have to know anything about history to enjoy an authentic Pizza Napoletana!

elite (adj) (n) /ɪˈlit/ a small group of the best
(be) granted (v) /ˈgrӕntɪd/ (be) officially given, awarded
pedigree (n) (adj) /ˈpedɪ‚gri/ a documented history
strict (adj) /strɪkt/ precise and rigorous

5 Read the labels from food packaging. Look at the example. Then write sentences using one of the modal verbs in parentheses.

Suitable for vegetarians

1

(can / don't have to)

Example:

Vegetarians can eat this product.

NOT SUITABLE FOR PEOPLE WITH NUT ALLERGIES

2

(don't have to / shouldn't)

DO NOT EXCEED THE RECOMMENDED DAILY INTAKE OF SALT

3

(can / shouldn't)

SAMPLE – NOT FOR SALE

4

(don't have to / not allowed to)

Heat thoroughly before serving

5

(can / have to)

NOT RECOMMENDED FOR DIABETICS

6

(allowed to / shouldn't)

6 Work in pairs. Look at these food items. Answer the questions.

| durian | eggs | fugu | hakarl |
| oysters | potatoes | red beans | steak |

1 Which of these food items have you eaten?
2 Do you know of any special treatment these things need before you can eat them?

7 🔊 **22** Listen to the conversations about the food items in Exercise 6 and check your ideas. Complete the notes.

1 durian: you're not allowed to ....
2 eggs: you should ....
3 fugu: .... are allowed to ....
4 hakarl: you have to ....
5 oysters: you can't ....
6 potatoes: you don't have to ....
7 red beans: must ....
8 steak: you can ....

> **ferment** (v) /fər'ment/ to let food or drink undergo a natural chemical reaction
> **peel** (v) /pil/ to remove the skin from fruits or vegetables
> **raw** (adj) /rɔ/ uncooked or not well-cooked

8 Pronunciation weak forms

a 🔊 **23** Listen to some of the information from the conversations in Exercise 7. Notice how *to* is not stressed. Repeat the sentences.

b Work in pairs. Decide if you (don't) have to do these things. Discuss with your partner.

> keep eggs in the fridge
> wash rice before you cook it
> eat fish on the day you buy it
> cook meat until it isn't pink

Speaking

9 Work in pairs. Choose a dish you both like. Do you agree on the following points? Make notes using modal verbs where necessary. Then tell the class about the dish.

- essential ingredients
- optional ingredients
- cooking method
- presentation
- when and where to eat the dish

> *We'd like to tell you the secret of a good paella.*

> *You can make it with seafood or meat, but we think it's better with seafood.*

fugu (puffer fish)

a durian

hakarl (shark meat)

oysters

6b Imaginary eating

Reading and listening

1 Work in pairs. Discuss the statements. Do you agree with them?

1 Self-confidence: the difference between a winner and a runner-up is in attitude, not skill.
2 Willpower: you can achieve anything if you think you can do it.
3 Train your mind: people who consider themselves to be lucky have more "lucky" moments.

2 Read the news item *Imaginary eating*. What does the imaginary eating technique consist of?

3 🎧 **24** Listen to two people discussing the news item. Are these sentences true (T) or false (F)?

1 Jack doesn't believe the claims in the news item but Lin does.
2 Lin is open-minded about the idea.
3 Both of them agree that willpower is important.
4 Lin thinks Jack should try out the technique.
5 Lin eats too many snacks.
6 Jack is going to buy some chocolate.

4 🎧 **24** Listen to the conversation again. Match the two parts of the sentences.

1 I'll believe it
2 If you don't train your mind,
3 I won't find out
4 When I want to eat a snack,
5 I'll never have to buy chocolate again
6 As soon as it starts working,

a if this technique works.
b I'll let you know.
c I'll try just imagining it.
d unless I try.
e when I see it.
f you won't be able to lose weight.

5 Read the comment at the end of the news item again. Do you agree with it? With your partner, write your own comment to add to the comments section.

Imaginary eating

Christine Dell'Amore
National Geographic News
December 9

Obesity rates are climbing fast and we need to find new techniques for controlling overeating. According to new research, "imaginary eating" could be one such technique. A psychologist in the US reports that if you imagine eating a specific food, your interest in that food will drop. And if you are less interested in that food, you'll eat less of it. Carey Morewedge explains that people often try to avoid thinking about food when they need to lose weight. However, this might not, in fact, be a good strategy. On the other hand, if you force yourself to think about chewing and actually swallowing food, you'll reduce your craving.

COMMENTS

👤 **Rpineapple23** *11:09 a.m. on December 12*
This study is more proof of how powerful our brain is. The better we are at using that power when making decisions and controlling certain behaviors (such as food cravings), the healthier we will become.

reply   **recommend**

craving (n) /ˈkreɪvɪŋ/ a strong feeling that you want or need something

Grammar first conditional

6 Look at these sentences and answer the questions.

    a I'll never have to buy chocolate again if this technique works.
    b If you don't train your mind, you won't be able to lose weight.

    1 Which tenses are used to make the first conditional?
    2 Where can *if* go in conditional sentences?
    3 Look at the position of *if* in the sentences. When do we use a comma (,)?
    4 Do the sentences refer to the past, the present, or the future? (More than one option is possible.)
    5 Find three sentences in the news item that use the first conditional pattern. Do the sentences refer to future possibilities or things that are generally true?

> ▶ **FIRST CONDITIONAL**
>
> | *If* + simple present | , | *will* + infinitive |
> |---|---|---|
> | *will* + infinitive | | *if* + simple present |
>
> For more information and practice, see page 164.

7 Look at the grammar box. Complete the sentences with the simple present and *will* + infinitive.

    1 If you ＿＿＿＿ (believe) in yourself, you ＿＿＿＿ (be) more successful.
    2 I ＿＿＿＿ (need) a lot of willpower if I ＿＿＿＿ (want) to give up chocolate.
    3 If you ＿＿＿＿ (not buy) snacks, you ＿＿＿＿ (not be able) to eat them.
    4 If you ＿＿＿＿ (find) any more information, ＿＿＿＿ (you / let) me know?
    5 If we ＿＿＿＿ (go) to the supermarket, we ＿＿＿＿ (check) the price.
    6 I ＿＿＿＿ (give up) junk food if you ＿＿＿＿ (do) too.
    7 If I ＿＿＿＿ (not try) it, I ＿＿＿＿ (never know).
    8 What ＿＿＿＿ (you / do) if your plan ＿＿＿＿ (not work)?

> ▶ *WHEN, AS SOON AS, UNLESS, UNTIL, BEFORE*
>
> We use the present tense after these words when we refer to future events.
>
> For more information and practice, see page 164.

8 Read the sentences and cross out any options that are not possible. In some cases, both answers are possible.

    1 You won't change *as soon as / unless* you make an effort.
    2 *As soon as / When* you make up your mind, you'll be able to act.
    3 I'll weigh myself *before / when* I start my diet.
    4 I'll keep trying *before / until* I see a change.
    5 You won't see any results *unless / when* you try hard.
    6 *If / Unless* you give up easily, you won't achieve your target.
    7 *If / When* you are ready to try, I'll be happy to help.
    8 It will be a while *before / until* you notice a difference.

Vocabulary and speaking a healthy lifestyle

9 Work in pairs. Match the verbs with the nouns to make strategies for a healthy lifestyle. You can match some verbs with more than one noun and some nouns with more than one verb. Add ideas of your own.

Verbs	Nouns
avoid	a new sport
change	an outdoor activity
cut down on	bad habits
cut out	computer and TV time
give up	fatty food
learn	heavy meals at night
reduce	junk food
take up	relaxation techniques
	smoking
	snacks between meals
	stress

> ▶ **WORDBUILDING phrasal verbs**
>
> Phrasal verbs with *down* and *up* often describe change.
> *cut down*   *give up*

10 Think of a specific result for each strategy from Exercise 9. Write sentences with the first conditional.

    Example:
    If you avoid heavy meals at night, you'll sleep better.

11 Work with a new partner. Act out two conversations. Try to motivate your partner.

    Student A: You've been told to change to a healthier diet.

    Student B: You've been told you spend too much time sitting around and need to get more exercise.

> *I have to change my diet, but I don't want to give up my favorite foods!*

> *You could try imaginary eating.*

6c A caffeine-fueled world

Reading

1 Work in groups. Discuss your answers to these questions.

  1 Is your lifestyle very different from that of your parents' generation? In what way(s)?

  2 What kind of comments do people in your age group make about work, relationships, time, and modern life?

  3 How much tea, coffee, or other beverages do you drink in a normal day?

2 Read the article on page 75 and choose the correct option.

The article is about caffeine and *children / daily life / science.*

3 Complete these sentences.

  1 Tea, coffee, soft drinks, energy drinks, and .... are all sources of caffeine.

  2 Caffeine is classified as a psychoactive ....

  3 In Europe, there are various regulations on the sale of .... drinks.

  4 Modern lifestyles depend on caffeinated .... and ....

  5 Caffeine changes the natural .... of the human body.

4 What are the effects of caffeine? Complete the table.

Beneficial effects of caffeine
makes you less tired
makes you ....
relieves ....
reduces asthma ....
increases ....

Harmful effects of caffeine
is mood-altering
is ....
raises ....
increases the .... of heart disease

5 Answer the questions based on the article.

  1 How have people's working patterns changed?

  2 What helped us adapt to those changes?

  3 What are the risks of not getting enough sleep?

  4 What is the caffeine paradox?

6 Work in pairs. Did any of the information about caffeine surprise you? Tell your partner.

Critical thinking **language clues**

7 Find words in the article that signal the following.

  1 introducing a contrasting idea (paragraph 2):
    .... , ... , ...

  2 introducing a consequence:
    .... , ... (paragraph 2)
    .... , ... (paragraph 3)

8 Identify the two contrasting ideas for each of the words from Exercise 7 item 1.

9 Work in pairs. Discuss the questions.

  1 Do you think caffeine is harmful, beneficial, neither, or both?

  2 Did you change your ideas about caffeine after reading the article?

Vocabulary and speaking **modern life**

10 Which things are typical of a 24-hour society?

daylight work schedules	indoor jobs
electric light	living by the clock
heart disease	a natural sleep cycle
high blood pressure	tiredness

11 Complete the slogans about modern life with these words. Where do you think the slogans are from?

all close day night on today

  1 We never ....

  2 See the movies of tomorrow ....

  3 Open .... hours.

  4 All .... breakfast served here.

  5 Late .... shopping every Thursday.

  6 "Always ...." broadband.

12 Work in pairs. Make notes about modern life under two headings: *good things* and *bad things.* You can use ideas from Exercise 10. Then work in groups and discuss how the pace of modern life affects you.

> *I'm lucky because I don't have to live by the clock at the moment. I suppose that will change when I start working full-time.*

> *Yes, it will! My problem is working under electric lights all day. It really makes me tired.*

> *Me too.*

A caffeine
-fueled world

Over the centuries, people have created many rituals to accompany the consumption of their favorite drinks, tea and coffee. Just think of the Japanese tea ceremony, British afternoon tea, or the morning coffee and coffee break ritual in countless societies. Why are these drinks so popular? The answer is their secret ingredient: caffeine. In the modern world, the new caffeine "delivery systems" are canned "energy" drinks. And the more modern our world gets, the more we seem to need caffeine. People have known for years that caffeinated drinks make you less tired and more alert. This dual power of caffeine to counteract physical fatigue and increase alertness is part of the reason why it is the world's most popular mood-altering drug. It is the only habit-forming psychoactive drug we routinely serve to our children (in all those soft drinks and chocolate bars). In fact, most babies in the developed world are born with traces of caffeine in their bodies.

Most people don't think twice about their caffeine intake. However, caffeine raises blood pressure and thus increases the risk of heart disease. The widespread use of caffeine is now a cause for concern among scientists and public health officials. One result of this concern is that you are not allowed to sell energy drinks in France or Denmark. And in other European countries, manufacturers have to label cans with warnings.

The United States has no such rule, but many canned energy drinks sold there carry warnings anyway. On the other hand, much of the research suggests that caffeine may have health benefits. Studies have shown it helps relieve pain, reduces asthma symptoms, and increases reaction speed. Despite this, a study in Ireland recommended that children and pregnant women, among other groups, shouldn't drink energy drinks.

But we need coffee—or Diet Coke® or Red Bull—to get us out of bed and back to work. "For most of human existence, the pattern of sleeping and waking has followed sunrise and sunset," explains Charles Czeisler, a neuroscientist at Harvard Medical School. "Then, the way we work changed from a schedule built around the sun to an indoor job timed by a clock, and consequently humans had to adapt. Electric light and caffeinated food and drinks allowed people to follow a work schedule set by the clock, not by daylight or the natural sleep cycle." Therefore, without caffeine, the 24-hour society of the developed world simply couldn't exist.

"Caffeine helps people try to override the human rhythm that is in all of us," says Czeisler. "Nevertheless," he says solemnly, "there is a heavy, heavy price to pay for all this extra wakefulness." Without adequate sleep—the conventional eight hours out of each 24 is about right—the human body will not function at its best physically, mentally, or emotionally.

But our caffeine use has created a downward spiral. People need caffeine to stay awake, but as Czeisler points out, "the main reason they can't stay awake is they don't get enough regular sleep—because they use caffeine."

---

counteract (v) /ˌkaʊntərˈækt/ to reduce the effect of something by acting against it
fatigue (n) /fəˈtiɡ/ the feeling of being extremely tired
traces (n) /ˈtreɪsɪz/ very small amounts of something

6d Eating out

Vocabulary restaurants

1 Work in pairs. Which are the most important things to consider when eating out? Does it depend on the occasion?

> the atmosphere in the restaurant
> the food choice and/or quality
> the prices and/or value for money
> the service

2 Put these stages in eating out (a–h) in order (1–8).

a make a
   reservation   *1*
b have an appetizer
c have dessert
d have an entree

e leave a tip
f look at the menu
g order something to
   drink
h pay the bill

3 Are these comments usually said by a customer (C), a waiter (W), or both (B)?

1 Are you ready to order?
2 Would you like something to drink while you decide?
3 What's that made from?
4 What do they taste like?
5 I think I'll try that.
6 Can I take your order now?
7 And I'll have the same.
8 And for your entree?
9 Does it come with vegetables?
10 And what about you, sir?
11 Certainly.

Real life describing dishes

4 🔊 **25** Listen to the conversation in a Jamaican restaurant. Check your answers from Exercise 3.

5 🔊 **25** Look at the expressions for describing dishes. Listen to the conversation again. How are the dishes in the photos described?

> ▶ **DESCRIBING DISHES**
>
> It's / They're a sort / type / kind of:
> *baked / boiled / fried dish /*
> *fruit / meat / fish / vegetable*
>
> It's / They're made from:
> *a kind of bean / meat / vegetables*
>
> It tastes / They taste:
> *bland / hot / salty / spicy / sweet*
>
> It's / They're a bit like:
> *fresh cod / potatoes / lamb*

6 🔊 **25** Which of the four dishes do the customers order? Listen to the conversation again and check your answers. Would you order the same?

Diner 1	Diner 2

7 Write a list of six dishes, vegetables, fruit, or other food that are either from your country or that you have eaten abroad. Make notes that describe each item. Use the expressions for describing dishes to help you.

Food	Taste

8 Work in groups of three. Take turns describing and guessing your mystery foods.

plantain fritters

akkra

ackee and saltfish

goat curry

6e A staff meeting

Writing a formal letter

1 The employees at a small company, Hardwick Health Solutions, have written to the owner. Read the letter quickly. What is its purpose? Choose the correct option (a–c).

a to accept a proposal
b to make a proposal
c to object to a proposal

Dear Mrs. Hardwick,

We are writing to express our concern at the plan to close the staff restaurant at the end of this month.

In our view, this action will have serious consequences for all the staff. If there is no on-site restaurant, employees will have to travel to the nearest town at lunchtime. This could lead to time-management and punctuality issues.

In addition, it is important for working people to eat a healthy meal at lunchtime. If the restaurant closes, this will result in many people eating snacks and sandwiches. This kind of food is not nutritious and therefore staff health and productivity could suffer.

Currently, the staff are not allowed to eat at their workstations. How will the closure of the restaurant affect this policy? Will there be plans for a kitchen or food area?

We request a meeting to discuss these issues at your earliest convenience.

Yours sincerely,

PJ Firth

PJ Firth
Staff Representative

2 Answer the questions about each paragraph.

Paragraph 1: What is the proposal?
Paragraph 2: What consequences of this plan are mentioned?
Paragraph 3: What additional consequences of the plan are mentioned?
Paragraph 4: What questions does the writer have?
Paragraph 5: What does the writer want to happen next?

3 Writing skill explaining consequences

a Find these words in the letter. They link causes and consequences. For each word, underline the cause and circle the consequence in the letter.

1 lead to (paragraph 2)
2 result in (paragraph 3)
3 therefore (paragraph 3)

b Complete the sentences with these words. Sometimes, more than one option is possible.

consequently	lead to	means	result in	so
therefore	thus			

1 We object strongly to this proposal. _____ , we will not be able to support it.
2 We welcome the new staff kitchen. This will _____ more people eating a hot meal.
3 The menu prices have gone up. _____ , fewer people will continue to eat in the cafeteria.
4 A new take-out place in this area _____ we'll have more choice.
5 We suggest changing the menu since this could _____ more customers coming in.
6 We reduced our prices and _____ increased the number of customers.

4 Prepare a letter supporting or objecting to one of these proposals. Make notes before you start. Use the questions in Exercise 2 to guide you.

- Your college is going to close the student cafeteria.
- A late-night take-out restaurant is going to open on your street.
- Your employer is going to ban food and drink in the workplace.
- Your college or workplace is going to install vending machines with healthy snacks only.

5 Write your letter. Follow the structure of the paragraphs in Exercise 2. Use these questions to check your letter.

- Is the style correct for a formal letter?
- Is the purpose of the letter clear?
- Is it clear what action you are recommending?

6 Exchange letters with your partner. Read your partner's letter. Take the role of the person it is addressed to. Are you going to take any action as a result of the letter? Write a short reply.

Eating this fish is like playing a dangerous game.

Before you watch

1 Work in groups. Look at the photo and discuss the questions.

   1 Where was the photo taken?
   2 Would you eat this fish in a restaurant?
   3 What does the caption suggest about the fish?

2 Mark the things you think you will see people doing in this video.

> buying fish   catching fish   cooking fish
> cutting fish   eating fish

While you watch

3 Watch the video and check your answers from Exercise 2.

4 Watch the first part of the video (to 02:49). Are these sentences true (T) or false (F)? Correct the false sentences.

   1 Puffer fish is very cheap.
   2 All restaurants in Tokyo serve fugu.
   3 Puffer fish toxin is 100 times stronger than cyanide.
   4 Chef Hayashi has a lot of experience preparing fugu.
   5 You have to have a special license to cook fugu in Japan.
   6 Between 1945 and 1975, 2,500 Japanese people died from eating fugu.
   7 Nobody dies from fugu poisoning any more.
   8 Most poisonings happen after people eat fugu in restaurants.

5 Watch the second part of the video (02:52 to the end) and answer the questions. Then compare your answers with a partner.

   1 What does Yuji Nagashima study? What does he hope to develop?
   2 How much of the toxin is enough to kill a person? What are the effects of the toxin?
   3 What treatment should a person who has eaten puffer fish poison receive?
   4 How much of the puffer fish does Chef Hayashi throw away? Which two parts does he say are poisonous?

6 Complete the information about Tom Caradonna. Then watch the whole video again and check your answers.

Tom has decided to eat [1] _____ in the famous Matsumoto restaurant in Tokyo. The restaurant is [2] _____ years old. Tom has heard stories about people [3] _____ when they eat fugu, but he is not worried. Chef Hayasahi tells Tom and Aki that everything will be [4] _____ . He shows them his fugu chef's [5] _____ . The meal that Tom and Aki eat has [6] _____ different dishes, and includes sake topped with a cooked fugu [7] _____ . During the meal, Tom laughs and says that he can still [8] _____ !

After you watch

7 **Roleplay an interview in a fugu restaurant**

Work in pairs.

Student A: A friend has invited you to eat in a fugu restaurant, but you are a little worried. Use the ideas below to prepare questions you want to ask the chef.

Student B: You are a chef in a fugu restaurant. Use the ideas below to prepare what you are going to say to a worried customer.

- chef's qualifications to prepare fugu
- how long chef has worked with fugu
- which parts are dangerous
- how much of the fish is dangerous
- what happens if you eat the poison
- what the restaurant does in an emergency

Act out the interview. Then change roles and act out the interview again. Do you want to eat fugu in this restaurant?

8 Work in groups. Discuss these questions.

   1 What traditional dishes do people like to eat in your country?
   2 Are any of these dishes dangerous or unusual?
   3 Do you think it is important to maintain the traditional dishes of a country?

---

concern (v) /kən'sɜrn/ worry
cute (adj) /kjut/ attractive
cyanide (n) /'saɪəˌnaɪd/ a type of poison
fin (n) /fɪn/ a thin triangular part of a fish's body that helps it to swim
fool (v) /ful/ make someone believe something that is not true
funeral (n) /'fjunərəl/ a ceremony for a dead person
gill (n) /gɪl/ the part of its body that a fish uses to breathe
paralyze (v) /'pærəˌlaɪz/ make something stop moving

poison (n) /'pɔɪzən/ a substance that can kill people if they eat it
poison (v) /'pɔɪzən/ kill or make a person sick with poison
puffer fish (n) /'pʌfər ˌfɪʃ/ a type of fish that can fill its body with air
regulations (n) /ˌregjə'leɪʃənz/ official controls
sake (n) /'sɑki/ Japanese rice wine
toxin (n) /'tɑksɪn/ poison
wear off (v) /'wear 'ɔf/ stop having an effect

UNIT 6 REVIEW

Grammar

1 Read the conversation between two friends who are cooking. Cross out the incorrect options.

A: Do you know how to make risotto?
B: Oh yes. I ¹ *show / will show* you if you want.
A: OK, great. Well, I think I've got everything I need. ² *Can / Must* I use this pan?
B: Yes, sure. You ³ *have to / don't have to* ask.
A: When the onion ⁴ *is / will be* ready, I add the rice.
B: Yes, then the liquid. But you ⁵ *must / have to* add it slowly. Don't add more until the rice ⁶ *absorbs / will absorb* it.
A: ⁷ *Am I allowed to / Should* I stir it all the time?
B: Yes, because if it ⁸ *sticks / will stick*, it will burn.
A: ⁹ *Should I / Do I have to* add salt?
B: You can if you want to, but you ¹⁰ *can't / don't have to*. And the risotto ¹¹ *can't / has to* rest for a while before you ¹² *eat / will eat* it.
A: ¹³ *Am I allowed to / Do I have to* taste it?
B: Of course you are. You made it!

2 Work in pairs. Check your answers from Exercise 1.

3 Work in pairs. Take turns to state an intention and start a "chain." Follow the example below. How many results can you give?

give up / start eating meat	open a restaurant
give up / start smoking	sell my car
join a gym	take a vacation

> *I think I'll go on a diet.*

> *If you go on a diet, you'll lose weight.*

> *If I lose weight, I'll have to buy new clothes.*

I CAN	
talk about obligation, prohibition, permission, and recommendation (modal verbs)	☐
talk about the future results of present and future actions (first conditional)	☐

4 Which three pairs of verbs have the same meanings?

cut down on	cut out	give up
learn	reduce	take up

5 Work in groups. Discuss the connections between these pairs of things and how people can avoid the health problems. Use the verbs from Exercise 4.

1 fatty food + heart disease
2 junk food + high blood pressure
3 living by the clock + stress
4 bad habits + tiredness

Vocabulary

6 Work in pairs. Tell your partner if you never, always, or sometimes do these things when you eat out. Explain your reasons.

make a reservation	leave a tip
have an appetizer	look at the menu
have dessert	order a drink
have an entree	pay the bill

I CAN	
describe different foods	☐
talk about healthy living and modern lifestyles	☐
order food in a restaurant	☐

Real life

7 Look at the photo and choose the correct caption (a–b).

a Sushi is a Japanese dish. It's a type of seafood dish, made with balls or squares of rice, seaweed, and raw fish.
b Ceviche is a Latin American dish. It's also a seafood dish, made by using the juice of citrus, in this case limes, to "cook" a mixture of raw fish and seafood.

8 Work in groups. Prepare descriptions of as many dishes from the list as you can.

baklava	borscht	wontons	couscous	
fondue	pad thai	gravlax	kebab	lasagna
paella	pizza	risotto	curry	tortilla

9 Compare your descriptions with other groups. Are there any dishes nobody is familiar with? Look at page 155 to find out what they are.

I CAN	
ask about and describe different dishes	☐

Speaking

10 Work in groups. Discuss the rules your parents set for meal times when you were growing up. Was/ Is it the same for all the family? Are/Will you be the same with your own children?

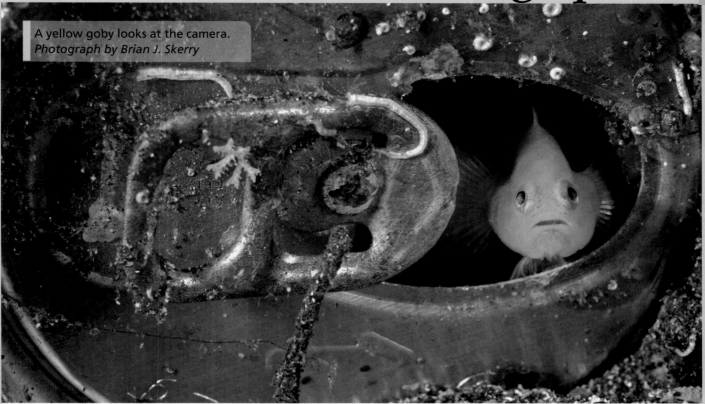

A yellow goby looks at the camera.
Photograph by Brian J. Skerry

FEATURES

1 Work in pairs. Look at the photo. Discuss the questions.

1 What can you see in the photo?
2 Where do you think this photo was taken?
3 Do you think this is the fish's natural habitat, a temporary shelter, or a permanent home?

2 Working in pairs, tell each other about your experiences with these living arrangements.

- leaving your parents' house to get some independence
- getting your own home and some privacy
- living with roommates, especially friends
- living at home with your parents

3 Work in groups. Discuss the questions.

1 Which is your favorite room at home?
2 How do different family members use different rooms?
3 Do you consider your home a private place, just for family, or do you often have friends over?

7a Homes

Vocabulary house features

1 Which of these features are important to you in your home? Why?

attic	balcony	closet
basement	fireplace	garage
garden	terrace	porch
central heating	your own room	

2 Look at the photos of four homes. Think of a question you would like to ask each homeowner. Work in pairs. Tell your partner.

Listening

3 🔊 **26** Marta Fereira is an architect and the presenter of the TV series *Home Planet*, about homes around the world. Read the questions (a–e) that viewers have sent her. Then listen and match Marta's replies (1–5) with the questions.

a Why are you so interested in traditional house design?   *1*
b We live in a new house that my dad calls a box. What do you think of the design of modern houses?
c What kind of factors influence house design?
d You mentioned shelters in your last show. What's the difference between a shelter and a house?
e How would you classify a Mongolian ger?

A ger belonging to Tuvan nomads in western Mongc
Photograph by David Edwards

The remains of homes carved into rock in Cappadocia, Turkey
Photograph by Joe Petersburger

A wooden house on stilts after floods in the Mekong River in southern Cambodia.
Photograph by Michael S. Yamashita

Modern terraced houses in Sabah, Borr
Photograph by Frans Lanting

4 **26** Listen again and complete the sentences.

1   Traditional designs are much better in _____ conditions.
2   A shelter is _____ than a permanent home.
3   You can put up a _____ quickly.
4   A ger isn't as solid as a _____ house.
5   A ger is easier to take down than a _____ .
6   The colder the climate, the warmer _____ needs to be.
7   Modern homes aren't necessarily the best _____ for every situation.
8   Modern homes in _____ are getting smaller and smaller.

Grammar **comparatives and superlatives**

5   Look at the sentences in Exercise 4. Underline:

1   the expression that describes a process of change.
2   the expression that explains how two things change in relation to each other.
3   the comparative and superlative forms of *good*.

▶ COMPARATIVES and SUPERLATIVES		
	short adjective/adverb *warm/easy/fast*	**long adjective/adverb** *expensive/efficiently*
comparative	*warmer/easier/faster* **(than)**	*more expensive/efficiently* **(than)**
–	*less warm/easy/fast* **(than)**	*less expensive/efficiently* **(than)**
–	*not as warm/easy/fast as*	*not as expensive/efficiently as*
=	*as warm/easy/fast as*	*as expensive/efficiently as*
superlative	*the warmest/easiest/ fastest*	*the most expensive/efficiently*
For more information and practice, see page 164.		

6   Look at the grammar box. What are the rules for the comparative and superlative forms of:

1   adjectives or adverbs with one syllable?
2   adjectives ending in -*y*?

7   Rewrite the sentences using the word(s) in parentheses so that the meaning is the same. Begin with the words in bold.

1   **Houses** aren't as appropriate for local conditions. (less)
2   **A cave house** is bigger than you think. (not as small)
3   **An igloo** is less cold inside than you might think. (not as cold)
4   The price of **new houses** goes up every year. (more and more expensive)
5   **My tent** is better than all the others in camp. (the best)
6   There are no houses as old as **this house**. (oldest)
7   **A house** on stilts survives better in floods. (easily)
8   A brick house is slower to put up than a ger. (**you can** / quickly)

Listening and speaking

8 **27** Listen to four people talking about where they live. Write the number of the speaker (1–4) next to the topics.

cleanliness	noise
housework	price
maintenance	size
neighbors	space

9   Pronunciation **as...as**

a **28** Listen to the word *as* in these sentences from Exercise 8. Is it strong or weak? Repeat the sentences.

1   We don't have **as** much money **as** people who are working.
2   I can't keep the place **as** clean **as** I'd like to because I have a full-time job.

b   Practice these sentences. Which speaker from Exercise 8 do you think says each sentence?

a   It's not as noisy as an apartment.
b   It isn't as expensive as a house.
c   It's as simple as it could be!
d   It's as clean as I can get it.
e   Apartments aren't as quiet as houses.
f   There aren't as many residents as there are in an apartment complex.

10   Work in groups of four. Use the ideas in Exercise 8 and discuss whether a house or an apartment is better for these people. Tell the class and give your reasons.

a group of students
a retired couple
a single person
a young family
a young married couple
an elderly person living alone

11   What about the people in your group? Which is better for you, a house or an apartment?

We've got two dogs, so for us a house is much better.

7b Before New York

Vocabulary in the city

1 Work in pairs. What kind of a place is New York? Try to describe New York in three words.

2 Complete the sentences with some of these words. Which sentences do you think are true of New York?

> atmosphere built-up crime financial modern
> neighborhoods open spaces polluted public transportation
> residents run-down skyscrapers traffic

1 The _____ is exciting and cosmopolitan.
2 There's an extensive _____ _____ system to get you from A to B.
3 It has an important business and _____ district.
4 Most of the buildings are very _____ .
5 It's one of the most _____ places you can live, with few open spaces.
6 The views from the _____ are spectacular, especially at night.
7 There's lots to do, both for tourists and _____ .
8 Some _____ are more dangerous than others.

3 Write sentences about places you know with the other words from Exercise 2.

Reading

4 Work in pairs. Discuss the questions. Then read the article *Before New York* and check your ideas.

1 What do you think New York was like before it became the city it is today?
2 What kind of people do you think lived there?
3 What kind of landscapes do you think you could see?

5 Read the article again. Answer the questions in your own words.

1 What's the connection between Eric Sanderson and the images accompanying the article?
2 What did Eric Sanderson aim to do with his project?
3 Why do you think the 2007 appearance of the beaver was symbolic to Sanderson?

Before New York

BY PETER MILLER

Of all the visitors to New York City in recent years, one of the most surprising was a beaver that showed up one morning in 2007. Although beavers used to be common in the area in the 17th century, there haven't been any for more than 200 years, says ecologist Eric Sanderson.

For Sanderson, the beaver's appearance was symbolic. For ten years, he's been leading a project to visualize what the New York area used to look like before the city transformed it. As Sanderson says, "There are views in this city where you cannot see, except for a person, another living thing. Not a tree or a plant. How did it get like that?"

In fact, long before the skyscrapers came to dominate the view, this place was a pristine wilderness where animals like beavers, bears, and turkeys would roam freely through forests, marshes, and grassland. Its ecology was as diverse as Yellowstone or Yosemite today. There used to be sandy beaches along the coasts and 56 miles of freshwater streams.

Sanderson's project has resulted in a 3-D computer model that lets you pick any spot in modern New York and see what used to be there. Take Fifth Avenue, for example. A family called Murray used to have a farm there, and in 1782, during the American Revolution, the British troops landed near it. Legend has it that Mrs. Murray offered the British officers tea while George Washington's troops slipped past them, down what is now Broadway. "I'd like every New Yorker to know that they live in a place with amazing natural potential—even if you have to look a little harder to see it," says Sanderson.

> **pristine** (adj) /ˈprɪstin/ pure, like new

Grammar *used to, would,* and the simple past

6 Look at the article and underline the sentences with *used to* and *would*. Do they refer to past habits and states or to single actions in the past?

7 Now find at least three examples of single actions in the past. What is the verb form?

> ▶ **USED TO and WOULD**
>
> **used to**
> 1 *Beavers, bears, and turkeys used to roam freely.*
> 2 *The Murray family used to have a farm here.*
> 3 *There didn't use to be any skyscrapers.*
> 4 *What did New York use to look like?*
>
> **would**
> *Beavers, bears, and turkeys would roam freely.*
>
> For more information and practice, see page 165.

8 Look at the grammar box and match the sentences with *used to* (1–4) with their uses (a–b). Which is the only use of *would*?

  a past states
  b past habits (repeated actions)

Computer Generated Image (top) by Markley Boyer
Photograph by Robert Clark

9 Rewrite the sentences using *used to* where possible.

  1 New York was a lot greener than it is now.
  2 There was a lot of forest and natural landscapes.
  3 The early residents didn't live in a large city.
  4 People hunted beavers for their skins.
  5 American troops fought a battle here.
  6 What was originally in the area where Fifth Avenue is now?

10 Complete the text with the simple past, *used to,* or *would* form of the verbs. In some cases, you can use more than one form.

I remember when I first ¹ _____ (move) to New York from California with my parents. I ² _____ (stand) in the street and stare up at the skyscrapers. They ³ _____ (be) taller than anything I'd ever seen. The streets ⁴ _____ (be) much busier than back in California and I ⁵ _____ (run) across from one side to the other holding my mother's hand. For the first few months, we ⁶ _____ (not /go) further than four blocks from home. My parents ⁷ _____ (not /own) a car in those days, so on Sunday mornings we ⁸ _____ (take) the subway to Central Park. We ⁹ _____ (have) breakfast at a great deli and then we ¹⁰ _____ (go) skating in the park. This ¹¹ _____ (be) all about twenty years ago. The city ¹² _____ (be) a lot more polluted and chaotic then. Nowadays, it's much more people-friendly.

11 Complete the sentences with the simple past, *used to,* or *would* so that they are true about you. Then work in pairs. Compare your sentences and ask follow-up questions about three of the sentences.

  1 Before I worked / studied here, I _____ .
  2 When I was in elementary school, I _____ .
  3 Before we moved here, my family _____ .
  4 I remember my first vacation. I _____ .
  5 Whenever I had a test at school, I _____ .
  6 In my family, on weekends we _____ .
  7 The first time I left home, _____ .
  8 As a child, I _____ .

Speaking

12 Is your town (or village or city) better now than it was in the past? Make notes for *then* and *now*. Then write at least six sentences.

13 Work in pairs. Compare your sentences. Are your views similar?

7c Sweet songs & strong coffee

Reading

1 Look at the information about Puerto Rico and complete the paragraph.

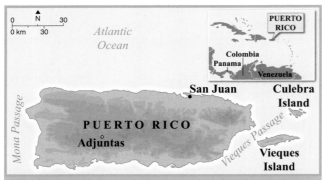

Adjuntas: population 4,980
Number of cinemas: 0
Number of stone benches in the town square: 65
Rank in the list of 20 top coffee-producing zones in
  Puerto Rico: 2nd

Puerto Rico, in the ¹ _____ , is made up of several ² _____ . The largest of these, also called Puerto Rico, is known as *Borinquen* from its indigenous *Taíno* name. The capital ³ _____ is San Juan. The official ⁴ _____ are Spanish, which gives it a third name, *La Isla del Encanto* (the Island of Enchantment), and English.

2 Read the article about Adjuntas on page 87 quickly. What is the article mainly about? Choose the correct option (a–c).

  a daily life and work
  b festivals and holidays
  c people and traditions

3 The author says about Adjuntas that "a deep love of the land and its customs runs through this place" (paragraph 1). Look at these examples (a–d) of this. Which paragraphs give this information?

  a Everyone takes part in tree-planting in the national park.
  b Local people acted against a plan to mine the local mountains.
  c Local singers still sing in traditional styles from centuries ago.
  d People show respect for the older generations in the community.

4 Read the article again. What does the author say about these things?

  1 the horses   3 Lala Echevarria's home
  2 the town square 4 Lauro Yepez's shop

5 Work in pairs. Find these expressions in the article. What do you think they mean?

  1 a coffee town (paragraph 1)
  2 good manners (paragraph 1)
  3 running water (paragraph 4)
  4 the love of her life (paragraph 4)
  5 ancestral islands (paragraph 5)
  6 to swap stories (paragraph 5)
  7 word spread fast (paragraph 5)
  8 a forgotten art (paragraph 5)

6 Have you ever been to a place where people still keep up old customs and traditions? Tell your partner about the place.

Critical thinking descriptions

7 Read three of the key features of descriptions. Then find an example of each one in the article.

  1 A description gives an account of what something is like.
  2 A description is factually accurate.
  3 The details of a description give the reader a clear picture of the subject

8 Work in pairs. Compare your examples from Exercise 7. Do you agree with each other's choices?

> **▶ WORDBUILDING verb → adjective**
> We can make adjectives from verbs by adding *-ing*.
> *surround + -ing → surrounding streets*
> *run + n + -ing → running water*

Speaking and writing

9 Work in pairs. Do you think Adjuntas is a good place for a vacation or to live? Tell your partner and give reasons using information from the article.

10 Imagine you are in Adjuntas. Write a postcard and send it to someone in your class.

By Linda Gómez

SWEET SONGS
& STRONG COFFEE

There's a dreamy atmosphere to Adjuntas, a coffee town in the Valley of the Sleeping Giant high in the mountains of Puerto Rico. A deep love of the land and its customs runs through this place, where people say their families have lived "since forever" and formal good manners rule daily life. You smell it in the surrounding streets, where food is cooked at roadside barbecues. You see it in the graceful horses paraded through town on holidays, and you feel it in the large, elegant square, with its fountains and stone benches.

Several decades ago, this love of the land motivated the local people to oppose a massive mining operation. The mountains surrounding Adjuntas are rich with gold, silver, copper, and zinc and the Puerto Rican government had reserved about 30 square miles for mineral exploitation.

People fought to protect the land despite the promise of jobs and money. They were saved by growing coffee and selling it throughout Puerto Rico. The profits helped the group persuade the government to transform the mining zone into a national park, El Bosque del Pueblo, which is now protected by law. Opened in 1998, the park runs a reforestation program allowing young and old to plant trees where land has been excavated. "Learning to manage the forest has been a kind of reincarnation for us," said Tinti Deya, a local resident. "We're like children doing everything for the first time, except in our case we're grandmothers."

Grandmothers are everywhere in Adjuntas and they're all respectfully addressed as Doña. Lala Echevarria, an 85-year-old great-great-grandmother, was born on the oldest street in town, where she still lives in a small, immaculate home. She grew up before electricity and running water, and remembers when the first car arrived in Adjuntas. "As a child, I used to spend all my time carrying water, finding firewood, looking after the chickens and the cows," she said. "There were sixteen of us. We would wash our clothes in the river and we used to cook on an open fire. At meal times, we kids would sit on the floor to eat." Doña Lala was working as a maid when she met and married the love of her life, Mariano the mechanic. They had thirteen children and shared 44 years before he died in 1983. She shows me the dozens of photographs of four generations of descendants that now fill her tiny home.

Traditions in Adjuntas go back centuries to the mountains of ancestral islands such as Mallorca, Tenerife, and Corsica. People play the old songs in the countryside and in little shops, like Lauro Yepez's place, where men meet to swap stories and have a drink. When I was there, troubadour Tato Ramos appeared and began to sing in a centuries-old flamenco style. Word spread fast. The shop filled with working-class men clapping, tapping, and nodding to the music. Ramos improvised songs about growing coffee, welcoming visitors, and ignoring parental advice, all topics requested by shop customers. "This is a forgotten art," said Yepez. "People give him a topic and he composes the song, in proper rhyme, on the spot."

Later, I played the recording I'd made for my 88-year-old Spanish father. His dark brown eyes twinkled with recognition. He nodded his head, smiled, and said, "Oh yes, this I remember, this I remember..."

firewood (n) /ˈfaɪərˌwʊd/ wood that is used as fuel
troubadour (n) /ˈtruːbəˌdɔr/ a traveling singer or songwriter

Real life expressing preferences and giving reasons

1 Work in pairs. Write a checklist of things to keep in mind when you are looking for somewhere to live.

2 🔊 **29** Listen to a conversation at a realtor's office. Does the woman mention the things on your checklist? What six things does she specify?

3 🔊 **29** Look at the expressions for expressing preferences. Listen to the conversation again and complete them.

> **▶ EXPRESSING PREFERENCES**
>
> I think **I'd rather** _____ than _____ , for now anyway.
> **I'd prefer** _____ _____ , but not too _____ .
> So, two bedrooms, and **preferably** with _____ _____ .
> **Would you rather** _____ places **or** _____ ones?
> To be honest, **I prefer** _____ to _____ .
> I have to say **I prefer living** _____ .
> I don't have a car. **I prefer to** _____ or _____ .

4 Work in pairs. Can you remember the reasons for the speakers' preferences? Compare your ideas. Then check the audioscript on page 178.

5 Pronunciation **rising and falling intonation**

a 🔊 **30** Listen and notice how the intonation rises then falls in this question.

Would you rather live in a town or a village?

b 🔊 **31** Listen and repeat these questions.

1 Do you prefer playing soccer or basketball?
2 Would you rather have tea or coffee?
3 Do you prefer summer or winter?
4 Would you rather go by car or by bike?
5 Do you prefer English or French?
6 Would you rather eat fish or meat?

c Work in pairs. Add at least six more pairs of items to the pairs in Exercise 5b. Take turns asking and answering about your preferences.

6 Work in groups of three. Where would you rather live? Ask and answer questions using these ideas. Explain your reasons. What do your choices say about the kind of person you are?

> In a new house or in an old one?
> In a city or a small town?
> In a downtown or in the suburbs?
> On the coast or in the mountains?
> In a historic area or in a new development?

7e Let's move to …

Writing a description of a place

1 Read the text. Where do you think it's from? Choose one of the options (a–c).

  a a personal blog
  b a realtor's website
  c a tourist information website

2 Read the text. How does the writer describe these things?

streets and buildings	stores	facilities
local residents	atmosphere	

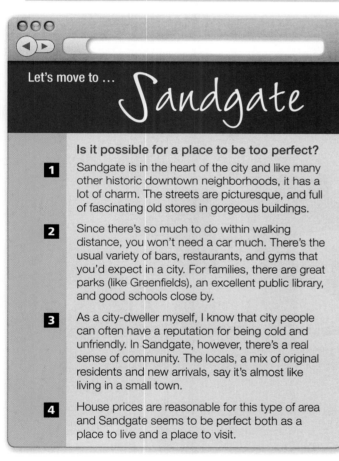

Let's move to … Sandgate

Is it possible for a place to be too perfect?

1 Sandgate is in the heart of the city and like many other historic downtown neighborhoods, it has a lot of charm. The streets are picturesque, and full of fascinating old stores in gorgeous buildings.

2 Since there's so much to do within walking distance, you won't need a car much. There's the usual variety of bars, restaurants, and gyms that you'd expect in a city. For families, there are great parks (like Greenfields), an excellent public library, and good schools close by.

3 As a city-dweller myself, I know that city people can often have a reputation for being cold and unfriendly. In Sandgate, however, there's a real sense of community. The locals, a mix of original residents and new arrivals, say it's almost like living in a small town.

4 House prices are reasonable for this type of area and Sandgate seems to be perfect both as a place to live and a place to visit.

3 Writing skill organizing ideas

a Read the text again. Write the number of the paragraph (2–4) next to the heading. There is one extra heading.

  a What kind of place is Sandgate?
  b Overall opinion?
  c What kind of people live there?
  d What is there to do there?

b Where is the best place in the text to include a paragraph with the extra heading from Exercise 3a?

Word focus *as* and *like*

4 Look at these two extracts from the text. Choose the correct option. Then find two more examples of *as* and *like* with the same meanings.

  1 …and like many other historic downtown neighborhoods, it has…
     It is similar to / It is many historic downtown neighborhoods.

  2 As a city-dweller myself, I know…
     I am similar to / I am a city dweller.

5 Find two other examples of *as* and *like* in the text. Match them with these meanings.

  1 because
  2 for example

6 Complete the sentences with *as* and *like*.

  1 _____ a life-long resident of my town, I take pride in our community.
  2 I love little parks _____ this.
  3 It's ideal _____ a vacation destination.
  4 Our public library is _____ a palace.
  5 _____ all good cafés, the one in my town has a great atmosphere.
  6 My studio, _____ yours, is small.

7 You are going to write a description of your own neighborhood. Take notes using the headings in Exercise 3a. Use these words or your own ideas.

a good range	a little limited	chaotic
close to…	easy access to…	elegant
excellent	modern	unfriendly
welcoming		

8 Decide on the order of the paragraphs in your description. Then write about 150–200 words.

9 Use these questions to check your description.

  • Are your ideas clearly organized into paragraphs?
  • Have you used *as* or *like* correctly?
  • Does your description give the reader a clear picture of your neighborhood?

10 Read a description a classmate has written about their neighborhood. Would you like to move there?

A special kind of neighborhood

The Mission is a successful neighborhood where new immigrants are welcome.

Before you watch

1 The Mission District is in San Francisco. Work in groups. Look at the photo and discuss the questions.

    1 What do you know about San Francisco?

    2 What does the caption tell us about the Mission District?

2 Write down at least five activities you think you will see people doing in the video.

While you watch

3 Check your answers from Exercise 2. What activities weren't on your list?

4 Complete the summary with these words.

mainly	began	immigrants
built	main	neighborhood

The ¹_____ church in the Mission District was ²_____ by the Spanish in 1791. Now the ³_____ is a central part of San Francisco because it is where the city ⁴_____ . Over the years, ⁵_____ have come here from Ireland, Germany, and Italy. In recent years they have come ⁶_____ from Mexico, and from Central and South America.

5 Watch the three sections of the video and answer the questions.

Music (01:10 to 02:12)

1 Who is Juan Pedro Gaffney?

2 How has his group helped people in Central America in the past?

Art (02:15 to 03:53)

3 What theme did Ray Patlan's work have in 1984?

4 What two things are the artists here fighting for?

Tradition (03:54 to 04:42)

5 Which church is Father Dan McGuire leader of?

6 What does he think immigrants bring to the area?

6 Match the sentence beginnings (1–6) with the endings (a–f).

    1 It's easy to see the style that

    2 The music of the Mission

    3 What happens is the murals

    4 It's great. It's like

    5 People see that they're

    6 The beauty of this particular parish is that

    a begin to reflect the community itself.

    b the different countries of Latin America come together here.

    c these recent additions give to the neighborhood.

    d not so different from each other.

    e deeply affects everyone.

    f coming home to a piece of art every day.

After you watch

7 **Roleplay interviewing a resident of the Mission District**

Work in pairs.

Student A: You are a journalist working for the local newspaper. You are going to interview a resident of the Mission District. Use the ideas below to prepare questions.

Student B: You have lived in the Mission District for a long time. Your parents were immigrants from Mexico. Use the ideas below to prepare what you are going to say to the journalist.

- where the resident's family originally came from
- the community
- the changes that have taken place over the years
- what's special about the area
- family life

Act out the interview. Then change roles and act out the interview again.

8 Work in groups. Discuss these questions.

    1 Which country would you choose to emigrate to? Why?

    2 What would you miss about your home country?

    3 Do you think most people emigrate because they want to, or because they have to?

---

bind (v) /baɪnd/ join closely
choir (n) /kwaɪər/ a group of singers
fairness (n) /ˈfeərnɪs/ justice, what is right
fit into (v) /ˈfɪt ˈɪntu/ adapt to
grow up (v) /ˈgroʊ ˈʌp/ become an adult
integrate (v) /ˈɪntəˌgreɪt/ become part of a community
jumping (adj) /ˈʤʌmpɪŋ/ (slang) very exciting

mural (n) /ˈmjʊrəl/ a painting on a wall
parish (n) /ˈpærɪʃ/ the area that a church serves
perform (v) /pərˈfɔrm/ put on a public show
powerful (adj) /ˈpaʊərfəl/ strong
raise (money) (v) /reɪz/ collect (money)
reflect (v) /rɪˈflekt/ show
vibrant (adj) /ˈvaɪbrənt/ full of energy

UNIT 7 REVIEW

Grammar

1 Work in pairs. Look at this photo taken in San Diego. What does it show?

2 Complete these comments about the photo with the comparative or superlative form of the adjective or adverb given. Use one, two, or three words.

1 "That's _____ thing I've ever seen!" (crazy)
2 "He has to hit the ball _____ than on a normal green." (carefully)
3 "The target isn't _____ you think." (far)
4 "It's actually _____ than it looks." (hard)
5 "Maybe he hits _____ from up there." (well)
6 "He can practice _____ he wants to." (often)
7 "He's _____ player in his club." (dedicated)
8 "He's getting _____ and _____ to the edge!" (close)

3 Complete the text with the simple past, *used to,* or *would* form of the verbs. In some cases, you can use more than one form.

| be | be | be | complain | live |
| make | not mind | not pay | play | |

When I ¹ _____ a kid we ² _____ soccer in the parking lot. I ³ _____ in an apartment complex and during the day the parking lot ⁴ _____ almost empty. There ⁵ _____ a sign "no ball games," but we ⁶ _____ any attention to it. Our parents ⁷ _____ but one neighbor sometimes ⁸ _____ about the noise we ⁹ _____ .

I CAN	
compare things and describe a process of change (comparative adjectives and adverbs, *as... as...*)	
describe how something stands out from the rest using superlative adjectives and adverbs	
talk about past states and past habits (*used to, would*)	

Vocabulary

4 Work in pairs. Which is the odd one out in each group? Why?

1 attic, basement, central heating
2 run-down, skyscrapers, traffic
3 balcony, fireplace, porch
4 built-up, polluted, residents
5 closet, garden, terrace

5 Work in groups. Discuss the questions.

1 What three things do you like and dislike about where you live?
2 Where did you use to live as a child? What was it like?

I CAN	
describe homes and their features	
talk about cities	
talk about places to live	

Real life

6 Choose the correct option. Then match the two parts of the exchanges.

1 A: *I'd rather / I prefer* to live on my own.
2 A: Where would you rather *go / to go*?
3 A: *I'd rather / I prefer* the country to the coast.
4 A: I prefer *living / live* near my family.
5 A: *I'd rather / I prefer* see a few more places first.
6 A: *I'd rather / I'd prefer* a bigger kitchen.

a B: What's wrong with this apartment?
b B: Are you looking for a roommate?
c B: I can show you a fantastic beach house.
d B: This apartment is nice. Are you going to take it?
e B: I don't feel like living downtown.
f B: Are you going to live near your work?

7 Work in groups. Say why you prefer each option. Give reasons for your answers.

fruit or cake	jazz or pop
mornings or evenings	rice or pasta
snow or sun	spring or fall

I CAN	
ask about preferences	
state preferences and give reasons	

Speaking

8 You are a realtor with an important house to sell: your own. Make notes about how you will describe your home's best features. Decide on a price. Then try to sell your home to one of your classmates.

Unit 8 Weird news

A flock of flamingos in the Gulf of Mexico
Photograph by Robert B. Haas

FEATURES

1 Work in pairs. Look at the photo. What is unusual about it? Do you think it is real or fake? Why?

2 Read the comments on the photo. What or who do the words in bold refer to?

1 If you look closely you can make **them** out.
2 **That**'s too much of a coincidence.
3 I've seen **this kind of thing** before.
4 I think **it**'s genuine.
5 You can see where **he** has added more flamingos.
6 Look at **the ones** at the top.

3 Work in groups. Have you ever been tricked by anything fake? How can you tell if these things are fake or genuine?

jewelry money paintings passports watches

8a Nature's mysteries

Vocabulary and listening the natural world

1 Work in pairs. You are going to listen to some audio clips from a website about mysteries in nature. Look at the photos from the website. Discuss them with your partner.

> *It looks like / reminds me of (a)…*

2 Work in pairs. You will hear these words in the audio clips. Complete the sentences with them.

ants	atmosphere	beetles	butterflies	flies
insects	nitrogen	oxygen	particles	predators
radiation	species	spikes	stem	

1 _____ and _____ are gases in the _____ .
2 Both _____ and _____ are flying _____ .
3 _____ is the name for energy in the form of rays or waves.
4 _____ and _____ live on the ground and in the soil.
5 Leaves and flowers grow from a plant's _____ .
6 _____ are tiny pieces of material.
7 _____ catch and eat other _____ .
8 Some plants have long, sharp _____ , like needles.

3 🔊 **32** Listen to the audio clips. Write the number of the clip (1–3) next to the words in Exercise 2.

4 🔊 **32** Listen to the clips again. Are the sentences true (T) or false (F)?

1 The colors are man-made lights.
2 The color of the lights depends on oxygen and nitrogen.
3 The orange ball is a butterfly egg.
4 One image uses a technique called macro photography.
5 Some plants can chase insects.
6 The Australian sundew plant traps flies on its sticky spikes.

5 What can you remember? Test each other.

1 What are the lights in the sky?
2 Why might butterflies lay eggs in places like this?
3 How do some plants catch animals?

Grammar modal verbs (2)

6 Match these sentences (1–4) with their uses (a–d).

1 The colors are so vivid that you think they can't be natural.
2 You imagine that they must be man-made.
3 This might be a painting or a work of art.
4 It may not seem logical, but there are indeed plants that catch insects.

a The speaker is certain something is true.
b The speaker is certain something is false.
c The speaker thinks it's possible something is true.
d The speaker thinks it's possible something is false.

> **SPECULATION AND DEDUCTION ABOUT THE PRESENT**

must	
might (not) / may (not) / could	+ base form
can't	+ be + -ing

| For more information and practice, see page 166. |

7 Look at the grammar box. Underline the modal verbs in the audioscript on page 178.

8 Read the text *Navigation in nature*. Cross out any options that are not possible.

Word focus *look*

9 Match the two parts of these sentences. Check your answers in the audioscript on page 178. Underline another expression with *look* that means the same as item 1.

1 The sky looks as though	a carefully.
2 The sky looks	b water.
3 The shiny drops look like	c it's on fire.
4 Look	d green.

10 Complete the sentences with an expression with *look* from Exercise 9.

1 You _____ great! Are you going somewhere special?
2 Mohamed _____ a model in that fine suit.
3 Joe _____ he hasn't slept all night.
4 You _____ angry! What's the matter?
5 You _____ you've had some good news.
6 I'll need to _____ closely at this contract.

Speaking

11 Work in two pairs within a group of four. You are photo editors at a magazine. You can't find the correct captions for your photos. Describe your photos to the other pair and find the correct caption.

Pair A: Turn to page 153. Look at the photos and captions.

Pair B: Turn to page 154. Look at the photos and captions.

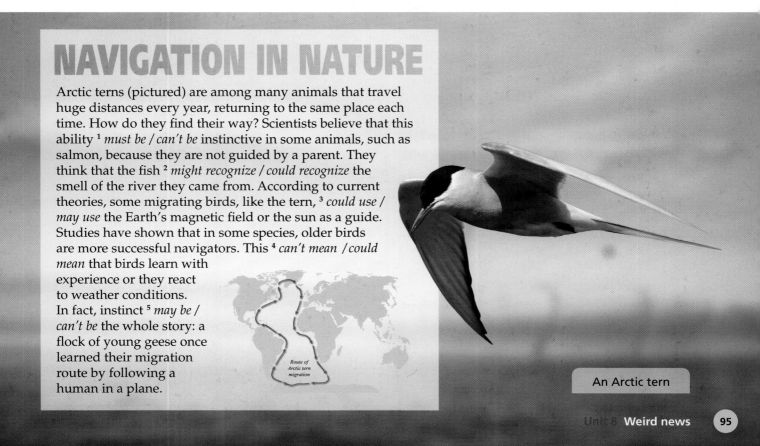

NAVIGATION IN NATURE

Arctic terns (pictured) are among many animals that travel huge distances every year, returning to the same place each time. How do they find their way? Scientists believe that this ability [1] *must be / can't be* instinctive in some animals, such as salmon, because they are not guided by a parent. They think that the fish [2] *might recognize / could recognize* the smell of the river they came from. According to current theories, some migrating birds, like the tern, [3] *could use / may use* the Earth's magnetic field or the sun as a guide. Studies have shown that in some species, older birds are more successful navigators. This [4] *can't mean / could mean* that birds learn with experience or they react to weather conditions. In fact, instinct [5] *may be / can't be* the whole story: a flock of young geese once learned their migration route by following a human in a plane.

Route of Arctic tern migration

An Arctic tern

8b Desert art

Vocabulary history

1 Are you interested in history? Complete the questions with some of these words. Then work in pairs asking and answering the questions.

> ancient belief century period prehistoric
> sacred society tradition

1 Do you enjoy visiting _____ monuments?
2 Which historical _____ interests you?
3 What do _____ cave drawings often show?
4 What do you think were the key historic events of the 20th _____ ?
5 Are there any historical sites with religious or _____ significance in your country?
6 Do you think we can learn from studying how _____ lived in the past?

Listening and reading

2 🔊 **33** Have you heard of the Nazca lines? Work in pairs. Try to answer the questions. Then listen to part of a radio show. Check your answers.

1 What are they?   5 How many are there?
2 Where are they?   6 How old are they?
3 How big are they?   7 How are they made?
4 What do they show?

> *I've never heard of them. But from the photo, they look as if they're drawings of something.*

> *I think they might be in South America, but I'm not exactly sure.*

3 Did any of the information surprise you? Is there any additional information you would like to know about the Nazca lines? Write two or three questions.

4 Read the article *Desert Art* and answer the questions. Does the article answer your questions from Exercise 3?

1 When did people discover the Nazca lines?
2 What ideas did people have about their purpose?
3 Why was water important to Nazca society?
4 What is the current theory about the significance of the lines?

5 Why do you think people are so fascinated by the Nazca lines?

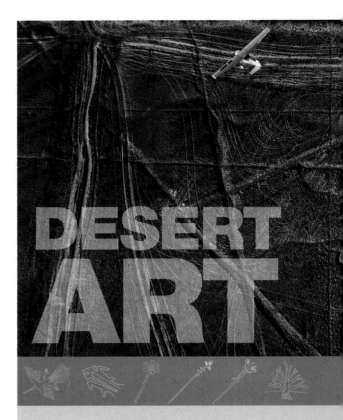

DESERT ART

The mysterious desert drawings known as the Nazca lines have puzzled people since they first become widely known in the late 1920s. Before air travel in Peru began, it was impossible to get a clear view of the giant drawings of the spider, monkey, and hummingbird. Yet the Nazca people who made these patterns 2,000 years ago couldn't have seen them from above.

One of the first formal studies of the lines was by Maria Reiche. She spent half a century working for their conservation and was convinced that the lines must have been part of an astronomical calendar. Other people thought they might have been ancient Inca roads or irrigation systems. The weirdest idea was that they could have been landing strips for alien spacecraft!

ceremonial (adj) /ˌserə'məʊniəl/ ritual and traditional
phenomenon (n) /fə'nɒmə,nɑn/ an unusual event or fact

▶ **WORDBUILDING noun → adjective**

We can make adjectives from nouns by changing the endings of the nouns.
mystery + *-ous* → *mysterious*
religion + *-ous* → *religious*
astronomy + *-ical* → *astronomical*
ceremony + *-al* → *ceremonial*

Spider
Photograph by Robert Clark

This region of Peru is one of the driest places on Earth and yet successful societies, including the Nazca, lived here. Water must have had an incredible significance to these societies, so perhaps the lines were related to it. We know that the Nazca River, which comes down from the nearby mountains, runs underground for about nine miles before suddenly resurfacing. This must have seemed an astonishing, even sacred, phenomenon to ancient societies. It has also become clear that there are other huge drawings in the area, not just the ones in the desert. Many are much older than the Nazca figures, so the same group of people can't have created them. It now seems that the Nazca lines may have been part of a long tradition of ceremonial activities connected to water and religious beliefs.

Grammar modal verbs (3)

6 Look at the grammar box. Find and number eight sentences with these forms in the article.

▶ SPECULATION AND DEDUCTION ABOUT THE PAST		
must		
might / may / could	*have*	+ past participle
can't / couldn't		
For more information and practice, see page 166.		

7 Answer the questions about the sentences (1–8) in the article.

1 Which sentences speculate about things that were possible?
2 Which sentences express certainty about the explanations they give?
3 Which sentences make a deduction based on logical information?

8 Rewrite the sentences about the Nazca using one of the words in parentheses. Check your answers with your instructor.

1 We know water wasn't easy to find. (*can't / must*)
2 It's possible the rivers dried up. (*might / may not*)
3 There's no doubt the lines were very important. (*could / must*)
4 Perhaps the lines had a religious significance. (*may / can't*)
5 It isn't logical that the animal drawings were roads. (*might / couldn't*)
6 Obviously the animals lived in the region. (*might / must*)
7 One possibility is that the Nazca people used simple tools. (*could / must*)
8 It seems clear that people maintained the lines carefully. (*might / must*)

Speaking

9 Work in pairs. Why do you think the Nazca lines were created? What do you know about these other mysterious sites?

The Sphinx	The Bermuda Triangle
Stonehenge	Petra
Rapa Nui	The Great Wall
Jamestown	

10 Work in groups. Look at the list of things archaeologists have found that date from around 2,000 years ago—the same period as Nazca society. What do they say about how people lived then?

a leather sandal
a circle of 6-foot granite "standing stones"
fragments of pottery with iron-based painted patterns
a metal pot containing cream with a fingerprint visible
pits dug in the ground, full of apricot and plum seeds
a bronze mirror in a grave
pots in the ground containing hundreds of coins
animal bones

11 Tell the class your ideas. Which ideas are the most interesting?

8c Lost and found?

Reading

1 Work in pairs. The disappearance of Amelia Earhart is one of aviation's greatest unsolved mysteries. Read the first article, *Where is Amelia Earhart? Three Theories*, on page 99. Find out what people think happened to her. Compare your answers.

2 Read the second article on page 99 quickly. Answer the questions.

1 Which of the three theories is the main article concerned with?
2 Which modern scientific technique might hold the key to the Earhart mystery?
3 If the project is successful, what will it prove?

3 Read the second article again. Answer the questions.

1 What is Justin Long's connection to the project?
2 Why can't the study use a sample of Earhart's hair?
3 What is the biggest problem facing the researchers on the new project?

4 Find these words in the articles. Look at how the words are used and try to guess their meaning. Then replace the words in bold in the sentences with these words.

log	profile	funding	reveal
archive	assumption	ensure	identical

1 The Science Council is **paying for** a study of wildlife in our area.
2 The tests **show** that the bones are human.
3 The museum has a huge **collection of documents** on the early days of flight.
4 We need to **make certain** that our results are correct.
5 The investigation is based on the **theory** that the sample is big enough.
6 Detectives often create a **description** of a suspected criminal.
7 These two samples are **exactly the same**.
8 The visitor **register** recorded twenty visitors yesterday.

5 Work in pairs. Complete the summary.

The new project aims to provide a way of testing ¹ _____ . The success of the project depends on several things. First, that the bone is from a ² _____ , not a turtle. Second, that Earhart's saliva still exists on ³ _____ . And third, that there is enough saliva to ⁴ _____ .

Critical thinking opinion or fact?

6 Read the definitions of *opinions* and *facts*. Then decide if the sentences from the articles are opinion (O) or fact (F).

Opinions are what people believe to be true. They can be a personal point of view or something that many people think.

Facts are items of information that we can check to prove or disprove.

1 Amelia Earhart […] was attempting a round-the-world flight in 1937.
2 Earhart could have landed on a different island.
3 According to Justin Long, Earhart's letters are the only items that are both verifiably hers and that might contain her DNA.
4 A 2009 study revealed that the sample [of hair] was actually thread.
5 Some scientists have suggested the Nikumaroro bone fragment isn't human at all.
6 About 99 percent of the nuclear genome is identical among all humans.

7 Find another fact and another opinion in the second article.

Speaking

8 Work in groups. Discuss your answers to the questions.

1 Why do you think Justin Long is involved in the project?
2 The bone fragment "might have been from one of Earhart's fingers." What other possibilities exist?
3 Is it certain that any saliva on the envelopes is Earhart's? Why?
4 Do you think the project will be successful? Why?

> In my opinion, Justin Long is involved because his grandparents were interested in Amelia Earhart.

Where is *Amelia Earhart?*

Three Theories

By Ker Than for National Geographic News

Amelia Earhart, the first woman to fly solo across the Atlantic Ocean, was attempting a round-the-world flight in 1937. She planned to land on the tiny Pacific Ocean island of Howland just north of the equator. She never arrived. Her fate, and that of her navigator Fred Noonan, remains one of aviation's greatest unsolved mysteries. Researchers have spent millions of dollars investigating the case and several books have been published that examined different theories.

The official US position is that Earhart ran out of fuel and crashed in the Pacific Ocean. The radio log from a US Coast Guard ship indicates that she must have been near Howland when contact was lost.

Another theory says that Earhart could have crashed on a different island, called Nikumaroro, and subsequently died since the island is uninhabited.

Yet another theory claims she was captured while on a secret mission to the Japanese-controlled Marshall Islands in the North Pacific and eventually returned to the US with a new identity.

Lost and found?
The missing pilot

February 18, 2011

Amelia Earhart's dried saliva could help solve the longstanding mystery of the aviator's 1937 disappearance, according to scientists who plan to take samples of her DNA from her correspondence. A new project aims to create a genetic profile that could be used to test recent claims that a bone found on the South Pacific island of Nikumaroro is Earhart's.

Justin Long, a Canadian whose family is partially funding the DNA project, points out that at the moment, anyone who finds fragments of bones can claim that they are Earhart's remains. Long, an Internet marketing executive, is the grandson of 1970s aviator Elgen Long, who with his wife wrote the 1999 book *Amelia Earhart: The Mystery Solved*. According to Justin Long,

Earhart's letters are the only items that are both verifiably hers and that might contain her DNA. Hair samples are one of the best sources of DNA, but no hair samples from Earhart are known. There was, in theory, a sample of Earhart's hair in the International Women's Air and Space Museum in Cleveland, US. However, a 2009 study revealed that the sample was actually thread.

The remains of Earhart, her navigator Noonan, and their twin-engine plane were never recovered. But in 2009, a group of researchers found a bone fragment on Nikumaroro that they believed might have been from one of Earhart's fingers. However, some scientists have suggested the Nikumaroro bone fragment isn't human at all but may instead belong to a sea turtle that was found nearby.

The new Earhart DNA project will be headed by Dongya Yang, a genetic archaeologist at Simon Fraser University

in Canada. Yang will work on four letters Earhart wrote to her family, out of more than 400 letters in the Earhart archive. Much of Earhart's correspondence was done by her secretary but the assumption is that Earhart must have sealed the envelopes of these personal letters herself.

Meanwhile, geneticist Brenna Henn of Stanford University said she knows of no other case where DNA has been collected from decades-old letters. But she said Yang's methodology "sounds reasonable." The problem is that about 99 percent of the genome is identical among all humans. If the team obtains little material, they have almost no power to discriminate between Earhart's DNA and anyone else's. To ensure that the DNA from the envelopes indeed belonged to Earhart, the team will compare it to DNA from Earhart's living relatives and DNA extracted from a letter written by Earhart's sister.

genome (n) /ˈdʒiːnoʊm/ the genetic information of each living thing
saliva (n) /səˈlaɪvə/ the liquid normally produced in your mouth

8d You're kidding me!

Real life reacting to surprising news

1 🔊 **34** Listen and choose the best headline (a–b) for each conversation.

1
  a **ESCAPED SHEEP TAKE OVER PARK**
  b **SHEEP IN GLOBAL WARMING SHOCK**

2
  a **FORGED EURO ALERT**
  b **USA TO JOIN THE EURO ZONE**

3
  a **FUEL PRICES TO DOUBLE NEXT WEEK**
  b **GAS PRICES SLASHED**

2 Can you remember? Answer the questions for each story.

1 What is the problem?
2 Does one of the speakers believe the other?
3 What is the date?

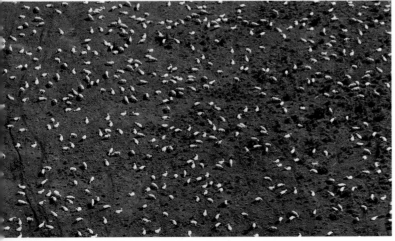

3 🔊 **34** Look at the expressions for reacting to news. Listen to the conversations again. Put the expressions in order (1–9).

> ▶ **REACTING TO SURPRISING NEWS**
>
> | | |
> |---|---|
> | Are you serious? | That can't be right! |
> | Are you sure? | They must have made a |
> | No way! | mistake. |
> | Oh yeah? | You're kidding me! |
> | Really? | You're pulling my leg! |

4 April Fools' Day (April 1) is a day when people play tricks on each other in many countries. Do you do anything similar in your country? Discuss with a partner.

5 Pronunciation **showing interest and disbelief**

a 🔊 **35** Listen to these expressions for reacting to news. Notice how the speaker's intonation rises to show interest and falls to show disbelief. Repeat the expressions.

Oh yeah? ↗   Come on! ↘

b Work in pairs. Take turns responding to these statements. Use the expressions in Exercise 3.

1 I'd love to go snorkeling in Antarctica.
2 A meteorite has crashed to Earth in the middle of Dubai.
3 I found a wallet full of money!
4 Biologists have discovered a parrot that can speak three languages.
5 I'm starting a new job tomorrow.

6 Work in pairs. Choose one of the other April Fools' Day headlines from Exercise 1. Decide what the hoax is. Make notes about the main points of the story. Invent as many details as you wish. Practice telling the story with your partner.

7 Work with a new partner. Take turns listening and reacting to your stories. Use the expressions for reacting to news to help you.

8e In the news

Writing a news story

1 Work in pairs. Read the news story. Do you think it is true or not? Explain your reasons to your partner.

2 Writing skill **structuring a news story**

a Read the introductory sentence in the news story again. Answer the questions.

1 What happened?
2 Who was involved?
3 Where did it happen?

b Read the main paragraph and find:

1 how the woman cut the cable.
2 four things that happened after she cut the cable.
3 two pieces of background information.

c Read the main paragraph again. How are the events and background details organized?

3 Vocabulary **-ly adverbs in stories**

a Find these adverbs in the story. Then match the adverbs with their meanings.

Adverbs

accidentally	unfortunately	temporarily
immediately	apparently	

Meanings

at once	by mistake	for a short time
it seems that	by bad luck	

b Cross out any options that are not possible.

1 *Apparently, / Quickly,* this type of incident is increasing in Georgia.
2 *Fortunately, / Incredibly,* nobody was hurt.
3 Internet service was *amazingly / gradually* restored across the region.
4 *Coincidentally, / Rapidly,* Internet service also failed in other regions last week.
5 Software providers say hackers *deliberately / sadly* sabotaged the service.
6 *Hopefully, / Slowly,* the police will release the woman because of her age.

c Work in pairs. Decide which of the sentences in Exercise 3b fit into the story and where they fit.

GEORGIAN WOMAN CUTS OFF ARMENIA'S WEB ACCESS

An elderly Georgian woman accidentally cut through an underground cable and cut off Internet service to all of neighboring Armenia.

The woman, 75, was digging for metal near the Georgian capital of Tbilisi when her shovel damaged the fiber-optic cable. Unfortunately, Georgia provides 90 percent of Armenia's Internet service so web users in the nation of 3.2 million people were left twiddling their thumbs for up to five hours. Large parts of Georgia and some areas of Azerbaijan were also temporarily affected. The damage was detected by a monitoring system and a security team immediately responded. The cable is protected, but apparently landslides or heavy rain may have left it exposed on the surface. The woman, called "the shovel-hacker" by local media, was arrested on suspicion of damaging property. She faces up to three years in prison.

4 You are going to write a hoax story or an April Fools' story. It can be invented or it can be a story you have heard. First, take notes about the main events and the background details of the story. Think about what, who, where, why, and how.

5 Write an introductory sentence to summarize the story. Then number your notes in the order you will write about them. Include at least three adverbs where appropriate.

6 Write your story in about 150–200 words. Include an interesting headline.

7 Work in pairs. Exchange stories. Use these questions to check your partner's story.

- Was the headline interesting?
- Are the facts of the story clear?
- Do you think the story is true?

Killer bees

One man believes that this foreign bee may cause problems for the whole rain forest.

Before you watch

1 Work in groups. Look at the title of this video and the photo and discuss the questions.

1 What do you know about bees?
2 Why do you think these bees are called "killer bees"?
3 What problems do you think they might cause for the rain forest?

2 The video is about a man who studies bees. What do you think you will see him doing in the video?

driving	getting stung by a bee
flying a plane	hiking in the rain forest
holding bees	putting his hand in a beehive
writing a journal	working with a beehive

While you watch

3 Watch the video and check your answers from Exercise 2.

4 Work in pairs. Choose one of the topics below. Watch the first part of the video (to 03:05) and make notes about David Roubik or bees. Then tell another pair what you found out about your topic.

David Roubik
1 Where and for how long has he studied bees?

2 Where does he work?

3 How many species of bees has he found in one square kilometer of the rain forest?

4 Why does he think there's a problem for the native bees?

Bees
5 How do bees benefit the rain forest?

6 Where do they live?

7 Why did people bring African honeybees to South America?

8 How did the experiment go wrong?

5 Watch the rest of the video (03:06 to the end). Are these sentences true (T) or false (F)? Correct the false sentences.

1 By 1982, the African bee was starting to make its home in Panama.
2 Roubik thinks the newspapers reported the story of the bees correctly.
3 The African bees are most dangerous to man.
4 Native bees are important because they pollinate the plants in the rain forest.
5 Native bees cannot compete with the stronger African bees.
6 Roubik visits the Mayan people because they have a lot of experience with bees.
7 Mayan farmers think the African bees are not a problem.
8 Fifteen years ago there wasn't much honey.

After you watch

6 Roleplay **interviewing a bee keeper**

Work in pairs.

Student A: You are an entomologist studying bees. Use the ideas below to prepare questions to interview a Mayan bee keeper.

Student B: You are a Mayan bee keeper. Use the ideas below to tell the entomologist your concerns.

- how long the farmer has kept bees
- how much honey there used to be
- how many native bees there are now
- the effects the disappearance of native bees is having on the local forests

Act out the interview. Then change roles.

7 Work in groups and discuss these questions.

1 Should human beings be permitted to experiment with nature to increase the production of food?
2 What are the risks of experiments like these? What are the advantages?

---

adaptable (adj) /əˈdæptəbəl/ able to change
canopy (n) /ˈkænəpi/ the top level in a rain forest
compete (v) /kəmˈpit/ try to be more successful
entomologist (n) /ˌentəˈmɑlədʒɪst/ a person who studies insects
force out (v) /ˈfɔrs ˈaʊt/ make a person or animal leave
hive (n) /haɪv/ a place where bees live
interact (v) /ˌɪntərˈækt/ have a relationship with
leading (adj) /ˈlidɪŋ/ most important
outlandish (adj) /aʊtˈlændɪʃ/ very strange

pollinate (v) /ˈpɑləˌneɪt/ carry pollen from one flower to another
repeatedly (adv) /rɪˈpitɪdli/ again and again
sting (v) (past: stung) /stɪŋ/ what an insect does when it injects a person with poison
spread (v) /spred/ move to cover a larger area
survive (v) /sərˈvaɪv/ continue living under difficult conditions
swarm (n) /swɔrm/ a large group of bees
take over (v) /ˈteɪk ˈoʊvər/ take control of something

UNIT 8 REVIEW

Grammar

1 Match the news headlines (1–3) with the comments (a–f). There are two comments for each headline. Choose the best option in the comments. Then work in pairs. Compare your answers.

1 **MAN CLAIMS TO BE 150 YEARS OLD**

2 **WEBSITE REVEALS LOCH NESS MONSTER PHOTOS**

3 **ASTRONOMERS FIND NEW PLANET**

a They *could / must* be fake.
b He *can't / must* be telling the truth.
c They *might have / must not have* used new equipment.
d It *can't have / might have* just appeared from nowhere.
e He *might / might not* be old, but not that old!
f They *might / must* be of a big fish.

2 Look at the photo of Stonehenge, a prehistoric site in southern England. What was Stonehenge used for? Check your ideas below.

the facts
- dated as 3-4,000 years old
- no written records from that period
- The larger stones weigh 25 tons. They come from about 19 miles away from the site.
- The smaller stones originate from Wales, 143 miles away.
- The circle is aligned with the sun's highest and lowest points in the sky.

the theories
- created by Merlin of King Arthur's court
- the ruins of a Roman building
- built by invaders from Denmark
- an alien landing area
- a sacred site
- a cemetery or burial site
- a scientific observatory

3 Work in pairs. Discuss the theories and decide what you think of each one. Then work with another pair. Which theory do you think is the most probable? Explain your reasons.

I CAN
speculate and draw conclusions about events in the present and past (modal verbs)

Vocabulary

4 Work in pairs. Write down two of these things.

1 gases: _____ , _____
2 insects: _____ , _____
3 words meaning "very old": _____ , _____
4 words for ideas in science or investigations: _____ , _____

5 Work in pairs. Answer as many questions as you can.

1 What is trick photography?
2 What part of a plant is the stem?
3 What kinds of things are sticky?
4 Name some animals that migrate.
5 What do irrigation systems do?
6 What's an archive?
7 What might be in someone's profile?
8 Is a hoax a person?
9 What kinds of things happen accidentally?

I CAN
talk about things from the natural world
talk about history

Real life

6 Test your memory. Can you remember ways of reacting to news using these words?

kidding	no	pulling	right	serious	sure

7 Work in groups. Each person needs six pieces of paper. Write surprising sentences about yourself (true and false) on the pieces of paper. Take turns reading your sentences out loud. Use appropriate expressions to react to the sentences about the other people and try to find out which sentences are true.

I CAN
react appropriately to surprising news

Speaking

8 Work in pairs. Tell each other the most surprising (true) thing you have read about or seen a report about in the last few months.

Venus Fort is a shopping mall in Tokyo designed to resemble a medieval European village. Every 30 minutes, there is an artificial sunset in the "sky" above the mall.

FEATURES

1 Work in pairs. Look at the photo and the caption. Compare the Venus Fort mall with places you usually go shopping.

2 Work in pairs. One of you is a market researcher and the other is a shopper. Take turns asking and answering these questions.

1 What have you bought today?
2 Who did you buy it for?
3 Have you been spending a lot of money?

3 Discuss the questions with your partner.

1 What's the best present anyone has ever given you?
2 What kinds of things do you and your family or friends buy for each other?
3 Do you buy these things for yourself or others?

> books / DVDs / CDs   clothes   electronics / gadgets
> jewelry   shoes   toiletries / cosmetics   other items

4 Work in pairs. Prepare a survey on shopping habits. Ask at least three other people your questions. Then compare the results.

9a Money talk

Vocabulary money

1 How are you with money? Mark the statements that are true about you. Check the meaning of any words in bold you are not sure about.

1 "I don't carry a lot of **cash**. I just use my **debit card**."
2 "I check my **bank statement** every week."
3 "I don't have any **credit cards** because I don't want to get into **debt**."
4 "I usually keep **receipts** for things in case I need to take them back."
5 "I like to do all my **banking** online."
6 "I know exactly how much is in my **savings account**."
7 "My electric **bill** is on **autopay**. I never have to remember to sit down and pay it!"
8 "I **borrowed** money to buy a new car last year."

2 Change the statements in Exercise 1 so that they are true about you. Then work in pairs. Compare your statements.

Listening

3 How do people usually pay (or pay for) these things in your country?

bus and train tickets	gas
household bills	rent / mortgage
cell phone	payments

4 🔊 **36** Listen to the radio show and mark the features of mobile banking that are mentioned.

1 It is a paper-free system.
2 It uses interactive voice menus.
3 You can transfer money from one person to another.
4 You can pay bills, buy goods, and manage your savings account.
5 You can text your bank with your instructions.

5 🔊 **36** Listen to the radio show again. Correct any factual errors. Do not change the words in bold.

1 There are approximately two billion cell phones in **the world** today.
2 A lot of people don't have easy access to **banks**.
3 With **the interactive voice system**, you can talk to your bank manager.
4 Algeria has **a new cell phone banking** plan.
5 In Afghanistan, the cell phone network covers **every town and city**.
6 The Afghan Army pays **all salaries** through cell phones.
7 The policemen in Afghanistan receive **their salaries** in cash.
8 **Each policeman** gets an email when he is paid.

6 Work in groups. What do you think are the advantages and disadvantages of cell phone banking?

Kabul residents pass advertising from a cell phone company.

Grammar noun phrases

7 Look at the words in bold in sentences 1–4 in Exercise 5. Match the words (1–4) with their uses (a–d).

a The first reference to this thing.
b These things in general.
c There is only one of this thing.
d The reference to this thing is known.

▶ ARTICLES IN NOUN PHRASES		
a/an		singular count noun
the	+	singular count noun, plural count noun, noncount noun
zero article		plural count noun, noncount noun
For more information and practice, see page 167.		

8 Look at the grammar box above. Then find the patterns in the audioscript on page 179.

9 Look at the grammar box below. Which word in bold in sentences 6–8 in Exercise 5 expresses ownership?

▶ DETERMINERS and POSSESSIVES IN NOUN PHRASES
Use *my, your, his, her*, etc. + noun to express ownership. Use *each, every to* refer to individual things and *all* to refer to a group of things.
For more information and practice, see page 167.

10 Read the tips and choose the correct option. Choose – if the sentence is already complete.

11 🔘 **37** Complete the sentences where necessary. Then listen and check.

1 I tried to save _____ money to get _____ new phone.
2 _____ model I wanted cost a fortune.
3 I gave up _____ chocolate, buying DVDs, and smoking.
4 I gave _____ money to _____ sister to take care of.
5 She told me how much I'd saved _____ week.
6 When I had enough, I went to buy _____ phone.
7 _____ store had _____ special offer.
8 I got _____ free upgrade with a new phone!
9 And I still had _____ cash I'd saved. Amazing!

12 Pronunciation linking

a 🔘 **38** Listen to these sentences from Exercise 11. Notice how the speaker links the words that start with a vowel to the final consonant of the previous word.

1 I tried to save money to get_a new phone.
2 The model_I wanted cost_a fortune.

b 🔘 **39** Underline the words that start with vowels in the other sentences in Exercise 11. Then listen and repeat the sentences.

Speaking and writing

13 Work in groups. Discuss the questions.

1 What do you think of the methods for saving money in Exercise 10?
2 What kind of things do you save up for?
3 What other methods for saving money can you recommend?

14 Work on your own. Write a short post for a website giving one tip for saving money.

Top Saving Tips

1 Make *a / each / –* list before you go shopping.
2 Put *a / the / your* small change in *a / the / your* jar.
3 Buy *every / the / their* supermarket's house brand products—they are usually cheaper!
4 Buy sale items that are near *its / their / your* expiration date.
5 Cut up *the / your / –* credit card.
6 Compare *each / every / –* prices before you buy *a / an / the* expensive item.
7 Unplug *every / their / all* electrical appliances when they are not in use.
8 Calculate how much you've saved *a / each / the* week to stay motivated.

9b The genuine article

Reading

1 Work in groups. Choose three items each person has with them (including clothes). How many questions can you answer?

1. Where was it made?
2. Who was it made by?
3. How was it made?
4. How did it get to the store?

2 Look at the website. Answer the questions.

1. Who is the woman in the photo?
2. What is her job?
3. What kind of products does she deal with?

3 Read the product information on the website. Match the products (1–4) with the consumer reviews (A–E) on page 109. There is one extra review.

THE GENUINE ARTICLE

Laura Morelli is our shopping expert. She gives advice on finding authentic products such as handmade crafts or fair-trade goods.

Click here to browse our list.
Read our consumer reviews!

- All fair-trade goods are bought directly from the producer.
- Our featured crafts have been made from sustainable resources.
- Many of the featured products can be ordered online.

PRODUCT DESCRIPTION:
1
This eco-basketball has been produced to the highest specifications for an all-weather, high-grip surface. After tax, profits are donated to children's charities.

Review (1 of 15)
By   SB
See also: Fair-trade sports soccer balls
         Venture snowboards

PRODUCT DESCRIPTION:
3
These handmade American cowboy boots are based on an original design but have been decorated with an explosion of color. A true work of art.

Review (1 of 8)
By   wichitaman
See also: Genuine Dutch clogs
         Fair-trade recycled tire sandals

PRODUCT DESCRIPTION:
2
These fair-trade cut flowers from Kenya have been grown free from chemical pesticides. Water-recycling methods are being introduced in many flower farms. Profits from these flowers will be used to support school projects for farm employees.

Review (1 of 5)
By   billbran
See also: Fair-trade beauty products

PRODUCT DESCRIPTION:
4
Turquoise jewelry from classic Navajo designs. Turquoise was being mined when the Spanish arrived in the area, and the Native Americans soon learned to mix Spanish silver with this beautiful mineral.

Review (1 of 23)
By   lisamay
See also: New England silver

A It's worth paying a little more for these. They last for ages, smell wonderful, and I get to help the people who grow them. It's a win-win situation!

B Absolutely gorgeous and incredibly practical. I'm so happy to be able to buy beautiful clothes that weren't made under sweatshop conditions.

C Excellent quality and so comfortable they can be worn all day. I love them.

D Great product. Great price. Great fun. And guilt free... knowing that no children were exploited so that my child could have a fun Christmas. It doesn't get any better!

E I was given a stunning set of matching rings, bracelet, and necklace. A gift that will be treasured forever! And it's great to support local craftsmen.

Grammar passive voice: all tenses

4 Look at these sentences from the website. Underline the main verb. Does the sentence give information about who or what does this action?

1 All fair-trade goods are bought directly from the producer.
2 Our featured crafts have been made from sustainable resources.
3 Many of the featured products can be ordered online.

5 Look at the grammar box. Find eight more sentences on the website with these patterns.

▶ PASSIVE VOICE: ALL TENSES		
(The goods)	are are being were were being have been can be will be	(ordered online).

For more information and practice, see page 168.

6 Which verbs do we use to form the passive?

7 Read about a fair-trade company. Choose the correct option.

Direct trade means that more of the final price ¹*pays / is paid* to the producers. We have a simple system. First, the coffee beans ²*take / are taken* to a central collection point by each grower. When the loads ³*have weighed / have been weighed*, the growers ⁴*get / are gotten* the correct payment. At the moment, we ⁵*are using / are being used* a standard shipping company to transport the coffee, but that arrangement ⁶*is reviewing / is being reviewed,* and next year specialized firms ⁷*will contract / will be contracted* to handle shipping. Once delivered, the coffee ⁸*can pack and sell / can be packed and sold* within a week.

8 Work in pairs. Write the passive form of the verbs. Then, underline the options you think are correct. Check your answers with your instructor.

1 Since its launch in 2003, 250 million *Nokia 1101 cell phones / Apple iPods* _____ (sell).
2 *Solitaire / Tetris* _____ (adapt) for 65 different platforms, making it the most successful computer game ever.
3 The work of *J.K. Rowling / Agatha Christie* _____ (translate) into more languages than that of any other author.
4 In 1986, the film *The Color Purple / Out of Africa* _____ (nominated) for eleven Oscars and didn't win any.
5 With 400 stores around the world, clothing brand *Ralph Lauren / Mango* _____ (wear) by more people than any other.
6 The first music video by *Justin Bieber / Lady Gaga* _____ (view) on YouTube over 500 million times.
7 Maps for the Xbox® game *Call of Duty / Grand Theft Auto* _____ (download) one million times in 24 hours when it went on sale.
8 A painting by *Picasso / Van Gogh* _____ (buy) at auction for $106 million in 2010.

9 Work in groups. Discuss the questions.

1 Do you know the products and people in Exercise 8?
2 Does anything in the sentences surprise you?

Speaking

10 Work in groups of four. Brainstorm as many brand names as you can. Then add what kind of product each item is and what alternative brands exist. Think of five reasons to buy famous brands and five reasons to buy alternative brands. Then turn to page 155.

9c The art of the deal

Reading

1 Work in pairs. Do you like bringing souvenirs back from trips? Discuss why you think people bring back items like these.

> brochures from galleries, museums
> decorative objects (pictures, ceramics)
> duty-free goods   locally made products
> postcards   T-shirts with slogans   used tickets

2 Read the article on page 111 quickly. Decide what kind of shopping experience (a–c) it describes.

  a   bargaining in local markets
  b   buying crafts directly from the maker
  c   choosing souvenirs for friends and family

3 Read the article again. Answer the questions.

  1   Who are the three main people in the article and why do they go to Morocco?
  2   What two things does Sam buy and how much does he pay for them?
  3   Which is Sam's most successful purchase?

4 Find these things in the article. How are they described? Complete the phrases.

  1 _____ juice
  2 _____ market
  3 _____ swords
  4 _____ fabrics
  5 _____ bones
  6 _____ lamps
  7 _____
                   bottle
  8 _____
    slippers

Critical thinking **testing a conclusion**

5 The writer concludes: "Mohamed will be proud." Is this conclusion justified? Look at the text again and underline the advice Mohamed gives to Sam.

6 Mark the pieces of Mohamed's advice that Sam follows. How effective was it? How do you know?

Speaking

7 You are a market trader. Choose four of these objects. Draw a picture of each object and think how you will describe it. Consider its origin, age, and material, and any interesting facts about it. Decide on a price for each object.

> boomerang bottle box clock coin figurine
> hat   lamp   rug stamp sword watch

8 Choose objects from Exercise 7 that you want to buy. Visit different traders and find out about the objects you want. Then choose which trader you will buy from.

> *This rug is lovely. How much is it?*

The
ART
of the
DEAL

By Andrew McCarthy

I'M IN MARRAKECH, the bustling heart of Morocco at the base of the Atlas Mountains, with my son, Sam. He's eight. We've come here with Mohamed, a friend who owns a store in our New York neighborhood. We're regular customers at Mohamed's store, where Sam can often be found negotiating with his friend. When they're not bargaining, they're chatting about swords, or camels, or the desert. "You need to come to Marrakech," Mohamed told me. "I'll show you around and teach Sam how to really get a bargain!" So here we are.

We meet up with Mohamed over a cup of mint tea at a table outside the tiny Café ben Youssef, deep in the medina, the old city of Marrakech. We're sitting in an area bordering the exotic stalls of the souk—marketplace. Vendors with carts offer freshly squeezed orange juice, others sell dates or figs. Nearby are the back-alley workshops that supply the goods to this world-famous market.

Later, as we stroll around, Mohamed introduces us to weavers and olive sellers, tile makers and rug merchants. He also begins the first of his bargaining tutorials for Sam.

"Everything in Morocco is open to negotiation, Sam. When you hear a price, the first thing you say is 'Too much—*bezaf*' and then walk away."

"But what if I like it?"

"When you see something you like, maybe a lamp, you ask about something else instead. Then, as you walk out, you ask, 'And how much is that lamp?' as though you'd just noticed it and aren't really that interested in it."

We turn a corner and are greeted with the scent of sweet-smelling orange blossoms. "Don't always give an offer. Make them continue to lower the price. Oh, and wear something Moroccan," Mohamed continues, as we enter a fairly large shop. Most of the stalls in Marrakech specialize in one thing, but not this one. Decorative and lethal-looking swords hang beside soft hand-dyed fabrics; large camel bones covered in writing sit beside massive copper lamps. It is here that Sam spots an ornate box. "Look, a treasure chest!" It's made of wood, and painted red and gold. He opens the lid, then closes it. "Cool." Then he spots a tall, cobalt blue, tear-shaped old perfume bottle. "Four hundred dirham," the shopkeeper pronounces. Fifty dollars. Sam says nothing. Whether he's too shy or is practicing Mohamed's bargaining technique, I can't tell. He eventually agrees to pay 200 dirham, about $24. I'd say the bottle is worth $10, at most. Clearly, his negotiating skills need a little work. "Just to get started, Dad," Sam reassures me as he pays for the bottle.

We spend a few days sightseeing around Marrakech, but Sam really has eyes for only one thing. Late one afternoon, we return to the shop where Sam saw the treasure chest. "You have returned. Very good." The shopkeeper places the chest on the floor. Sam runs his fingers over it.

The shopkeeper speaks. "Give me 2,500."

Sam shakes his eight-year-old head. "Eight hundred."

"I like your *babouches*," says the merchant. Sam's wearing a pair of bright yellow, Moroccan men's slippers. He ignores the comment.

"You're very good. I'll take 1,800 dirham," the merchant announces.

"One thousand."

Both are silent. Neither blinks. What happens next, happens fast.

"Fifteen hundred, and it's yours."

"Twelve hundred."

"Thirteen hundred."

"Yes!"

The deal is done. Mohamed will be proud.

blink (v) /blɪŋk/ open and close your eyes very quickly
merchant (n) /ˈmɜrtʃənt/ someone who sells things
vendor (n) /ˈvendər/ someone who sells things
workshop (n) /ˈwɜrkˌʃɑp/ a place where people make things

Real life buying things

1 🔊 **40** Listen, then answer the questions for each conversation.

1   What kind of store is it?
2   What does the customer want to buy?
3   Does the customer buy the item?

2 🔊 **40** Look at the expressions for buying things. Listen to the conversations again. Mark each option that is used by the customer (C) and the salesperson (S).

> ▶ **BUYING THINGS**
>
> Can I look at this silver chain?
> Could I see this silver chain?
> It's on sale, actually; 20 percent off.
> I wanted / I was looking for something more delicate.
> Can she return it if she doesn't like it?
> May I have a gift receipt?
> Excuse me, do you work here?
> What's / Do you have the reference number or the model name?
> Let me see if it's in stock.
> That model is currently on backorder.
> How much do you charge for delivery?
> How much does gift-wrapping cost?
> We accept payment / You can pay by card or in cash.

Vocabulary shopping

3 Work in pairs. Can you remember the question and response for each word? Check your answers in the audioscript on page 179.

available	in stock
cash registers	model name
delivery	receipt
exchange	reference number
gift-wrapping	return

4 Work in pairs. Choose one of the conversations from Exercise 1. Take a role each. Look at the audioscript on page 179 and memorize the conversation. Then close your books and practice the conversation.

5 Take the roles of a customer and a salesperson. Choose two of these items and act out two conversations. Use the expressions for buying things to help you.

> an item of furniture for your new home
> clothes for your father's birthday
> toiletries for your sister
> a DVD for a friend
> a kitchen appliance for your brother
> clothes for yourself
> a new car for yourself
> a tablet for your grandmother

9e For sale

Writing an eBay ad

1 Work in pairs. Have you ever bought or sold anything on eBay? Read these headings from the guidelines to sellers. Why is this information useful to buyers?

- information about the seller
- item condition
- item description
- item photo
- payment methods
- shipping details
- starting price
- reason for selling

2 Read the eBay ad and find the information from Exercise 1.

3 **Writing skill** **relevant and irrelevant information**

a Sellers on eBay are advised to give as much information about the item as possible. Read the description of the rug. Cross out three sentences in the description of the rug that do not give relevant information.

b Which of these sentences give relevant information for this ad? Where do they fit in the ad?

1 I've had it for about two years.
2 It looks great in my living room.
3 I've cleaned it regularly.
4 We're moving next month.
5 We are near downtown Boston.

4 Prepare an ad for something you want to sell. Use these headings and make notes.

- item
- age
- size/shape
- condition
- reason for selling
- starting price

5 Write your ad and give your contact details. Use these questions to check your ad.

- Have you given honest information about the item to prospective buyers?
- Is there any other information you could add to help the sale?

6 Publish your ad in the classroom. Read the other ads and bid on any item you want to buy.

A ROUND ORANGE DEEP-PILE RUG

Zoom	Enlarge

Item condition:	Used
Starting bid:	**$10.00**
Postage:	Free local pick-up
Payments:	*PayPal*, cash on receipt

Habitat "Africa" rug in orange. Hand-woven deep-pile round wool rug. Measures 8 feet across.

This rug is in used condition. It was a gift from my parents. It has some marks, but otherwise it is in good condition. I think that with a professional steam cleaning, it will freshen up really well.

Selling because we're moving to a new house and are changing the color scheme. New house is in the country, so we are going to have rustic-themed decor.

The rug currently retails for $200 new. It's such a shame to throw it away, so I hope that I can sell it rather than recycle it.

Payment within three days of end of auction or cash on receipt. Local pick-up preferred.

Beginners pay more.

Before you watch

1 Work in groups. Look at the title of this video and the photo and discuss the questions.

  1 Who are the people in the photo?
  2 What do you think they are doing?
  3 What do you think the caption means?

2 Mark what you think you will see in this video.

a taxi	a cup of tea
a hotel	a metal table
caftans	a police officer
carpets	dates and apricots
a donkey	a man carrying vegetables

While you watch

3 Check your answers from Exercise 2. Number the things in the order you see them in the video.

4 Complete the sentences with the correct option.

  1 Buying and selling in the market is:
    a quick and not very personal.
    b slow and very impersonal.
    c face-to-face and personal.
  2 A fez is:
    a a kind of drink.
    b the name of a person from Fez.
    c a kind of hat.
  3 Beginners at bargaining pay:
    a 20 or 30 percent more.
    b 50 percent more.
    c 100 percent more.
  4 Bargaining is:
    a a way to cheat customers.
    b a test to find who is the best bargainer.
    c a way to make people pay cash.
  5 The real test for customers is:
    a the restaurant.
    b the carpet shop.
    c the night market.
  6 According to Gonnie, the secret of bargaining is:
    a to watch what the Moroccans do.
    b not to get angry.
    c to pretend not to be interested.

5 Match the people (1–6) with what they say (a–f).

  1 the narrator
  2 Vincent
  3 Ahmed
  4 the carpet salesman
  5 Chakib
  6 Bo

  a For this money I can't leave it.
  b You want to buy a camel for the price of a donkey?
  c This is business, Moroccan-style.
  d The Moroccans are very good at bargaining and they say they are the best in the world.
  e Everyone comes with an intention to bargain.
  f We don't have a really fixed price.

After you watch

6 **Roleplay bargaining in a Moroccan market**

Work in pairs.

Student A: You are a market vendor. Use the ideas below to make notes.

- What things do you sell?
- What prices are you going to charge?
- Make a list of your items and their prices.

Student B: You are a tourist. You are at a stall in a Moroccan market and you want to buy three items. Make a deal with the vendor.

Act out the conversation. Student A: try to get as good a price as you can. Student B: bargain!

When you have finished, change roles and act out a new conversation with different items and prices.

7 The narrator says that "vendors aren't trying to cheat customers" but that "it's all part of the game." What do you think that means? Do you agree?

8 Work in groups and discuss these questions.

  1 Have you ever bargained over the price of something? Where? For what?
  2 Do people bargain for things in your country? What things?
  3 Which do you prefer: bargaining, or a system of fixed prices? Why?

---

alley (n) /ˈæli/ a narrow street or passage
bargain (v) /ˈbɑrgɪn/ negotiate a price
cheat (v) /tʃit/ make someone pay too much

pressure (v) /ˈprɛʃər/ try to make a person do something
vendor (n) /ˈvɛndər/ a person who sells things
watch out (v) /ˈwɑtʃ ˈaʊt/ be careful

UNIT 9 REVIEW

Grammar

1 Work in pairs. Which of these things do you consider when you buy electronic goods? Which is the most important factor?

- brand
- design
- ease of use
- energy use
- price
- size
- style (shape, color, materials)

2 Complete the text with articles, determiners, and possessive adjectives where necessary.

THE GREEN GUIDE

Shopping Tips: televisions

1 _____ days when **2** _____ TVs came in two types, **3** _____ color or black and white, are long gone. TVs today use several technologies and **4** _____ one has **5** _____ different level of energy efficiency.

Many people change **6** _____ TV because they want **7** _____ bigger screen. But bigger TVs use a lot more energy. **8** _____ US Department of Energy says **9** _____ energy from **10** _____ TVs in America is enough to provide power to **11** _____ home in the state of New York for **12** _____ year. Giant plasma screen models can be the most energy-hungry appliance in **13** _____ home.

One major factor in **14** _____ TV power use is the picture setting. **15** _____ TV's picture settings can make a surprising difference, sometimes cutting **16** _____ total by as much as 50 percent. On the other hand, **17** _____ 52-inch LCD uses twice the power of **18** _____ 32-inch model.

3 Work in pairs. Do you have any of these products with you today? Match the products with their raw materials and countries of origin. Then describe the process from the raw material to the final product.

Products	Raw materials and countries of origin
a bar of chocolate	wheat – Canada
a pair of jeans	lithium – Chile
a sandwich	gold – South Africa
jewelry	flowers – south of France
cell phone batteries	cotton – Egypt
perfume	cocoa beans – Ghana

4 Work with other pairs. Compare your ideas. Try to complete any information you are not sure about.

I CAN
use articles, determiners, and possessive adjectives ☐

describe how products are made (passives) ☐

Vocabulary

5 Write and number (1–6) six types of stores you go to regularly. Then work in pairs. Choose a number and your partner will say the store with this number on his/her list. You have 30 seconds to name six things you can buy there. Take turns.

6 Match words from A and B to make compound nouns.

A bank   credit   debit   savings

B account   card   statement   transfer

7 Work in pairs. What could a salesperson or customer say using each of these words?

available	delivery	exchange	gift-wrapping
in stock	receipt	return	

I CAN
talk about everyday things we buy ☐

talk about ways of paying for things and banking ☐

ask for and give product and sales information ☐

Real life

8 Work in pairs. Take turns being the customer and the salesperson in a store. Act out conversations in which you buy each of the things in the photos.

I CAN
buy and sell items in a store ☐

Speaking

9 Work in groups. Discuss the questions.

1 What could you not live without? Why?
2 Do your favorite possessions have monetary or sentimental value?
3 What was your best or worst purchase ever?

Unit 10 No limits

On the annual *Marathon des Sables,* keeping the sand out of your face can be a problem.
Photograph by Pierre Verdy

FEATURES

1 Work in pairs. Look at the photo and the caption. What other problems do you think runners like this face?

2 "Ultrarunning" is running a race that is longer than the standard 26-mile marathon, often under challenging conditions. Does ultrarunning appeal to you? Why?

3 Work in groups. Discuss the questions.

1 Other extreme sports include bungee jumping, BASE jumping, cave diving, and free climbing. Have you tried any of them?
2 Why do you think people push themselves to the limit?
3 What do you think of people who try to overcome their body's limits in other ways (like cosmetic surgery, anti-aging medicines, etc.)?

> **BASE** /beɪs/ stands for four kinds of fixed objects from which you can jump: buildings, antennas, spans (bridges), and earth (cliffs)

10a The bionic woman

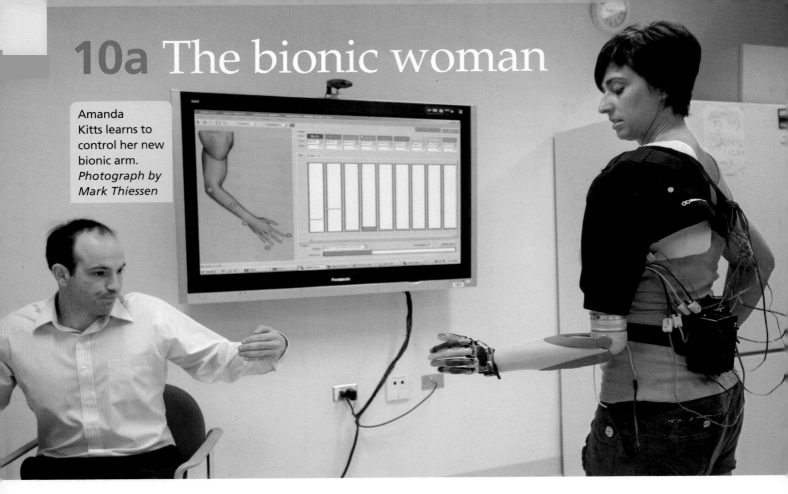

Amanda Kitts learns to control her new bionic arm.
Photograph by Mark Thiessen

Listening

1 🔊 **41** Listen to part of a TV preview show. Mark the three things the documentary is about.

bionic devices	growing new organs
cosmetic surgery	anti-aging treatments
face transplants	

2 🔊 **41** Match the two parts of the sentences. Then listen again and check.

1 *The Bionic Woman* was a TV series
2 The documentary is about a woman
3 Doctors have developed a process
4 Amanda Kitts is learning to do things
5 Bionics can help people
6 There'll be a time

a that we take for granted.
b when blind people will use bionic devices to see.
c in which the character was part machine and part human.
d which grows new organs.
e who have lost limbs.
f whose arm was amputated.

3 What do you think the advantages of a bionic limb are compared with a traditional artificial limb? Tell your partner.

Grammar **defining relative clauses**

4 Look again at the sentences in Exercise 2. The second part of the sentence is the defining relative clause. It begins with a relative pronoun. Answer the questions.

1 Who or what does the information following the relative pronoun refer to?
2 Which relative pronouns have the same meaning?
3 In which sentence is it possible to leave out the relative pronoun?

5 Look at the grammar box. Choose the correct option.

A defining relative clause gives *essential / additional* information about something.

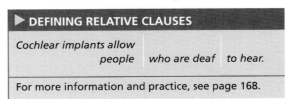

▶ DEFINING RELATIVE CLAUSES		
Cochlear implants allow		
people	who are deaf	to hear.

For more information and practice, see page 168.

6 Underline other defining relative clauses in the audioscript on page 180. How many defining relative clauses are there?

7 Look at the diagram of a bionic body. Complete the captions. You can use one relative pronoun twice.

1 cochlear implants allow people _____ are deaf to hear

2 temporary artificial hearts for people _____ are waiting for transplants

3 prosthetic arms _____ can receive signals from the brain

4 the first replacement hips—from a time _____ bionics was an idea from science fiction

5 healthy area of bone _____ the bionic limb is attached

6 bionic limbs _____ movement mimics the body's natural steps

8 Cross out any relative pronouns that are optional and insert any that are missing. Then check your answers with your instructor.

1 Amanda Kitts has a bionic arm receives signals from her brain.

2 A hospital is a place where patients are treated.

3 I don't like the medicine that I have to take.

4 People have burn injuries can benefit from face transplants.

5 Organ regeneration can help patients kidneys are diseased.

6 The doctor who we saw in the film is a pioneer in bionics.

Vocabulary and speaking
medicine

9 Work in pairs. Choose the best option.

1 Several people were *injured / wounded* in the accident.

2 It's just a small cut. It will *treat / heal* naturally.

3 What time is your doctor's *appointment / date*?

4 They can't *cure / heal* this yet, but they can relieve the symptoms.

5 Where does it *hurt / pain*?

6 The *healing / treatment* has some unpleasant side effects.

7 The doctor is *controlling / monitoring* the patient's condition.

8 The injection isn't *hurtful / painful*.

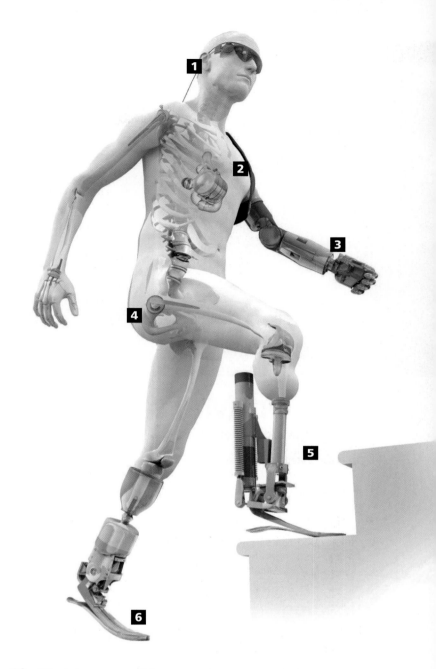

10 Work in groups. Take turns choosing a word and then giving its definition.

surgeon injection
botox operating room blood test
accident emergency
scan ambulance stitches
donor crutches
surgery technician ward
X-ray paramedic first aid

Botox is something that celebrities use to make themselves look younger.

LATER DOMES FOR GARDENS
AND HABITATION

FACTORIES EMITTING SUPER
GREENHOUSE GASES

HABITATION
MODULE
COMMUNITY

EARTH
RETURN
VEHICLE

HABITATION
MODULE

EARLY DOMES FOR
GARDENS

| YEAR ZERO | 100 YEARS | 200 YEARS | 600 YEARS |

1 THE THOUSAND-YEAR project might begin with a series of eighteen-month survey missions. Each crew making the six-month journey from Earth to Mars would add a small habitation module to the base.

2 AN EARTH-LIKE ATMOSPHERE could be made. First, the carbon dioxide that is now frozen in the ice would be released. Maybe mirrors could focus sunlight on the ice to do this.

3 WITH ENOUGH carbon dioxide, the temperature would go up and rain would fall. Algae and microbes could survive and transform the rocky surface.

4 FLOWERING PLANTS could be introduced when the microbes had created soil. This would add oxygen to the atmosphere. Forests might even grow.

Life on Mars?

Making the red planet go green

If we tried to, could we really transform the frozen surface of Mars into a place where humans could live? And should we?

The first question has a clear answer: Yes, we probably could. Most of the work in "terraforming," says NASA planetary scientist Chris McKay, would be done by life itself. "We wouldn't have to build Mars, just modify its atmosphere," McKay says. "If we warmed it up and threw in some seeds, plants would grow there."

Enthusiasts such as Robert Zubrin, president of the Mars Society, dream of Martian cities. Zubrin, an engineer, believes civilization cannot succeed without limitless expansion. He also thinks that if we transformed Mars—a horrifying idea to some—we might learn to manage our limited Earth better. But if I were an astronaut, I wouldn't be happy about that six-month journey!

Reading

1 Work in pairs. Do you think these statements are true (T) or false (F)? Find the answers on the webpage.

1 Mars is bigger than Earth.
2 Earth is hotter than Mars.
3 Earth is closer to the sun than Mars.
4 Martian days are longer than Earth days.

2 Look at the picture. Answer the questions.

1 What process does the picture illustrate?
2 Why is it red on the left and green on the right?
3 What is the purpose of the structures shown?

3 Match the captions (1–4) with the stages in the process (a–d).

a changing the atmosphere
b introducing simple organisms
c setting up places to live
d creating conditions for plants to grow

4 Read the text *Life on Mars?* and look at the picture again. Answer the questions.

1 How long would it take to transform the environment on Mars?
2 What is the key to the process?
3 What would be the benefits of transforming Mars?

5 Work in groups. Discuss the statements.

1 "I think we'll need to colonize other planets if we don't change our habits on Earth."
2 "I don't think the ideas described here will work."
3 "I'd like to live on Mars."

> ▶ **WORDBUILDING suffixes -ful, -less**
>
> We can add *-ful* to the end of a noun to mean "with" and *-less* to mean "without."
> a *painful* injection   *limitless* expansion

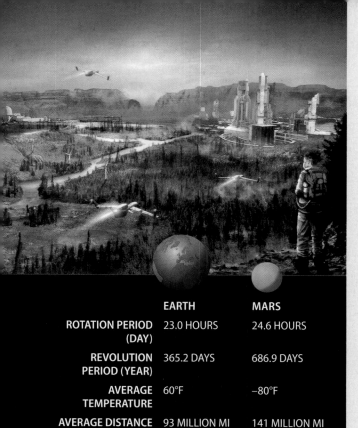

	EARTH	MARS
ROTATION PERIOD (DAY)	23.0 HOURS	24.6 HOURS
REVOLUTION PERIOD (YEAR)	365.2 DAYS	686.9 DAYS
AVERAGE TEMPERATURE	60°F	–80°F
AVERAGE DISTANCE FROM THE SUN	93 MILLION MI	141 MILLION MI

Grammar second conditional

6 Look at these sentences from the text. Which verbs are used to make the second conditional?

1 If we warmed it up and threw in some seeds, plants would grow there.
2 But if I were an astronaut, I wouldn't be happy about that six-month journey!

7 Look at the sentences in Exercise 6 again. Choose the correct options.

1 The second conditional refers to situations in *the past / the present or the future*.
2 The second conditional refers to *improbable / real* situations.

> ▶ **SECOND CONDITIONAL**
>
> | *If* + simple past, | *would could (not) might* | base form |
> |---|---|---|
>
> For more information and practice, see page 169.

8 Look at the grammar box. Find the patterns in the text and the captions. What is the difference between *would, could,* and *might*?

9 Look again at statement 1 in Exercise 5. Why is the first conditional—and not the second conditional—used?

10 Complete the questions. Then answer the questions using information from the text and the captions.

1 If we _____ (have) to transform Mars, what _____ (be) the first stage?
2 How long _____ it _____ (take) for astronauts to reach Mars?
3 _____ it _____ (be) possible to change the atmosphere on Mars?
4 What _____ (happen) if the ice on Mars _____ (melt)?
5 How _____ the temperature _____ (change) if carbon dioxide _____ (increase)?
6 What _____ we _____ (learn) from changing the environment on Mars?

11 Complete the sentence with your own ideas. Then work in pairs. Compare your sentences.

If we transformed Mars,
we could... people would... it might...

12 Work in two pairs in a group of four.

Pair A: Make a list of positive aspects of these situations.

Pair B: Make a list of negative aspects.

- living in a habitation module on Mars
- being an astronaut on a long space voyage
- being an astronaut on the International Space Station
- going on a space-tourism trip into the Earth's orbit

13 Compare your ideas in your group. Which experience would be the best / the worst?

If you lived in a habitation module, you'd be safe from any danger.

Yes, but your life would be very restricted.

Speaking

14 Work on your own. Think of a new place to live. Write down five reasons why you'd like to live there. Then work in groups. Take turns telling your group the reasons, but don't say the place. Can they guess before you give all of the reasons?

I'd love to live in this place. I'd never be cold again.

15 Think about your answers to the questions. Then tell the class.

1 If you could start a new life, what things would you change, and how?
2 What would you miss about your old life?

10c Two journeys, two lives

Reading

1 How much do you know about these people? Choose the option (a–c) you think links them.

   a They broke "unbreakable" records.
   b They were successful in the face of huge obstacles.
   c They became rich and famous in their chosen careers.

Galileo	Nelson Mandela
Helen Keller	Oprah Winfrey
Martina Navratilova	Roald Amundsen

2 Work in pairs. You are going to read about two people who overcame obstacles in their lives.
Student A: Read about Diane Van Deren.
Student B: Read about John Dau.
Make notes to answer these questions.

   1 Who?
   2 Where?
   3 When?
   4 Distance covered?
   5 Time taken?
   6 Food and drink?

3 Tell your partner about the story you read. Use your notes to help you. Ask your partner at least one question about their story.

4 Now read your partner's story. Is the story what you expected to read? Did anything surprise you?

Critical thinking **reading between the lines**

5 Work in pairs. Using the information in the stories and your own interpretation of them, discuss the questions.

   1 Why did they begin their journeys?
   2 Did they run through choice or necessity?
   3 What have they achieved for themselves as a result of their journeys?
   4 What have they achieved for others as a result of their journeys?

6 Read the quotes. Who do you think said each one: Diane Van Deren or John Dau? Why?

   1 "I think people refuse to try things because they fear failure."
   2 "All I have to think about is my body."
   3 "There have been many impossible situations in my life, but I keep trying."
   4 "You can't give up."

7 Do you know of other people who have overcome obstacles to achieve in unexpected ways?

Word focus *take*

8 Look at these extracts from the stories. What do the expressions with *take* mean? Choose the correct option (a–c).

   1 Diane Van Deren was […] **taking part** in the Yukon Arctic Ultra.
     a leaving   b participating   c winning
   2 She […] had a kiwi-size piece of her brain **taken out**.
     a removed   b repaired   c returned
   3 […] a journey that had **taken** him **more than** half of his life.
     a been farther than b been longer than c been faster than
   4 Dau […] **took care of** a group of younger children.
     a controlled   b played with   c protected

9 Work in pairs. What do the expressions with *take* mean in these sentences?

   1 The Yukon Arctic Ultra takes place every two years.
   2 Diane Van Deren took up running after an operation to cure her epilepsy.
   3 Diane Van Deren couldn't take off her boots because they had frozen to her feet.
   4 John Dau's plane to New York took off from Nairobi airport.
   5 The fighting in Sudan took away John Dau's childhood.

Speaking

10 You are going to nominate an inspirational person for a prize. Choose someone from one of these categories. Make short biographical notes about the person and the reasons why you find them inspirational. Then give your presentation.

- art, music, and fashion
- business and academia
- movies and television
- local life
- science and medicine
- sports and adventure
- technology

Diane Van Deren

ON FEBRUARY 19, 2009, DIANE VAN DEREN WAS ONE OF A DOZEN RUNNERS TAKING PART IN THE YUKON ARCTIC ULTRA, A 400-MILE RACE ACROSS FROZEN TUNDRA IN THE MIDDLE OF WINTER. Not a single woman had ever completed it. With temperatures of 30 degrees below zero and only seven hours of daylight each day, it's probably the toughest race in the world. But, then, there is no woman like Diane Van Deren.

Twelve years earlier, Van Deren, a former professional tennis player, had a kiwi-size piece of her brain removed to treat her epilepsy. The operation was successful, but she noticed a strange side effect: she could run without stopping for hours.

At the start of the Arctic Ultra, icy winds froze Van Deren's water supplies, so she had nothing to drink for the first hundred miles. She kept going by sucking on frozen fruit and nut bars. On the eleventh day, the ice beneath her feet cracked open and Van Deren fell up to her shoulders into a freezing river. She managed to climb out but her soaked boots froze to her feet.

Yet somehow through it all, Van Deren remained positive. This was perhaps helped by another curious by-product of her operation. "I have a problem with short-term memory. I could be out running for two weeks, but if someone told me it was day one of a race," she jokes, "I'd say, Great, let's get started!"

On February 26, 2009, exactly twelve years after her surgery, Van Deren crossed the finish line of the Arctic Ultra. She was one of eight finishers—and the first and only woman.

> **by-product** (n) /ˈbaɪ ˌprɑdəkt/ a result that was not planned
> **epilepsy** (n) /ˈepɪˌlepsi/ an illness affecting the brain

John Dau

IN 2001, JOHN DAU BOARDED A PLANE TO NEW YORK. IT WAS THE BEGINNING OF ONE TRIP BUT THE END OF A JOURNEY THAT HAD TAKEN HIM MORE THAN HALF OF HIS LIFE. In 1987, aged thirteen, Dau fled his home in southern Sudan, running from the soldiers sent to destroy his village. He met up with a small group of boys like himself and together they walked for weeks to reach a refugee camp in Ethiopia. "I was barefoot and wearing no clothes; at night the desert was so cold. We thought about our parents all the time," remembers Dau. The boys had no food and nothing to drink. "We chewed grass and ate mud to stay alive."

Moving through hostile territory, the boys walked by night and slept by day. Eventually they reached the camp, where Dau spent the next four years. As one of the older boys, he led and took care of a group of younger children that eventually numbered 1,200. But Dau was forced to run again when the camp came under threat. Along with 27,000 other boys, he set off to walk back to Sudan. To get there they had to cross the Gilo River. "Rebels were shooting at us, so we had to dive into water infested with crocodiles," Dau recounts.

Thousands of boys were eaten, drowned, shot, or captured, and only 18,000 of them made it into Sudan. But the area was soon attacked, so Dau and the other "Lost Boys" of Sudan set off south again, this time to a camp in Kenya. By now, Dau had walked almost 1,000 miles.

Ten years later, Dau was one of a handful of Lost Boys sponsored to study in the US. A new kind of journey was about to begin.

> **rebel** (n) /ˈrebəl/ a soldier fighting against a government
> **refugee camp** (n) /ˈrefjʊʤi ˌkæmp/ a temporary home for people who have left their country of origin

10d First aid

Vocabulary injuries

1 Work in pairs. Complete the table with the things that cause these injuries. Some things can cause more than one injury. Add at least one more cause of each injury.

Allergic reactions	Cuts and bruises	Sprains and breaks

> blades and knives
> falling off something
> eating the wrong food
> insect bites
> tripping or falling
> wasp and bee stings

2 For each injury, decide with your partner what is the best thing to do.

Real life talking about injuries

3 🔊 **42** Look at the expressions for describing injuries. Which expressions refer to the injuries in Exercise 1? Listen and check.

> ▶ **TALKING ABOUT INJURIES**
>
> **Describing injuries**
> I'm feeling a little sick.
> I've been stung.
> It doesn't hurt.
> It hurts when I move it.
> It looks a little swollen.
> It might need stitches.
> It's just a sprain.
> It's painful.
> That looks nasty!
> You might have broken something.
> It's nothing.
>
> **Giving advice**
> If I were you, I'd go to the emergency room.
> I would keep an eye on it.
> I wouldn't just ignore it.
> You should put some antihistamine lotion on it.
> You'd better wash it right away.
> Why don't you go and see Rosana?
> It might be worth getting it X-rayed.
> You should get it looked at.
> Have you tried putting lotion on it?

4 🔊 **42** Listen to the conversations again. What advice is given in each case? Check your answers in the expressions for giving advice.

5 Pronunciation *and*

a 💿 **43** Listen and notice how *and* is linked to the word before it and how the *d* isn't pronounced. Repeat the expressions.

> A and E
> cuts and bruises
> sprains and breaks
> wasp and bee stings
> bites and stuff
> go and see Rosana

b Link words from A with words from B using *and*. Practice saying the pairs of words.

> **A** | day | doctors | eyes | food |
> | hands | mind | rich | fruit |

> **B** | body | drink | ears | famous |
> | night | nurses | nuts | knees |

6 Work as a class. You will be assigned a role as a patient or a doctor.

Patients: Choose one of the injuries below and think about how you will describe it to the doctor. Then visit each doctor and describe your problem. Who gives the best advice?

Doctors: Look at the list of injuries and think about appropriate treatment. Then listen to each patient and give advice. Which is the hardest case to treat?

> a deep cut on your thumb from a kitchen knife
> a painful ankle after jumping off a trampoline
> feeling sick after being stung by a wasp
> multiple cuts and bruises after a mountain biking accident
> strange skin rash after eating out
> neck and shoulder pain after falling off a horse

10e What do you think?

Writing a personal email

1 Who do you turn to when you need advice about these things? Work in pairs. Compare your ideas.

> car trouble
> difficulties at work
> financial problems
> personal problems
> relationship dilemmas

2 Read the email. Choose the best option (a–c).

  a The writer is asking for information about a job opportunity.

  b The writer is getting in touch with an old friend.

  c The writer needs some help making a decision.

3 Is the style of the email formal, neutral, or informal? Underline the words or expressions that show this.

4 What advice would you give to Kate? Tell your partner.

5 Writing skill linking ideas (2)

a Complete the table with the highlighted words from the email that belong in each group.

clearly	....
naturally	....
in fact	....
to be honest	....
Before I forget	....
Incidentally	....
Anyway	....
Well	....
All the same	....
Even so	....
However	....

Hi there,

Thanks so much for the get well card! I'm feeling a lot better now, actually. And I've been meaning to write to you for a while—I want your advice about something.

I have the chance to spend a year on a project in the South Pacific. (I know, it sounds like paradise—I bet you wish you were me!) It's a job in a community health center on Vanuatu. I'd have to do some training if I took the job, of course. I can do basic first aid, but I'd need to know more than that.

The thing is, I'm not sure if I should go. It would mean giving up the job I've got now, obviously. But I wouldn't mind that—it's not that great a job! And I've often thought about a career in nursing…

So, what do you think?

Hope all is well with you. By the way, were you able to sell your car?

Take care,

Kate

b Complete the sentences with suitable expressions. There is more than one possibility.

  1 Your problem sounds familiar. _____, I had to make a similar decision once.

  2 You'd miss your family at first, _____ .

  3 I hope I've helped you a little! _____, how's your sister?

  4 That's what I did. _____, I hope I've helped.

  5 It could be interesting. _____, it's going to be hard.

6 Think about a problem you need help with. Write an email to someone in your class.

7 Use these questions to check your email. Then send your email to someone in your class.

  • Have you used a variety of linking expressions?

  • Have you used them correctly?

8 Write a reply to the email you have received.

Simply walking is more tiring than
doing the same activity at sea level.

Before you watch

1 Work in groups. Look at the photo and discuss the questions.

   1   What is the person in the photo doing?
   2   Do you need any special qualities to do this?
   3   Why do you think walking is more tiring in the mountains than at sea level?

2 You will see people doing lots of activities in this video. Mark the activities you think you will see.

dancing	crossing a river
cooking	looking after animals
sailing	hiking in the mountains
flying	playing an instrument
ringing a bell	climbing rocks

While you watch

3 Watch the video and check your answers from Exercise 2.

4 Match the people (1–3) with how they adapt to living at high altitude (a–c).

   1   Tibetans   a   Scientists are not sure.
   2   Andeans   b   They breathe faster.
   3   Ethiopians   c   They have more hemoglobin in their blood.

5 Answer the questions.

   1   What causes mountain sickness?

   2   What has Dr. Aldenderfer been studying?

   3   What three things did ancient people need to be able to do with fire?
      a
      b
      c

   4   What might data from DNA studies tell us about how people adapt to high altitude?

6 Complete the sentences with words from the glossary. Check your answers with the video.

   1   A person takes in less oxygen with each _____ .
   2   Native people of the South American Andes developed a different _____ for living in thin mountain air.
   3   Ancient people were attracted to mountain heights by the _____ of good hunting.
   4   Humans also needed clothes for _____ ... clothes that were warm enough to protect the wearer from the _____ cold.
   5   The first _____ needed to make complex clothing, such as _____ , appeared as people were moving into the high altitudes of Tibet.

After you watch

7 Roleplay **planning a hiking trip**

a Work on your own. You are going on a hiking trip in the Andes. Plan what you need to do before you go, what to take with you, and how long you want to go for.

b Work in pairs. Compare your ideas with your partner and try to agree on as many points as you can. Do you think your partner will be a good hiking companion?

8 At the beginning of the video, the narrator says: "Even with the best equipment, mountain climbing can be hard work." What does that mean? Does having too much equipment take away from the challenge and adventure of climbing?

9 Work in groups and discuss these questions.

   1   Are there any places with extreme living conditions in your country?
   2   Do people live in these places?
   3   How have they adapted to living there?

---

adapt (v) /əˈtrɪbjut/ change something to make it suitable for a new situation
attract (v) /əˈtrækt/ make someone become interested in something
attribute (v) /əˈtrɪbjut/ say that something is responsible for something else
breath (n) /breθ/ a lungful of air
breathe (v) /brið/ take air into your body
enable (v) /enˈeɪbəl/ make a person able to do something
hemoglobin (n) /ˈhiməˌɡloʊbɪn/ substance in red blood cells that carries oxygen
hunting (n) /ˈhʌntɪŋ/ the activity of chasing and catching wild animals

hypoxia (n) /haɪˈpɑksiə/ the feeling of being sick and short of breath when you are at high altitude
intense (adj) /ɪnˈtens/ very great or extreme
lungs (n) /lʌŋz/ the organs in your chest used in breathing
needle (n) /ˈnid(ə)l/ a long thin pointed instrument with a hole at one end that is used to join pieces of fabric
proof (n) /pruf/ evidence that shows something is true
prospect (n) /ˈprɒspekt/ the possibility that something exists or might happen
protect (v) /ˈprɒspekt/ keep something safe
strategy (n) /ˈstrætədʒi/ a way to achieve an objective
survival (n) /sərˈvaɪvəl/ staying alive
tool (n) /tul/ a piece of equipment you use to make something

UNIT 10 REVIEW

Grammar

1 Work in pairs. Look at the photo. Under what circumstances would you do this activity?

2 What would you do if you were in this situation and:

- you got to the top and were too scared?
- had to go first?
- were the last one there?
- it was your first time?
- you felt sick?

3 Work in pairs. BASE jumping from this spot is illegal.

Student A: You are one of the people in the photo. Think about why you do this sport.

Student B: You are a park ranger who is in the valley. Think about the possible consequences.

Act out the conversation that takes place when Student A lands.

4 Work in pairs. For each of these things, agree on a definition and an example. Then compare with another pair.

a life-threatening situation	bravery
a dangerous place	extreme sports

I CAN	
give descriptions or definitions of things that include essential information (defining relative clauses)	☐
talk about improbable situations in the present or the future (second conditional)	☐

Vocabulary

5 Work in pairs. Which is the odd one out in each group? Why?

1 camp, home, hotel, plane
2 blood test, heal, scan, X-ray
3 algae, mirror, plants, seeds
4 pain, paramedic, technician, surgeon

6 Work in pairs. Answer as many questions as you can.

1 How might you sprain your ankle?
2 What would you do if a bee stung you?
3 What can people be allergic to?
4 Have you ever broken a bone?
5 Would you consider cosmetic surgery?
6 Do you know anyone who is afraid of injections?
7 What would be the worst thing about being an astronaut?
8 Who or what lives in a colony?

I CAN	
talk about the body and injuries	☐
talk about medicine and emergency medical treatments	☐

Real life

7 Choose the correct option. Then decide what injury or illness each piece of advice could refer to.

1 You should *get / getting* an X-ray.
2 You'd better *call / calling* an ambulance.
3 It might be worth *go / going* to the doctor's.
4 Have you tried *take / taking* antihistamines?
5 If I were you, I'd *put / putting* some lotion on it.

8 Work in pairs. Act out two conversations using advice from Exercise 7.

I CAN	
describe injuries and give first-aid advice	☐

Speaking

9 Work in groups. What do you have more confidence in: modern, alternative, or traditional medicine? Does it depend on the type of health problem?

Unit 11 Connections

This woman speaks *Koro*, a language that has just been "discovered" by linguists. *Photograph by Chris Rainier*

FEATURES

1 The photo shows someone being interviewed about the languages spoken in her region. Which of these parts of a newspaper do you think the interview would appear in?

business section	national news
opinion	politics and society
entertainment	sports pages
features	weekend edition
front page	world news

2 Work in pairs. Read the comments about newspapers. Think of at least two ways to complete each comment.

1 "I get the headlines on my cell phone, so…"
2 "I don't read the paper. It's too…"
3 "I don't believe everything I read because…"
4 "I turn straight to the sports pages even though…"

3 Work with a new partner. Prepare a survey on media habits. Use the comments from Exercise 2 to come up with questions. Ask at least three other classmates your questions. Then compare your results.

11a The last "uncontacted" tribe?

Reading

1 Work in groups. Look at the headline and the photo with the news item. Discuss the questions.

   1 What do you think the photo shows?
   2 Where might you expect to find isolated tribes?
   3 What might threaten such tribes?

2 Read the news item. What role do these organizations play in the story?

   1 Funai
   2 Survival International
   3 the government of Peru
   4 the BBC

3 Find the following information in the news item.

   1 three reactions to the photos the first time they were published
   2 what happened the second time the images were published

4 Work in pairs. Which of these things led to the story having more impact the second time?

   a a change in the Peruvian government policy
   b the involvement of the BBC
   c the changing nature of digital communication, e.g., viral videos
   d the video footage as well as photos
   e the increase in people with Internet access

The *last* "uncontacted" tribe?

In 2008, in order to draw attention to illegal logging on the Brazil-Peru border, the Brazilian department for indigenous groups' affairs (Funai) released photos of an "uncontacted" Amazonian tribe. Funai said that the tribe was under threat because of the logging. At the time, some people asked if the tribe was truly "uncontacted." The NGO Survival International said that they were confident that the photos were genuine.

The Survival International spokesman, David Hill, explained that his organization wasn't suggesting that the tribe had never had any contact with the outside world, but that they now lived without it. Nevertheless, the Peruvian government suggested that the story was no more than a strategy by groups opposed to development of the area's resources. Fast forward two years, by which time about 50 percent of the Peruvian Amazon had been contracted to oil and gas developers. The photos were republished to coincide with previously unseen footage of the tribe shown in a BBC documentary. This time, the images went viral. Survival International said the images had spread across the world within minutes. Their website had over a million hits in three days. The images provoked a worldwide reaction on Facebook, YouTube, and Vimeo. A typical post asked why nobody had done anything to save these tribes. Three days later, the Peruvian government announced that they would work with the Brazilian authorities to stop illegal logging in the area. The contractors in the area were unavailable for comment. But as a Funai spokesperson said later, one image had had more impact than one thousand reports.

> **logging** (n) /ˈlɒgɪŋ/ cutting down and transporting trees
> **viral** (n) /ˈvaɪrəl/ an Internet communication that people send on to lots of other people

One of the world's last uncontacted tribes
Photograph by Gleison Miranda

Grammar **reported speech**

5 Look at the highlighted sentences in the article. Choose the actual words.

1 Funai said, "The tribe *is / was* under threat because of the logging."
2 People asked, "*Is / Was* the tribe truly uncontacted?"
3 Survival International said, "*They / We* are confident that the photos are genuine."

6 Underline six other examples of reported speech in the news item. How do verbs, question forms, and pronouns change when words are reported?

▶ REPORTED SPEECH

They said (that)	
He asked if/whether	they would print it.
She asked why/how	

For more information and practice, see page 170.

7 Change the reported words in the news item to the actual words. Work in pairs. Compare your answers.

8 With your partner, match the quotes about the story (1–6) with the people who you think said them (a–d). Then report the words in the style of the news item.

1 "We took the photos to show that these people exist."
2 "How many tribes like this are there?"
3 "The term 'uncontacted' is more of a media word than a scientific term."
4 "Do unseen tribes exist?"
5 "There is no evidence they exist."
6 "If we don't save these tribes, this will happen to all of us."

a a language expert
b an anonymous poster
c a Funai spokesperson
d a Peruvian government official

9 Read about the first contact some tribes had with outsiders. Complete the text with the correct form of the verbs for reported speech.

In the Survival International video *Stranger in the Forest,* tribal people of Brazil spoke of their first contact experiences. One man recalled that his father ¹ _____ (make) friends with three white men and ² _____ (help) them, but that illnesses ³ _____ (follow) quickly. Another explained that although they ⁴ _____ (have) their own forest diseases, they ⁵ _____ (not / kill) like measles or malaria. A young man said that the people who ⁶ _____ (die) had knowledge that he ⁷ _____ (need) and that he ⁸ _____ (not / have) any way of getting this knowledge now. He said that if the forest ⁹ _____ (not / mark) as theirs, the outsiders ¹⁰ _____ (take) it all. The final speaker told the filmmakers that his group ¹¹ _____ (be) now small as a result of contact with outsiders and asked them how they ¹² _____ (can stop) this from happening again.

Speaking and writing

10 Work in two pairs within a group of four.

Pair A: Turn to page 153 and follow the instructions.

Pair B: Turn to page 154 and follow the instructions.

11 In the group, act out the dialogues. Then write a short news item about what happened to the other pair.

12 Compare your report with the original news item.

Vocabulary **communications technology**

1 Complete the sentences with some of these words. Then write your own questions with the other words.

blog	broadband	ebook	Flickr®
Skype™	texting	tweet	Twitter
WiFi	YouTube		

1 Do you follow anyone on .... ?
2 Do you prefer .... or calling your friends?
3 Do you know how to upload photos to .... ?
4 Do you think you pay a lot for your .... connection?
5 Do you use .... to talk to people?
6 Have you ever written a .... ?

2 Work in pairs. Ask and answer your questions from Exercise 1.

Listening

3 Work in pairs. Read the headlines. What do you think the stories are about? Write one sentence for each headline.

1 **Company fires workers by text**

2 **YouTube or "UFOtube"?**

3 **How to enjoy tomorrow's solar eclipse**

4 **Email alert warns of traffic chaos**

5 **Tweet your way around the world**

4 🔊 **44** Listen and write the number of the conversation next to the headline. There is one extra.

5 ▶ **44** Listen again and choose the correct option (a–c).

1 The journalist asks her Twitter followers _____ .
   a to meet her for breakfast
   b to send in photos
   c to suggest things to do
2 The blog reminds readers _____ .
   a not to bookmark the eclipse page
   b not to use telescopes
   c to check the weather
3 The company told people _____ .
   a not to show up for work
   b not to use text messages
   c to come to work early on Monday
4 The politician has invited aliens _____ .
   a to come to his house
   b to meet him
   c to watch his video

6 Work in groups. What do you think about the media used in each case in Exercise 4?

1 Was it appropriate? Was it effective? Was it innovative?
2 What other ways are there to communicate this information?
3 How do you use these media?

Grammar reporting verbs

7 Complete these sentences from Exercise 5. Then underline the reporting verbs.

1 The journalist asks her Twitter followers
   _____ .
2 The blog reminds readers _____ .
3 The company told people _____ .
4 The politician invited aliens _____ .

8 What follows the reporting verbs in Exercise 7? Choose the correct option (a–c).

a the word *that*
b a verb
c a noun

9 Which verb form is used for the reported words?

10 Write the direct speech for the reported speech in Exercise 7. Sometimes, more than one answer is possible.

▶ REPORTING VERBS: PATTERNS		
ask / tell / remind / invite	someone	(not) infinitive
promise / offer		(not) infinitive
For more information and practice, see page 171.		

11 Match the words in these sentences with the reporting verbs in the grammar box. Then write sentences reporting what the people said.

1 Marta to Amy: "Don't forget to turn off your cell phone."
2 Jose to Marta: "Can you set up my email?"
3 Amy to Jose: "Come and watch the movie on our new flat screen TV."
4 Marta to Amy: "Plug in the battery charger first."
5 Jose to Marta: "I can upload those photos to the computer for you."
6 Amy to Jose: "Don't worry, I'll turn it off when I'm done."

▶ REPORTING VERBS: THOUGHTS
Verbs like *realize, think, wonder,* and *know* have the same pattern as *say* and *ask*.
For more information and practice, see page 171.

12 Look at the audioscript on page 181. Underline reported thoughts with the verbs *realize, think, wonder,* and *know*.

13 Pronunciation contrastive stress

a ◑ **45** Listen to these exchanges from two of the conversations in Exercise 4. Notice how the words in bold are stressed. Repeat the exchanges.

1 A: It's a great idea to use Twitter for something like that.
   B: I didn't realize Twitter could be useful for **anything**!
2 C: It says here there's an eclipse tomorrow, did you know?
   D: Tomorrow? I thought it was **today**.

b ◑ **46** Listen to four other exchanges. Repeat the exchanges.

Speaking

14 Work in pairs. Have you ever done any of these things? Tell your partner.

- made a promise you couldn't keep
- offered to do something without thinking about the consequences
- invited someone to do something and later regretted it
- asked someone to do something and it turned out badly

I once promised to buy my brother a car.

Wow, that's generous. So what went wrong?

11c Digital connections

Reading

1 Are these things "communication"? Think about your answers. Then discuss your answers with the class.

1 An author writes a book. It is read by 10,000 people.
2 A celebrity has 100,000 followers on Twitter.
3 A TV news program is watched by one million viewers.
4 You have 500 friends on Facebook.

2 Work in pairs. Say what you think these terms mean. Read the article on page 135 and underline the terms. Check your ideas.

> the printing press
> connecting tools
> digital communication
> social networking
> digital media
> new media

3 Read the article again. Choose the correct option (a–c).

1 The invention of the printing press was important because:
   a books became easy to produce.
   b people had greater access to information.
   c it was a powerful tool.
2 What is Wesch's main area of interest?
   a Social networking
   b Digital technology
   c Internet videos
3 What does Wesch say about Internet relationships?
   a They are the same as family relationships.
   b They are not like real relationships.
   c He doesn't understand them.
4 What does Wesch say about digital media?
   a People should find new uses for these applications.
   b Social networking has no useful purpose in the real world.
   c Connecting to more and more people has no real value.

Critical thinking summarizing

4 Read the summary of Wesch's ideas. Choose the correct options.

Michael Wesch suggests that changing the way we communicate with each other [1] *can change / cannot change* the relationships we have with other people. He thinks words like "community" [2] *still have / might not have* the same meaning when they are used about people who are only connected to each other digitally. He also thinks that we [3] *have always been able / have not started* to use social networking to its full potential.

5 Find examples in the article that support the three ideas in the summary in Exercise 4.

6 Do you agree with what Wesch says? Tell the class your reasons.

Word focus *time*

7 Find three expressions with the word *time* in the article. Which one(s) refer to:

a an occasion / occasions?   b a historical period?

8 Work in pairs. Match the two parts of the exchanges.

1 Do you remember the time before color TV?
2 In ten years' time, all books will be digital.
3 I was going to call you, but I didn't have time.
4 It's time to go.
5 Why is your phone buzzing?

a I know! I've been really busy too.
b I don't know. It does it all the time.
c Hang on. I'm not ready yet.
d That soon? I don't agree.
e No! I'm not that old.

Speaking

9 Read the questions and make notes of your ideas.

1 Could we manage in the modern world without digital communication?
2 Is it possible to be addicted to things such as texting, Twitter, or Facebook?
3 Are there any potential dangers in the way we use digital media?

10 Work in groups. Discuss the questions in Exercise 9. Did you change your mind about anything during the discussion?

> I think that …

> Well, I thought that … , but now …

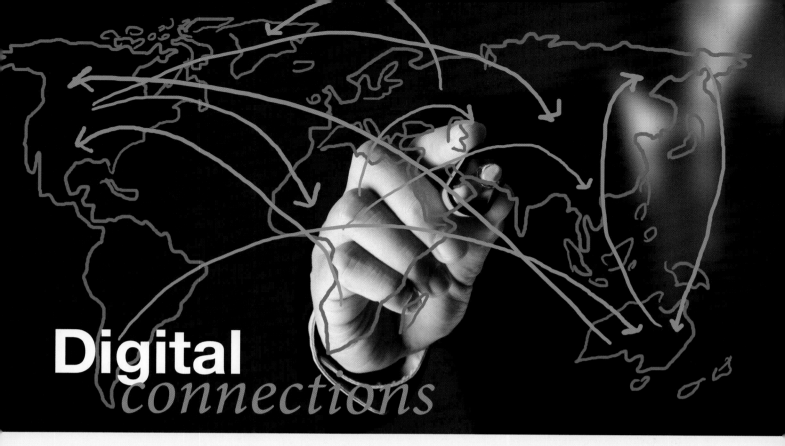

Digital connections

Technology is connecting us in ways never seen before in human history. How will that change our societies, our relationships, ourselves?

That's the question that interests Michael Wesch. The last time communications technology had such a wide-ranging impact was 500 years ago with the invention of the printing press. Being able to print texts instead of writing them by hand transformed the world. It changed the way people could communicate with each other. Suddenly, multiple copies of books could be made quickly and easily. As more books became available, ideas spread much more rapidly. But what will be the impact of digital technology, the most powerful connecting tool we have ever seen?

Michael Wesch argues that communication is fundamental to our relationships, so it follows that a change in the way we communicate will change those relationships. Wesch, a university professor, explores digital communication in his work. In particular, Wesch and his students look at social networking and other interactive Internet tools like YouTube. When people create and share personal videos on YouTube, anyone anywhere can watch them. Wesch says that this leads to some people feeling a sort of deep connection with the entire world. But it's not a real relationship; it's not the same as the connection you feel with a member of your family. In fact, as Wesch says, it's a relationship without any real responsibility that you can turn off at any moment. So does it make sense to talk about a YouTube "community"?

Wesch himself experienced the impact of digital media when he created and posted his own short video on YouTube. It attracted immediate attention and has been viewed millions of times. In his video, he tells us that webpages get 100 billion hits a day and that a new blog is started every half second. He asks us to think about the power of this technology and how we use it. What could we do with it? What is its potential?

Wesch isn't interested in what new media was originally designed for, but in how it can be used in other ways. For example, social protests such as gathering signatures for online petitions can now be done using Facebook. He says that it's important to end up in control of the technology, not vice versa.

Outside of the university, in the real world, Wesch believes it's crucial for people to be able to use the new environment of digital media for the greatest possible impact. "It's the tragedy of our times that we are now so connected we fail to see it. I want to believe that technology can help us see relationships and global connections in positive new ways. It's pretty amazing that I have this little box sitting on my desk through which I can talk to any one of a billion people. And yet do any of us really use all the potential that's there?" ∎

petition (n) /pəˈtɪʃən/ a written request signed by many people, usually to ask for action by an authority
potential (n) /pəˈtenʃəl/ what something could become

11d Can I take a message?

Real life telephone messages

1 🔊 **47** Listen, and complete the notes.

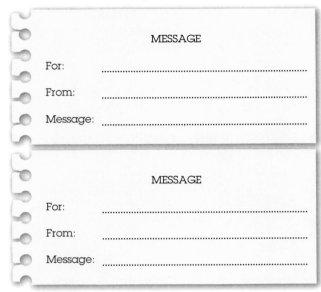

```
              MESSAGE

  For:      ..................................................

  From:     ..................................................

  Message:  ..................................................
```

```
              MESSAGE

  For:      ..................................................

  From:     ..................................................

  Message:  ..................................................
```

2 🔊 **47** Look at the expressions for telephone messages. Listen to the telephone calls again. Mark the expressions the speakers use.

> ▶ **TELEPHONE MESSAGES**
>
> **Introductions**
> This is a message for Raj Singh.
> Could I speak to Jess Parker, please?
> Is Jess there?
> Can I take a message?
> Could I leave a message?
>
> **Message content**
> Can you ask her to call me?
> It's about the apartment.
> I'm returning her call.
> I'd like to speak to her as soon as possible.
>
> **Caller's details**
> I'm at 617-555-1212.
> My number is 617-555-1212.
> Can I take your name, please?
> Can I ask who's calling?
>
> **Endings**
> I'll try and call you later.
> I'll call back.
> I'll let her know that you called.
> She'll get back to you.

3 🔊 **48** Listen to the messages that are passed on to Raj and Jess. Answer the questions for each person.

   1 How many messages are passed on in total?
   2 What is the mistake in the messages from Exercise 1?

4 Work in pairs.

Student A: Give the correct message for Raj to your partner.

Student B: Give the correct message for Jess to your partner.

5 Pronunciation **polite requests with *can* and *could***

a 🔊 **49** Listen to these requests from the second telephone call in Exercise 1. Notice how the speaker's voice rises on *please*.

   1 Could I speak to Jess Parker, please?

   2 Can I take a message?

b Work in pairs. Practice making requests with *can* and *could* using these ideas. Pay attention to sounding polite.

   1 give me your name / number / address
   2 leave my name / number / address
   3 ask him/her to call me back / get in touch / give me a call
   4 make an appointment
   5 call sometime

6 Work in pairs. Look at the audioscript on page 181 for the second telephone call in Exercise 1. Take a role each. Memorize the conversation. Then close your book and practice the conversation. Change roles and repeat the conversation.

7 Work in pairs. You are going to leave a message for someone in your class. Use the expressions for telephone messages to help you.

Student A: Choose a classmate (Student C). Decide what your message is. "Call" Student B and leave the message for Student C.

Student B: Take the message for Student C.

Then change roles.

8 Work in a new pair with the classmate you took the message for. Give this person the message.

11e A community meeting

Writing a report of a meeting

1 Read the notes taken at a residents' meeting to discuss the inclusion of their street on Google Street View. Answer the questions.

1 Ms. Macy and Mr. Ross are against the idea. What issues did they mention?
2 What points did other residents make?
3 What action did the residents decide to take?

2 Writing skill using notes to write a report

a Read the first paragraph of the report of the meeting. Answer the questions.

1 Which part of the notes does this paragraph correspond to?
2 What are the main differences between the language used in the report and the language used in the notes?

b Write these notes as full sentences. Use the word(s) in parentheses and make any other necessary changes.

> 1 next meeting Nov 2 (on)
> 2 absent: Mr. & Mrs. Watts (and)
> 3 call Thurs. / Fri. (or)
> 4 2 street lights (second)
> 5 address? (what)
> 6 ask library, town hall, etc. (and so on)
> 7 not a big problem + easy to solve (in addition)

3 Imagine you were at the residents' meeting. Use the rest of the notes to complete the report. Write full sentences and add any additional details you think are relevant.

4 Work in pairs. Exchange your reports and compare what you have written. Use these questions to check your reports.

- Is the factual information the same?
- Are there any differences in the way you have reported the meeting?

> *Residents' meeting Oct 11*
> *1 GOOGLE STREET VIEW*
> *1.1 concern about Street View & privacy:*
> *— news story about cat on Street View (Ms. Macy)*
> *— house numbers / people's faces visible (Mr. Ross)*
>
> *1.2 other viewpoints:*
> *— satellite image sites — more detail +*
> *this info already widely available (Ms. Falco)*
> *— burglars — don't need Street View!*
> *(Mr. & Mrs. Lund) (general agreement here!)*
>
> *1.3 questions:*
> *can a street opt out of Street View?*
> *are we covered by any privacy laws?*
> *legal situation?*
>
> *Action:*
> *Ms. Falco to investigate (contact Google, other*
> *residents' associations, etc.) and get back to us.*

Residents' meeting October 11

The first item on the agenda was Google Street View. Several residents expressed their concerns about Google Street View and privacy. For example, Ms. Macy said she had read about a woman in New York being able to see her cat through her apartment window on Street View. Another resident, Mr. Ross, was worried that house numbers or people's faces would be visible.

They were two women with one goal.

Before you watch

1 Work in groups. Look at the photo and the title of this video and discuss the questions.

1 What do you think was the women's goal?
2 Why were they doing this?
3 What kind of problems do you think they had?

2 Write down four ways of keeping in contact with people when you travel. How do you think the women kept in contact with others on their trip?

While you watch

3 Watch the video and check your answers from Exercises 1 and 2.

4 Watch the video again. Number these things in the order you first see them in the video.

a	a dog	e	a bowl
b	sunglasses	f	icicles
c	boots	g	gloves
d	a tent	h	a map

5 Are these sentences true (T) or false (F)? Correct the false sentences.

1 Liv and Ann wanted to be the first women to ski across Antarctica.
2 They wrote a book about their adventure.
3 Ann believes there's nothing left to explore.
4 Winds were not a problem for the women.
5 They used hot water to warm their fingers.
6 They communicated with people from other countries by radio.
7 People told the women about what they wanted to do with their lives too.
8 Their next goal is to cross the Arctic Ocean.

6 Match the sentence beginnings (1–6) with the endings (a–f).

1 The crossing had been completed only once before
2 You never know how you're going to be
3 The hardships got worse
4 Liv and Ann shared their story
5 What we ended up getting
6 Despite their remote location,

a with people from 150 countries through an online journal.
b when they arrived in Antarctica.
c the women still felt connected with people around the planet.
d in your moment of truth.
e by a team of two male explorers.
f were other people's dreams.

After you watch

7 Roleplay **a video interview**

Work in pairs.

Student A: Imagine you are skiing across Antarctica. Read the information below.

- You are going to connect to an Internet video link to answer questions about your trip from people in different countries.
- Write down some of the experiences you want to talk about, for example: the training, the weather, the food.
- Answer the questions people ask you.

Student B: You are going to talk to an explorer who is skiing across Antarctica. Read the information below.

- You are going to connect to an Internet video link where you can ask the person questions.
- Write down the questions you want to ask the person, for example: about their training, the weather, the food.
- Ask your questions.

Act out the interview. When you have finished, change roles and act out the interview again.

8 Ann Bancroft says: "There's certainly *you* to explore, you know, internally. And these trips draw out new things in you as an individual." What do you think she means? What kinds of new things do you think people learn on extreme journeys like this one?

9 Work in groups and discuss these questions.

1 What parts of the world are still left to explore?
2 Are there any parts of your country you would like to explore?
3 Who would you go with on an extreme journey? Why?

---

achieve (v) /əˈtʃiv/ be successful in doing something
demanding (adj) /dɪˈmændɪŋ/ very hard
draw out (v) /ˈdrɔ ˈaʊt/ bring out
goal (n) /goʊl/ objective
hardship (n) /ˈhɑrdˌʃɪp/ something that makes life difficult
overcome (v) /ˌoʊvərˈkʌm/ succeed in dealing with a problem
prior to (phrase) /ˈpraɪər tu/ before
relate to (v) /rɪˈleɪt tu/ have something in common with
remark (v) /rɪˈmɑrk/ comment
remote (adj) /rɪˈmoʊt/ far from other people
share (v) /ʃeər/ tell other people about
struggle (n) /ˈstrʌgəl/ a fight or battle
tire (n) /taɪər/ the rubber part that goes around the outside of a wheel
undertake (v) /ˌʌndərˈteɪk/ do something difficult
unparalleled (adj) /ʌnˈpærəˌleld/ unique
unpredictable (adj) /ˌʌnprɪˈdɪktəbəl/ changing a lot

UNIT 11 REVIEW

Grammar

1 Work in pairs. Do you agree with these statements?

1 Cell phones are dangerous.
2 Children shouldn't use cell phones.
3 Fears about health problems and cell phones are unnecessary.

2 Read the news item. Does it support the statements in Exercise 1?

NEW DOUBTS OVER CELL PHONES

New doubts have been raised over the safety of cell phones, according to a report published yesterday.

Back in the 1990s, when cell phones first appeared, few people asked if there were any health risks. Within a decade, cell phone ownership had exploded, and several groups suggested that their overuse was dangerous and could lead to an increased risk of cancer. Now, with about five billion users worldwide, there is still no definitive evidence of this. Still, several governments have told people to limit the time and frequency of their cell phone calls, and reminded parents not to allow their children to use them. In fact, health professionals said recently that the danger to young people had become a mental, not a physical, health issue. According to Eric Schmidt, Google's executive chairman, there are now only two states for children: "asleep or online." Yesterday's report said that vulnerable young people were becoming addicted to the online world and unable to cope with the challenges of the real world.

3 Find six reporting verbs in the text. Write what people actually said. Then compare with your partner.

4 Work with a new partner. Tell him/her what you thought about the statements in Exercise 1 and whether the news item surprised you.

I CAN	
report people's words (reported speech)	
use appropriate verbs to report people's words (reporting verbs)	

Vocabulary

5 In which section of a newspaper would you find information about these things?

1 an in-depth interview with a musician
2 changes in the government
3 currency exchange rates
4 national sports results
5 traffic problems
6 the newspaper's opinions of events
7 TV programming
8 a volcano eruption in the South Pacific

6 Work in pairs. Tell your partner if and how you keep in touch with these people.

cousins	immediate family
current friends	old school friends
old colleagues	people you met on vacation
grandparents	

I CAN	
talk about news media	
talk about communications technology	

Real life

7 Work in pairs. Put the sentences from one half of a telephone conversation (a–e) into a logical order. Then act out the conversation, adding the other person's words.

a Thanks. I'll try and call him later, anyway.
b It's about the books he ordered. He asked me to call him.
c OK. Well, could I leave a message?
d Yes, I'm at 555–1212 until about five.
e Is John Liu there, please?   1

I CAN	
leave, take, and pass on telephone messages	

Speaking

8 What was the most recent news story you heard? Tell your partner:

- where you read or heard the story.
- why you remember it.
- what people involved in the story said.

Unit 12 Experts

Cormorant fisherman, China
Photograph by Chris McLennan

FEATURES

1 Work in groups. Look at the photo and the caption. The fisherman uses the cormorants, a type of bird, to help him catch fish. How do you think this works?

2 Some types of animals are "experts" at certain tasks. What do you know about these animals? Discuss in pairs.

> dogs falcons beavers sharks bees chameleons

3 Do people work with any of the animals in the list above? Why and how?

4 Work in groups. Discuss the questions.

1 Think of three ancient traditions from your country. Have they died out or do people still follow them?
2 What skills and expertise do people have now in things that didn't exist in the past?

12a Experts in the field

Vocabulary expeditions

1 Work in pairs. How can these people or things help you on an expedition?

backpack	dried food
equipment	guide
GPS	hammock
machete	setting up a camp
sleeping bag	tent

2 Think of three more things you think would be essential on an expedition. Tell your partner and explain your reasons.

Listening

3 Read about Emma Stokes and Beth Shapiro. Answer the questions.

1   What are their areas of expertise?
2   What kind of places have they traveled to?
3   What kind of things could cause problems in those areas?

4 Work in pairs. You are going to listen to the stories of two uncomfortable experiences Emma and Beth had. First, decide which story you think these words come from.

bite	bones	deserted
eaten alive	eye-opener	flatten
go crazy	mammoth	mummies
net	remote	steps
trumpeting	tusks	

5 🔊 **50** Listen to the stories. Check your answers from Exercise 4.

6 🔊 **50** Listen again. Answer the questions.

1   Who was Emma with?
2   What woke her up?
3   What had they done wrong?
4   What happened to the camp?
5   What was Beth hoping to find in Siberia?
6   What was the place where she set up camp like?
7   What was the problem there?
8   How did they try to deal with the problem?

Emma Stokes is a wildlife researcher who has coordinated projects to protect gorillas and tigers. She's used to tough conditions like cutting a path through the forest or sleeping out in a hammock. Her first expedition was to an African forest, where she had an unexpected experience.

Beth Shapiro is a biologist and a leading authority on extinct mammal species. Much of her work is done in the field, particularly in Siberia. It's often a challenge to find animal remains. But on her first visit there, it was a living animal that caused the problem.

7 Read the comments. Who do you think said each one: Emma or Beth?

1 "We could have been killed."
2 "We could have gone there at a different time of year."
3 "We couldn't have avoided the insects."
4 "We should have checked the area before we camped."
5 "We should have taken more repellent."
6 "We shouldn't have put up our tents in that spot."

8 Have you ever had a similar experience? Tell your partner.

> ▶ **WORDBUILDING prefix** *in-*
>
> We can add *in-* to the beginning of a word to mean "not."
> *inappropriate* place
> *inadequate* nets

Grammar *should have* and *could have*

9 Look again at the comments in Exercise 7. Match the comments (1–6) with the meanings (a–d).

a This was the right thing to do, but we didn't do it.
b This was the wrong thing to do, but we did it.
c This was possible, but it didn't happen.
d This was impossible and it didn't happen.

> ▶ *SHOULD HAVE* **and** *COULD HAVE*
>
> | *should (not)* *could (not)* | *have* + past participle |
> |---|---|
>
> For more information and practice, see page 171.

10 Look at the grammar box. Complete the story about being treated by a traditional healer with *should (not) have* and *could (not) have* and past participle forms.

I'm an anthropologist and once when I was working in a remote area, I ate something ¹ I _____ (eat). I was pretty sick. ² I _____ (feel) any worse, actually! I suppose ³ I _____ (have) some medicine with me, but I didn't. Anyway, the local healer brought me the strongest of their local medicines. ⁴ I _____ (take) it immediately, but it smelled so bad that I didn't, and of course I got much worse. So the next day I accepted the medicine and after a few terrible days, I got better. Then I found out what the medicine was! I really think ⁵ I _____ (die) without it, though.

11 Pronunciation *should have* and *could have*

a 🔊 51 Listen to the sentences. Notice how *should have* and *could have* sound like one word.

b 🔊 51 Listen again and repeat the sentences.

Speaking

12 Work as a class. You will be assigned a role as an amateur or an expert.

Amateurs: Look at the list of activities and think about a time you had a problem with one of them. What went wrong? Try to find an expert who can tell you what you should have done. Who gives the best advice?

Experts: Choose the activity that you know most about. Think about some of the typical things people do wrong and why. Then listen to the amateurs. What is the most common problem?

> cooking
> driving
> first aid
> fixing things
> going to an important social event
> starting a new job
> traveling somewhere new
> visiting a foreign country

> *I was making a cake for a special occasion once and it didn't rise.*

> *Did you use baking powder? You should have added it to the flour.*

12b The man who ate his boots

Reading

1 Work in pairs. You are going to read a review of a book about Arctic expeditions called *The Man Who Ate His Boots*. Discuss the questions.

1 What kind of environment is the Arctic region?
2 What challenges do explorers face there?
3 How much do you know about the lifestyles of people who live in the Arctic?

2 Read the first paragraph of the book review. Find the following information.

1 the reason for the expeditions
2 the fate of the expeditions
3 two words to describe the explorers

3 Read the whole review. Are these sentences true (T) or false (F)?

1 The explorers learned a lot from the local Inuit people they met.
2 Canvas tents were an appropriate type of shelter.
3 The explorers wore inadequate clothing.
4 The explorers pulled their own sleds.
5 The explorers had no access to vitamin C to prevent scurvy.

4 What do you think the title of the book refers to? Tell your partner.

THE MAN WHO ATE HIS BOOTS is a fascinating account of expeditions that went wrong. The book examines the 19th century search for a route to Asia via the Northwest Passage through the Arctic Ocean. Author Anthony Brandt describes the many attempts by both land and sea that ended in failure and tragedy, including the lavish 1845 expedition led by Sir John Franklin. Brandt shows how these brave, yet sometimes foolish, explorers could have avoided starvation, frostbite, and even death if they had copied the survival techniques of the local Inuit people. Some of the more surprising details the book reveals include:

IGLOOS   The explorers, despite repeatedly watching the Inuit build igloos, insisted on using canvas tents. Tents freeze in sub-zero temperatures and give little insulation to anyone inside them. If they had learned to build igloos, the explorers would have been warm even in the worst Arctic weather.

SEALSKIN   If the explorers had worn sealskin and furs like the Inuit, they wouldn't have suffered from the frostbite that was common among them, but rare among the Inuit.

DOG TEAMS   Why didn't the British use dog teams to pull their sleds? Hauling sleds themselves was a tradition among many explorers right into the early 20th century. It cost Scott and his men their lives on their return from the South Pole in 1912.

The British did get something right, however, when Captain Edward Parry grew salad vegetables in boxes on board his ship. It was known that fresh vegetables and fresh meat prevented scurvy, although at that time the reason for this (vitamin C) had not been discovered. Parry's men wouldn't have been as healthy if they hadn't eaten the salads.

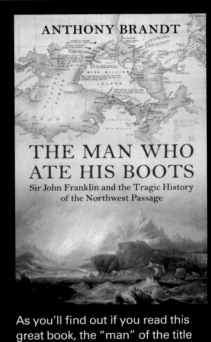

ANTHONY BRANDT

THE MAN WHO ATE HIS BOOTS
Sir John Franklin and the Tragic History of the Northwest Passage

As you'll find out if you read this great book, the "man" of the title had to eat more than his boots in the end.

canvas (n) /ˈkænvəs/ a type of cotton used in tents and sails.
frostbite (n) /ˈfrɒstˌbaɪt/ irreversible damage to the body caused by freezing conditions, usually affecting toes and fingers
lavish (adj) /ˈlævɪʃ/ extravagant, luxurious, excessive
scurvy (n) /ˈskɜrvi/ an illness caused by lack of vitamin C
starvation (n) /stɑrˈveɪʃən/ death or loss of strength caused by not eating

Grammar **third conditional**

5 Look at these sentences from the review. Which verbs are used to make the third conditional?

1 If they had learned to build igloos, the explorers would have been warm.
2 Parry's men wouldn't have been as healthy if they hadn't eaten the salads.

6 Look at the sentences in Exercise 5 again. Answer the questions.

1 a Did the explorers learn to build igloos?
  b Were they warm?
2 a Were Parry's men healthy?
  b Did they eat salads?

▶ THIRD CONDITIONAL		
If + past perfect,	would could (not) might	have + past participle
For more information and practice, see page 172.		

7 Look at the grammar box. Find two more third conditional sentences in the review. Why is the conditional in the first sentence formed with *could*?

8 Rewrite the sentences using the third conditional and any words in parentheses.

1 The British got frostbite because they wore inadequate clothing. (furs)
   If they'd worn furs, they wouldn't have gotten frostbite.
2 The men were exhausted because they pulled their own sleds. (dogs)
3 The sleds were heavy because the men took unnecessary items. (essential items)
4 Some men got scurvy because they didn't eat enough fresh food. (Inuit food)
5 They became ill because they didn't know their canned food was poisonous.
6 One expedition got stuck in the ice because they believed the Arctic Ocean couldn't freeze. (ask local people)
7 The expeditions weren't successful because they didn't follow local customs.

9 Work in pairs. Match the pairs of sentences. Then write a new sentence using the third conditional with *would, could,* or *might*.

1 We should have planned everything better.
2 We got lost.
3 We couldn't ask for help.
4 The local people gave us directions.
5 We forgot to check the museum opening times.
6 We couldn't get into the museum.

a We got there too late.
b The vacation was a disaster.
c We didn't know how to read the road signs.
d We found the way back to the main road.
e We should have taken a phrase book.
f We didn't buy tickets ahead of time.

Speaking

10 Think of three times in your life when you had to decide on a course of action, whether it was important or trivial. Think about the answers to these questions.

1 Was it easy or difficult to decide what to do?
2 How did you decide?
3 What would/could have happened if you had done something different?

11 Work in pairs. Tell your partner about your decisions. Ask your partner follow-up questions. Would you have done the same things?

> When we were in high school, we had to choose which foreign language to study.

> Oh, so did we. What were your options?

> Well,...

12c The legacy of the samurai

Reading

1 How much do you know about the samurai? Work in pairs. Try to answer the questions.

1 Who were the samurai?
2 Where were they from?
3 When did they live?
4 What did they do?

2 Before you read about the samurai, look at these words. Work in pairs and make connections between the words.

army	combat	duty	enemies
fighting	generals	martial arts	opponents
soldiers	sword	warrior	weapon

An army is made up of soldiers.

3 Read the article about the samurai on page 147. Check your answers from Exercise 1. Find the words in Exercise 2.

4 According to the article, are these statements true (T) or false (F)?

1 The early samurai were similar to medieval European knights.
2 The samurai eventually died out following their defeat in battle.
3 Samurai warriors had a wide range of cultural interests.
4 The military skills of the samurai have been lost.
5 The legacy of the samurai has spread outside of Japan.

5 Find these words in the article. Look at how they are used and try to guess their meaning. Then replace the words in bold in the sentences with these words.

savage	battle-weary	unarmed	overcoming
appeal	lone	fierce	threat

1 I don't understand the **attraction** of swords.
2 I think I am **winning against** my opponent.
3 That boxer is **intense and aggressive**.
4 The army was **exhausted after the attack**.
5 The battle was **exceptionally violent**.
6 We fought **without any weapons**.
7 What was the main **danger** to the success of the samurai?
8 The police say they are looking for a **single, unaccompanied** gunman.

Critical thinking **relevance**

6 Which of these sentences could be included as additional information? Where should the sentences go in the article?

1 His words might easily have been spoken by a Bushido master from three centuries ago.
2 The samurai promised to be loyal to these men, who needed soldiers to keep their power.
3 Samurai also played *Go*, a board game about territorial conquest.
4 The classic movie *Seven Samurai* by Japanese director Akira Kurosawa has been described as one of the most influential movies ever made.

Word focus *go*

7 Look at these sentences and choose the correct meaning (a–b) of the expressions with *go*.

1 The original samurai **went into battle** on horseback.
    a fought   b sat
2 Things **didn't go well** for the samurai.
    a didn't move   b weren't good
3 Samurai fighting skills **went into decline**.
    a improved   b weakened
4 He's asked if he'd like to **go back in time**.
    a return home   b return to the past

8 Work in pairs. What do the expressions with *go* mean in these sentences?

1 The battle plan went wrong and ended in disaster.
2 The battle went on for six days non-stop.
3 The number of injured soldiers is going up daily.
4 Suddenly, everything went quiet.
5 We've decided to go ahead with our plan.
6 I'm going to have a go at flower arranging.

Speaking

9 Would you like to go back in time and experience life in a different age and country? Or would you prefer to live in the future? Think about the following points.

- when and where
- why that time appeals to you
- your role or position in that society
- opportunities
- possible dangers

10 Work in groups. Ask questions to find out about your classmates' time-traveling choices. Which is more popular: the past or the future?

THE LEGACY OF THE SAMURAI

Samurai history

The samurai (the word means "one who serves") were the elite warrior class of Japan for nearly 700 years. In the tenth century, the imperial court in Kyoto tried and failed to organize a conscript army. If the court had succeeded, the wealthy landowners might not have employed private soldiers, and the samurai might never have existed. The original samurai were chivalrous warriors who went into battle on horseback, challenging opponents to ritualized combat. Their customs would have been familiar to a medieval European knight if they had ever met each other. Later, as armies became larger and the fighting more savage, most samurai trained for hand-to-hand combat. However, during a long period of peace in Japan, things didn't go well for the samurai and eventually, in the 1860s, they lost their position of power in Japanese society.

Bushido

Bushido is the warrior's code. It was first written down as a kind of self-help manual during the long period of peace when samurai fighting skills went into decline. The martial arts tradition continues in Japan to this day. Millions of Japanese children still practice the classic warrior skills of sword fighting (kendo), archery (kyudo), and hand-to-hand, unarmed combat (jujitsu) at school. But Bushido is also a code of ethics: honor, loyalty, and sacrifice. As Terukuni Uki, a martial arts teacher, explains, "Here we teach the spirit of winning, but it's not so much defeating an opponent as overcoming one's own self. These days it seems everyone is looking for someone to blame rather than focusing on himself. Our message here is that if you try hard, at kendo or anything else, you will enjoy life."

Samurai identity

The samurai's sword symbolized the authority and luxury of the warrior class. It was both a weapon and an art object. This double identity mirrored the samurai themselves. They were warriors, but they also socialized with painters, playwrights, and intellectuals. Samurai generals practiced calligraphy, did flower arranging, and went to the theater. But of all their cultural activities, the tea ceremony was the most important. The ceremony of making and drinking tea was another ritual, almost a meditation. It was carried out in a small room where swords were forbidden, even to samurai, and it must have been very appealing to battle-weary warriors.

Samurai today

What explains the samurai's timeless appeal? He is one of the world's greatest action figures. He's the lone swordsman who kills dozens of enemies in the name of duty and individual glory. He's the cowboy, the knight, the gladiator, and the *Star Wars* Jedi all rolled into one. The samurai have inspired hundreds of movies, video games, comic books, and TV dramas. In Japan, each spring, men put on samurai armor and reenact famous battles. These "weekend samurai" look fierce and realistic, but, with their plastic goggles and blunt swords, they wouldn't have been a threat to the real thing. Asked if he would like to go back in time, one of them replies, "I romanticize those times, but I also fear them. It was live or die."

---

archery (n) /ˈɑrtʃəri/ the sport or fighting skill using bows and arrows

calligraphy (n) /kəˈlɪgrəfi/ the skill or art of decorative writing

chivalrous (adj) /ˈʃɪvəlrəs/ courteous and considerate

conscript (n) /ˈkɑnˌskrɪpt/ a soldier who is called up to fight by the authorities

knight (n) /naɪt/ a soldier of high social status

ritualized (adj) /ˈrɪtʃuəˌlaɪzd/ a way of doing something that follows a formal ritual or pattern

12d I'm so sorry!

Real life making and accepting apologies

1 Work in pairs. Do people apologize a lot in your culture? Would you apologize in these situations?

- arriving late for a meeting
- forgetting someone's name
- serving food a guest doesn't like
- not liking the food someone cooks for you
- taking someone's chair in a café
- not greeting a colleague
- breaking or losing someone's possession
- handing in work after a deadline
- losing something that belongs to someone else

2 You are going to listen to three conversations in which people apologize. Look at the expressions for making and accepting apologies. What do you think the three conversations are about?

> ▶ **MAKING AND ACCEPTING APOLOGIES**
>
> **1**
> I'm really sorry you've gone to all this trouble.
> There's no need to apologize—it's not a problem.
> It's my fault. I'll make you something else.
> **2**
> I couldn't help it—I slipped.
> Don't blame me—this floor is slippery.
> Look, it was an accident! It could have happened to anyone.
> It's not your fault. Sorry I got upset.
> **3**
> I'm so sorry to keep you waiting.
> Don't worry about it—that service is terrible.
> Sorry about that!
> It's just one of those things—buses are unreliable!

3 🔊 **52** Listen to the three conversations and check your ideas from Exercise 2.

4 🔊 **52** Listen to the conversations again. Then answer the questions.

1 What is the problem?
2 What are the relationships between the people? Write the number of the conversation (1–3) next to the speakers.
   a a married couple
   b a guest and a host
   c two classmates
3 How is the situation resolved?

5 Work in pairs. Do you think all of the expressions for making and accepting apologies would be appropriate in each of the three relationships?

6 Work in pairs. Take turns speaking and responding using an appropriate expression.

1 Excuse me. This is a no-smoking area.
2 I'm so sorry. I forgot to bring your book back.
3 Excuse me. That seat is taken.
4 You should have told me you didn't eat garlic!
5 Why is there no milk left?
6 I'm really sorry I didn't tell you I was coming!
7 Excuse me. Please wait your turn.
8 Sorry, we don't accept credit cards.

7 Work in pairs. Choose one of the problems in Exercise 1 or use your own idea. Decide what your relationship is and take a role each. Prepare a conversation that includes at least one apology.

8 Act out your conversation in front of another pair. Can they identify the situation and the relationship?

12e How to behave...

Writing a website article

1 Work in pairs. Have you ever spent time in an English-speaking country? Tell your partner three things (apart from the language!) you found strange or different there.

2 Read the article from a website that arranges host families for foreign-language students in the United States. What do you think of the advice? Does any of it surprise you?

HOW TO BEHAVE WITH A HOMESTAY *family*

I've stayed with several families in the US and each of them has been different. But there are some key things I can pass on to get the best out of your stay. I hope these things are useful!

- Even though you are a paying guest in their home, take a small gift for your hosts. You'd expect a gift from a guest, I'm sure.
- Your stay is not just about learning English. Americans will expect you to show an interest in American culture.
- Take some photos from home so you can talk to your hosts about the photos. Taking the photos will give you more opportunities to actually speak English, too.
- You're not a tourist, so don't behave like a tourist. Your host family will be getting on with normal life. Normal life is what you are there to experience!
- And finally, remember the importance of being punctual (two o'clock means two o'clock!), polite (be careful with expressions you've picked up from pop music and movies!), and sociable (join in with things—at least the first time).

3 Writing skill **revising**

a Look at this list of seven things that you should use to check your writing. Has the writer of the website article already checked all the things?

- grammar
- linking words
- organization
- relevance
- spelling
- style
- vocabulary

b The writer can improve the article by not repeating some words. Look at the first line of the article. Who or what does *them* refer to?

c Replace the rest of the highlighted words in the article with these words. There is one extra word.

It	one	She	That	the same
their	them	there	they	This

4 Work in groups. You are going to write an article for students coming to your country. First, brainstorm ideas. Use the categories below or ideas that are more relevant to your culture.

- celebrations
- dress
- food
- formality
- greetings
- house rules
- meal times
- money
- personal hygiene

5 Work on your own. Choose three to five ideas from your list in Exercise 4. Write an article of 150–200 words.

6 Use the list in Exercise 3a to check and revise your article.

7 Exchange articles with the other members of your group. Which were the most common topics?

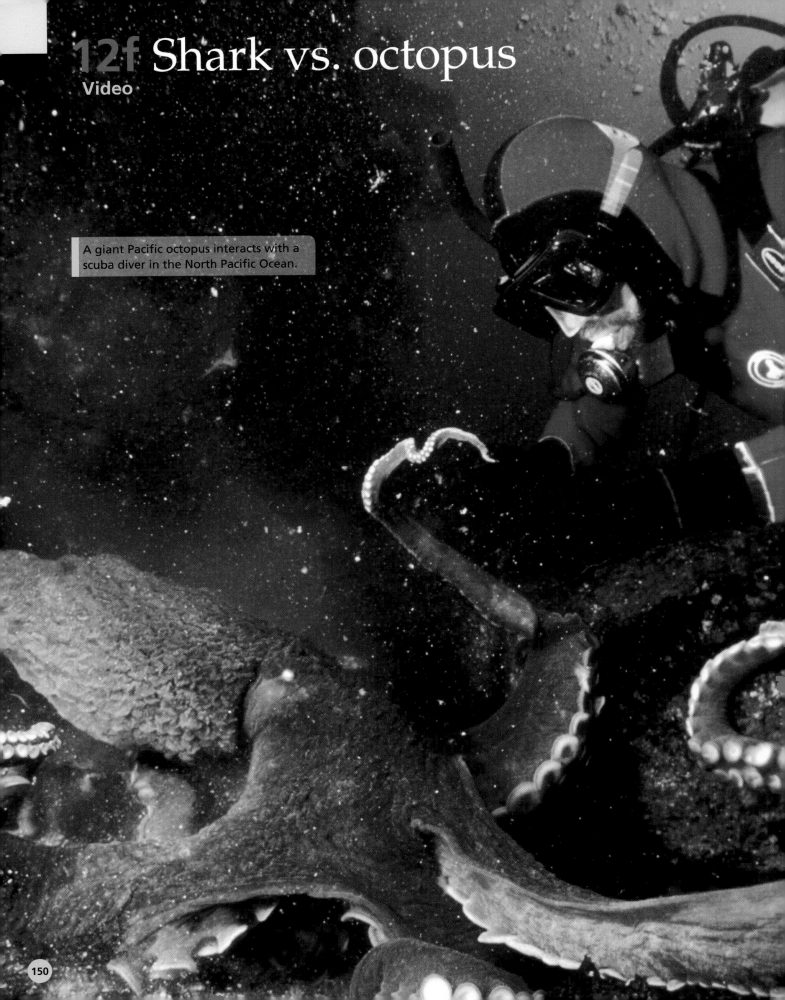

A giant Pacific octopus interacts with a scuba diver in the North Pacific Ocean.

Before you watch

1 Work in groups. Look at the photo and discuss the questions.

   1 What is unusual about this animal?
   2 How would you feel if you were the diver? Why?
   3 Which animal would frighten you more: an octopus or a shark? Why?

2 Work in pairs. You are going to watch an encounter between an octopus and a shark. What do you think will happen? Compare your ideas with another pair.

While you watch

3 Watch the video and check your answers from Exercise 2.

4 Work in pairs. Watch the first part of the video (to 01:40). Make notes about your animal. Then tell your partner.

Student A: the spiny dogfish shark
1 usual food

2 how it gets its name

3 usual behavior

Student B: the giant Pacific octopus
4 three ways it keeps itself safe from predators

5 usual food

5 Watch the whole video and answer the questions.
   1 Where are these animals?

   2 What was happening at the aquarium?

   3 What was the explanation?

   4 Why was the behavior of the octopus a surprise?

   5 How does the octopus kill sharks?

6 Complete the summary with these words.

bodies	creature	killing	predator
responsible	tank	welfare	

Although the spiny dogfish shark is a
¹_____ , octopus is not its regular prey, otherwise the aquarium staff wouldn't have put the two animals in the same ²_____ . But when ³_____ of sharks began appearing at the bottom of the tank, the staff became worried about the sharks' ⁴_____ . The giant Pacific octopus is an extraordinary ⁵_____ , but nobody expected it would be ⁶_____ for ⁷_____ the sharks.

After you watch

7 **Roleplay an interview with an expert**

Work in pairs.

Student A: You are an expert in octopus behavior. You were part of the team of divers that filmed the shark–octopus encounter. Use the ideas below to prepare what you are going to say to an interviewer.

Student B: You are a presenter on a TV wildlife show. You are going to interview the person who filmed the shark–octopus encounter. Use the ideas below to prepare questions.

- why the video was made
- what were the expectations
- feelings while filming
- any problems
- any surprises
- why the video is important

Act out the interview. Then change roles and repeat the interview.

8 Work in groups and discuss these questions.
   1 If you had to kill something to eat it, would you? Or would you prefer to go hungry?
   2 Do you think we should eat things if we aren't prepared to kill them ourselves?

---

aquarium (n) /əˈkweəriəm/ a type of zoo for marine animals
camouflage (v) /ˈkæməˌflɑʒ/ to use coloring that is the same as an animal's surroundings so it becomes more or less invisible to predators
crab (n) /kræb/ a marine animal with a hard shell
dismiss (v) /dɪsˈmɪs/ to reject something or somebody
fearless (adj) /ˈfɪərlɪs/ brave, courageous, not afraid
flexible (adj) /ˈfleksəbəl/ able to bend easily
humble (adj) /ˈhʌmbəl/ not special or important

ink (n) /ɪŋk/ dark liquid, named after writing ink, that some animals produce
pack (n) /pæk/ a group of animals, such as dogs or wolves
school (n) /skul/ a group of marine animals, such as fish
spine (n) /spaɪn/ a sharp, needle-like part on an animal's body
sucker (n) /ˈsʌkər/ part of an animal's body that is used to help them stick to things
welfare (n) /ˈwelfeər/ the condition or health of people or animals

UNIT 12 REVIEW

Grammar

1 Complete the article.

Steve Winter won the Wildlife Photographer of the Year 2008 award for this photo of a snow leopard at night. What makes this photo so extraordinary? First, patience. Steve spent ten months on this assignment. If he ¹ _____ (be) in a hurry, he ² _____ (not get) his shots. Second, dedication. Steve camped out for six weeks at 30 degrees below zero, conditions in which he ³ _____ (freeze) to death! Next, cooperation. Steve credited the knowledge of local experts Tashi Tundup and Raghu Chundawat, without whom he ⁴ _____ (not be able) to do the project. Finally, the animal itself. Steve says the photo "was a real collaboration between the snow leopard and myself." And it's true. Imagine how differently the photo ⁵ _____ (turn out) if the snow leopard ⁶ _____ (not go) hunting, slowly and silently, on that snowy night.

2 Work in pairs. Think about the story you have just read. Read these sentences. Make comments about the story using the words in parentheses. Then discuss your comments.

1 His first camera was a gift from his father on his seventh birthday. (if)
2 The snow leopard has a reputation for being impossible to find. (might)
3 Steve didn't get any shots until he moved higher up the mountain. (should)
4 National Geographic commissioned the assignment from Steve. (not)

I CAN	
talk about things that did not happen (*should have* and *could have*)	
talk about the hypothetical results of things that did not happen (third conditional)	

Vocabulary

3 Complete the words. They are all connected with expeditions. Which ones have you used?

1 types of shelter: i_____ , t_____
2 things for carrying gear: b_____ , s_____
3 things to sleep in: h_____ , s_____ b_____
4 local people who can help you: g_____ , h_____
5 alternatives to fresh food: c_____ food, d_____ food

4 Work in groups. What do you think:

- people get out of joining in battle reenactments?
- people learn from doing martial arts?
- is the appeal of violent movies or video games?

I CAN	
talk about things you need on expeditions	
talk about things connected with martial arts	

Real life

5 Work in pairs. Complete the exchanges with these expressions. Then continue the conversations.

Don't worry about it.	No, it's my fault.
It's not your fault.	Well, don't blame me!

1 A: I'm so sorry I forgot to call you last night.
  B: _____ I wasn't at home anyway.
2 A: Oh, no. We haven't got any orange juice left.
  B: _____ I don't even drink it.
3 A: I'm really sorry about getting upset yesterday.
  B: _____ I shouldn't have shouted!
4 A: Sorry about the problem the other day.
  B: _____ You did nothing wrong.

I CAN	
make and accept apologies	

Speaking

6 Work in groups. You work at a new school for teenagers and must create a code of conduct for them. Make a list of appropriate and inappropriate behaviors.

7 Work in two pairs in a group of four. One of the students at the school is in danger of being expelled.

Pair A: You are the student's teachers. Explain what the student has done wrong and what the consequences are.

Pair B: You are the student's parents. Try to persuade the school to reconsider.

UNIT 1b, Exercise 9, page 13

Pair A: The Blue quiz

Ask Pair B the quiz questions without the options. Give them 5 points if they can answer the question immediately. Give them 1 point if they need to hear the options. The answer is in bold.

Pair B will then ask you the yellow questions.

1 Where do the Tuareg—or "blue people"—originally come from?
   a the Kalahari desert
   b the Namib desert
   c the Sahara desert
   They are an ethnic group in West Africa. The men traditionally wear blue.

2 Who lives in the Blue House in South Korea?
   a the president
   b the king
   c the prime minister
   It's the official residence and it has a blue-tiled roof.

3 What is the name of the country where the Blue Nile begins?
   a Sudan **b Ethiopia** c Uganda
   It originates in Lake Tana, then joins the White Nile to form the Nile river.

4 Which part of the US is famous for "the blues" (music)?
   a the West Coast
   b the Deep South
   c the Midwest
   The name comes from "the blue devils," meaning sadness and melancholy.

UNIT 3b, Exercise 10, page 37

Pair A

Read the solution to puzzle A. Pair B will ask you questions to solve it. Then ask Pair B questions to solve puzzle B.

> **Solution to puzzle A**
> The people on the yacht decided to have a diving competition. When they were all in the water, they discovered they had forgotten to put a ladder down the side of the yacht. They couldn't get back onto the yacht, so they drowned.

UNIT 8a, Exercise 11, page 95

Pair A

Decide what you think each photo shows. Then describe your photos to Pair B and find the correct captions.

1 What/Where could it be? Why?
2 What/Where can it not be? Why not?
3 What can you say for certain about the photo? Why?

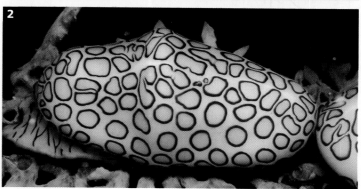

Two of these captions are for Pair B's photos. Listen to their descriptions of the photos and find the correct captions.

a A macro shot of a banana plant stem is magnified 32 times.
b A blue cod swims past sea pens—tiny animals which live in colonies shaped like branches.
c The space shuttle *Endeavour* lifts off from Cape Canaveral, Florida, leaving a trail of smoke.

UNIT 11a, Exercise 10, page 131

Pair A

Read the news story. Write a short dialogue between the man and a rescuer. Practice your dialogue so that you are ready to act it out for Pair B. Then turn back to page 131.

> A walker who got lost in the hills was rescued this weekend after taking a photo with his phone and emailing it to the Volunteer Rescue Service. The man had fallen and was injured, but with no maps he couldn't tell the rescuers where he was. He took the photo after advice from the rescue team, who then recognized his location immediately.

UNIT 1b, Exercise 9, page 13

Pair B: The Yellow quiz

Pair A will ask you the blue questions. You will get 5 points if you can answer the question immediately. You will get 1 point if you need to hear the options.

Then ask Pair A the yellow questions.

1   Which fruit does the California Yellow Fruit Festival celebrate?

   a   the lemon
   b   the pineapple
   c   the banana
   Every September, Ventura County, California, holds a two-day lemon festival.

2   Which sport gives a yellow jersey to the winner?

   a   golf
   b   horse racing
   c   cycling
   The Tour de France race takes place every year.

3   Where do yellow taxi cabs come from originally?

   a   Chicago   b   New York   c   Washington
   Mr. Hertz started the Yellow Cab Company (in 1915) because yellow is the easiest color to see from a distance.

4   Where can you see the house that inspired Van Gogh's *Yellow House* painting?

   a   Holland   b   Spain   **c   France**
   Van Gogh spent the summer of 1888 in Arles, in the south of France.

UNIT 3b, Exercise 10, page 37

Pair B

Ask Pair A questions to solve puzzle A. Then read the solution to puzzle B. Pair A will ask you questions to solve it.

> **Solution to puzzle B**
> The man had fallen into the Dead Sea. This is actually a saltwater lake. The salt density is so high that you can easily float on the surface.

UNIT 8a, Exercise 11, page 95

Pair B

Two of these captions are for Pair A's photos. Listen to their descriptions of the photos and find the correct captions.

a   A man walks on cooled red lava at the Nyiragongo volcano in the Democratic Republic of the Congo.
b   A man collects the salt after the water has evaporated from a stream in Peru.
c   A flamingo tongue mollusc feeds on a blue-violet sea fan.

Decide what you think each photo shows. Then describe your photos to Pair A and find the correct captions.

1   What/Where could it be? Why?
2   What/Where can it not be? Why not?
3   What can you say for certain about the photo? Why?

UNIT 11a, Exercise 10, page 131

Pair B

Read the news story. Write a short dialogue between Adam and Corey. Practice your dialogue so that you are ready to act it out for Pair A. Then turn back to page 131.

> A message in a bottle which was put into the Atlantic Ocean in Florida has reached Ireland. Adam Flannery, aged 17, found the bottle which had been sent by high school student Corey Santos. The message gave Corey's contact details and asked the finder to get in touch with details of where the bottle ended up.

UNIT 4d, Ex 8, page 52

Student A: Choose a request (1–12). You are going to make this request.

Student B: Find the request for your partner's number. Choose an appropriate situation (a–d) for this request. You are going to respond to it.

Act out a conversation in this situation. Use the expressions for making and responding to requests on page 52 to help you. Take turns making and responding to requests.

Requests
1 You want to sit down.
2 You can't make out the phone number on a letter.
3 You don't know where the company buildings are.
4 You want an application form sent in the mail.
5 You need a pen.
6 You need a taxi.
7 You need to know the time.
8 You want help with an application form.
9 You need a ride somewhere.
10 You want to leave your coat somewhere.
11 You want to wash your hands.
12 You want to use the phone.

Situations
a You're with a friend.
b You're at a company's reception desk.
c You're in an interview.
d You're on the phone.

UNIT 5 Review, Exercise 8, page 68

Role 1
The most traveled airline pilot

Role 2
Wildlife conservationist of the year

Role 3
Writer of travel guides for independent travelers

UNIT 6 Review, Exercise 9, page 80

Baklava   A rich, sweet pastry with chopped nuts and syrup or honey. From Turkey, the Caucasus, and central Asia.

Borscht   A soup popular in many Eastern and Central European countries. Main ingredient: beetroot.

Couscous   From North Africa. A dish of semolina served with a meat or vegetable stew.

Curry   A south and southeastern Asian dish made with lamb, fish, or chicken on rice with a savory, spicy sauce.

Fondue   Popular in Switzerland and France originally. Pieces of bread are dipped into melted cheese.

Goulash   A Hungarian meat soup or stew, flavored with paprika.

Gravlax   Raw salmon cured in salt, sugar, and the herb dill. From Scandinavia.

Kebab   Cubes of meat (or fish) on a skewer, cooked over an open fire. Originally from Central and Western Asia.

Lasagna   A dish of pasta sheets layered with cheese, meat, and tomato sauce, and baked in the oven.

Pad thai   A stir-fried dish of rice noodles, scrambled eggs, peanuts, shrimp, and vegetables.

Paella   A rice dish originally from Valencia, Spain. Rice is cooked in a shallow dish with meat or seafood. Saffron flavors and colors the rice.

Tortilla   1 A type of flatbread made from corn or wheat in Central America.   2 A potato omelette from Spain.

Wontons   Chinese dumplings stuffed with ground pork, spices, and vegetables and usually fried.

UNIT 9b, Exercise 10, page 109

Work in two pairs within your group of four.

Pair A: Prepare a two-minute presentation on why it's better to buy famous brands. Give examples from your list in Exercise 10 on page 109.

Pair B: Prepare a two-minute presentation on why it's better to buy alternative brands. Give examples from your list in Exercise 10 on page 109.

Give your presentations to the class or to another group. Then take a class vote to find out how many people are going to try alternative brands.

UNIT 1

Simple present and present continuous

Form

Simple present

Affirmative	Negative
I/You/We/They **work**.	I/You/We/They **don't work**.
He/She/It **works**.	He/She/It **doesn't work**.

Interrogative	Short answer
Do I/you/we/they **work**?	Yes, I/you/we/they **do**. No, I/you/we/they **don't**.
Does he/she/it **work**?	Yes, he/she/it **does**. No, he/she/it **doesn't**.

Present continuous

Affirmative	Negative
I'**m working**. ('m = am)	I'**m not working**.
You'**re**/We'**re**/They'**re working**. ('re = are)	You/We/They **aren't working**. (aren't = are not)
He'**s**/She'**s**/It'**s working**. ('s = is)	He/She/It **isn't working**. (isn't = is not)

Interrogative	Short answer
Am I **working**?	Yes, I **am**. No, I'**m not**.
Are you/we/they **working**?	Yes, you/we/they **are**. No, you/we/they **aren't**.
Is he/she/it **working**?	Yes, he/she/it **is**. No, he/she/it **isn't**.

Use

We use the simple present to talk about:
- things that are always or generally true.
  Water freezes at 0° Celsius.
  Lucas doesn't paint portraits of people.
- things that are regular actions.
  Carla goes to an art class every Thursday.
  Does he go to the gym every day?
- permanent situations.
  He lives in Peru.
  They wear a uniform at work.

We use the present continuous to talk about:
- things that are in progress at the time of speaking.
  They're eating lunch now.
- temporary situations or situations happening "around now."
  I'm studying art at the moment.
- a situation that is in the process of change.
  People are wearing cheaper clothes nowadays.

Stative verbs

We usually use the simple present with stative verbs such as *like, love, hate, want, believe, know, sound, taste,* or *understand* to talk about states such as thoughts, senses, emotions, and possession. We don't usually use these verbs in the continuous form.
Isabel loves swimming.
He doesn't understand French.
Remember, some verbs can have both stative and dynamic meanings.
That guy looks great—I love his outfit!
Everyone is looking at him—he's wearing a great outfit!

We often use these time expressions with the simple present: *always, never, every day, on Mondays.* With the present continuous, we often use these time expressions: *at the moment, (right) now, this week, this summer.*

Practice

1 Complete the sentences with the simple present or present continuous form of the verbs.

1 They sometimes ____work____ (work) late.
2 _____ you _____ (want) to see the new color scheme for the office? It's red!
3 Irene _____ (study) Picasso's blue paintings at the moment.
4 I _____ (not like) that color at all!
5 It's fall and the trees _____ (change) color.
6 Tiger Woods is in the final round so he _____ (wear) his famous red shirt.
7 _____ Shui _____ (know) anything about South America?
8 This jewelry _____ (not come) from Africa. It's from Indonesia.

Question forms

Form

To form questions in the simple present we use *do* and *does* with the main verb.
Do you **eat** meat?
Does he usually **work** on Saturdays?

When we use a question word (like *what, where, who*) the question word comes in front of *do* and *does*.
What do they want to do?
Where does she study English?

We invert the subject and the verb when we make questions with *be* and modal verbs.
Are they in the kitchen?
Can she ride a bicycle?

When the question word is the subject of the question, we don't invert the subject and the verb.
Who likes this artist?
What is making that strange noise?

Common question words are: *who, what, when, where, why, how, which, how much/many.* You cannot form subject questions with *where, when, why,* or *how.*
Where do you live? (Not ~~Where you live?~~)
When does it start? (Not ~~When it starts?~~)

Use

We begin questions with *do/does, am/is/are, have/has,* and modal verbs when we want a *yes/no* answer, which is often very short.
Does he **live** in London? *Yes, he does./No, he doesn't, but he is moving there soon.*
Do they **like** *soccer? No, they don't.*
Is he *in France now? No, he isn't./Yes, he's there until next week.*
Can they **come** *on Monday? Yes, they can.*

We use question words when we want more information.
When *does the bus arrive? It usually gets here at four o'clock.*
Who *lives in that yellow house? Mr. Johnson lives there.*

Practice

2 Complete the questions.

1 *Where does* Ahmad _____ *live?_
    He lives in Dubai.
2 _____ they _____ to work?
    They go to work by bike.
3 _____ the women always _____ in bright colors?
    No, they don't. They only dress in bright colors at festivals.
4 _____ working?
    No, I'm not. I'm checking my email.
5 _____ these lovely yellow flowers?
    Susana bought them.
6 _____ I _____ to the movies tonight?
    Yes, you can. What's playing?
7 _____ Nanoko always _____ that orange necklace?
    She wears it because orange is the color of happiness. She's Japanese.
8 _____ blue shirts _____ Alex
    _____?
    He has about twenty blue shirts.

UNIT 2
Present perfect
Form

We form the present perfect with the simple present of the verb *have* + past participle.

Affirmative	Negative
I've/You've/We've/They've **arrived.** ('ve = have)	I/You/We/They **haven't arrived.** (haven't = have not)
He's/She's/It's **arrived.** ('s = has)	He/She/It **hasn't arrived.** (hasn't = has not)

Interrogative	Short answer
Have I/you/we/they **arrived?**	Yes, I/you/we/they **have.** No, I/you/we/they **haven't.**
Has he/she/it **arrived?**	Yes, he/she/it **has.** No, he/she/it **hasn't.**

We add *-ed* to regular verbs to form the past participle: *arrive → arrived, work → worked, play → played, start → started.*
Note the spelling rules for other regular verbs:
*   for verbs ending in *-e*, we add *-d*: *die → died, lie → lied*
*   for verbs ending in *-y* (after a consonant), we change the *-y* to *i* and add *-ed*: *try → tried, study → studied*
*   for verbs ending in vowel + consonant (not *-w, -x* or *-y*), we double the consonant: *stop → stopped, jog → jogged*
Some verbs have irregular past participles, for example: *do → done, find → found, have → had, know → known, make → made, meet → met*

Use

We use the present perfect:
*   to talk about a situation that started at some time in the past and continues into the present.
    *I **have played** in this band for three years.* (I am still playing in the band.)
*   to talk about a past action with results in the present situation that we want to emphasize.
    *They **have** recently **improved** this theater.* (The present situation is that the theater is better now.)
*   to talk about situations in the past when there is no time reference given.
    *Zap Mama **have had** several hits in Belgium.*
*   when a time reference includes the present.
    *We've **heard** a lot of great music **today**.*

When we are interested in a specific time in the past, we use the simple past:
*Zap Mama **had** several hits in Belgium **last year**.*

We use the present perfect with *since* and *for* to talk about how long a situation has continued. We use *since* with the point of time when the activity started, for example, *since Monday, since ten o'clock, since January, since I was a boy.*
*I've played the piano **since 2002**.*
We use *for* to talk about a period of time, like *for an hour, for three days, for two months, for a long time.*
*The band has played at the same festival **for five years**.*
Note that we do not use the simple present with *for* and *since* when the activity started in the past. We say:
He's been here since noon. (Not *~~He's here since noon.~~*)

We often use the present perfect with *already, just,* and *yet* to talk about actions that happened recently, or actions that have not happened but we think will happen soon.
*I've **already** seen his new music video.*
*We've **just** been to see U2 in concert.*
*I haven't been to the opera **yet**, but I'd like to go one day.*

Practice 2/15/18

1 Complete the sentences with the present perfect form of the verbs, and choose *for* or *since*.

1 I _have worked_ in this theater (for) / since twenty years. (work)
2 The band has sung this song at every concert *for* / (since) they started. (sing)
3 I haven't been to the ballet *for* / (since) I was a child. (not be)
4 They have written their own songs (for) / since many years. (write)
5 We haven't seen Eric Clapton play live *for* / (since) 2005. (not see)
6 The theater company has worked very hard (for) / since six months. (work)
7 Has their manager called again *for* / (since) yesterday morning? (call)
8 Bob Dylan has toured the world continuously (for) / since many years. (tour)

Verb patterns: *-ing* form and infinitive
Form

-ing form	
verb + *-ing*	I **like playing** the violin.
-ing as the subject	**Playing** the guitar is magical.
preposition + *-ing*	They are **good at dancing.**

infinitive	
verb + infinitive	He **wants to play** the violin.
adjective + infinitive	This music is **easy to play.**

Use

We use the *-ing* form of the verb:
- after certain verbs such as *like, love, enjoy, prefer.*
  *I **love listening** to jazz.*
  Other verbs that are followed by the *-ing* form are: *can't help, consider, dislike, enjoy, finish, hate, imagine, involve, keep, mention, mind, don't mind, miss, postpone, practice, report, risk, stand, can't stand, suggest.*
- as the subject of the sentence: ***Dancing** is great exercise.*
- after a preposition: *I'm pretty quick **at learning** English.*

After certain verbs we use the infinitive form of another verb. This is often to talk about hopes, intentions, and decisions.
*He offered **to help** me.*
*They didn't want **to work** in the evening.*
Common verbs that are followed by an infinitive are: *afford, agree, aim, appear, arrange, attempt, can't bear, decide, demand, expect, hope, intend, learn, manage, need, offer, plan, prepare, promise, refuse, seem, want, wish, would like.*

Practice

2 Choose the correct option.

1 They like *to meet* / (meeting) new people.
2 That music is cheerful *to listen* / (listening) to.
3 We always enjoy *to see* / (seeing) good movies.
4 We want (to visit) / *visiting* the new art gallery.
5 *To act* / (Acting) in plays is very enjoyable.
6 Jose's really good at *to tell* / (telling) stories.
7 Do you need (to buy) / *buying* the tickets?
8 Penelope remembered *to be* / (being) on stage when she was a child—she was terrified!

UNIT 3
Simple past and past continuous
Form
Simple past

Affirmative	Negative
I/You/He/She/It/We/They **worked.**	I/You/He/She/It/We/They **didn't work.**

Interrogative	Short answer
Did I/you/he/she/it/we/they **work?**	Yes, I/you/he/she/it/we/they **did.**
	No, I/you/he/she/it/we/they **didn't.**

We add -ed to regular verbs to form the simple past:
play → played, jump → jumped.
Note the spelling rules for other regular verbs:

- for verbs ending in -e, we add -d: realize → realized
- for verbs ending in -y, we change the -y to i and add -ed: carry → carried
- for verbs ending in vowel + consonant (not -w, -x, or -y), we double the consonant: plan → planned

Some verbs have an irregular affirmative form in the simple past:
do → did, go → went, see → saw

We use did and didn't to form questions and negatives.
Did you go fishing when you were at the beach?
Brad **didn't** swim in the pool yesterday.

Note that the simple past form of be is I/he/she/it was and we/you/they were. The negative forms are wasn't and weren't. We invert the subject and verb when we make questions.

Past continuous

We form the past continuous with the simple past of the verb be + the -ing form of the verb.

Affirmative	Negative
I/He/She/It **was working**.	I/He/She/It **wasn't working**. (wasn't = was not)
You/We/They **were working**.	You/We/They **weren't working**. (weren't = were not)

Interrogative	Short answer
Was I/he/she/it **working**?	Yes, I/he/she/it **was**. No, I/he/she/it **wasn't**.
Were you/we/they **working**?	Yes, you/we/they **were**. No, you/we/they **weren't**.

Use

Simple past

We use the simple past:

- to talk about a finished action in the past when there is a clear reference to a specific time or when the time is understood from the context. We often use a time phrase (yesterday, last week, ten years ago).
  I **visited** France last year.
  Did you **watch** the documentary yesterday?
- to describe a sequence of actions in a story.
  I **jumped** into the water and **swam** to the shore.
- for a single or repeated action in the past.
  I **went** to the lake. He **rode** the bus every day.

Past continuous

We use the past continuous:

- to describe an action in progress in the past. The past period (such as last week, last Monday) has finished.
  Last Friday **we were swimming** in the sea.

- to talk about an unfinished action in the past.
  I **was writing** a letter to my friend. (I probably didn't finish the letter.)
  I **wrote** a letter to my friend. (I finished the letter.)
- to describe a situation or the background to a story.
  The sun **was shining** in through the window.

Simple past and past continuous

We use the past continuous with the simple past to talk about two actions that happened at the same time in the past or when one action in progress (past continuous) was interrupted by another action (simple past). We can join the tenses with the words when, while, so, and because.

I met a group of tourists
↓
time ————————————————→
I was traveling through India

While I **was traveling** through India, I **met** a group of tourists.
What **were** you **doing** when you **heard** the news?
They **were enjoying** the boat trip, so they **didn't get off** the boat.

We can use when with both the simple past and the past continuous. We also often use while with the past continuous.
Remember, we don't use stative verbs (such as be, like, believe, understand) in the continuous form.

Questions in the past

- Questions in the past continuous ask about activities before an event: What **was** the crocodile **doing**? (before it started to come towards you)
- Questions in the simple past ask about activities after an event: Where did you go? (after you saw the crocodile)

Practice

1 Choose the correct option.

1 What *was happening* / (*happened*) after you *fell* / (*were falling*) in the water?
2 While Mateo *swam* / (*was swimming*) in the sea, a shark suddenly (*appeared*) / *was appearing*.
3 Kayley *jogged* / (*was jogging*) by the river when she (*lost*) / *was losing* her keys.
4 It *didn't rain* / (*wasn't raining*), so they (*didn't take*) / *weren't taking* their raincoats.
5 It (*was*) / *was being* too hot to do anything, so everyone *slept* / (*was sleeping*).
6 When we (*arrived*) / *were arriving* at the resort, the sun *shone* / (*was shining*).
7 The girls *surfed* / (*were surfing*) when they (*saw*) / *were seeing* a dolphin.
8 Where *was* / (*did*) the crocodile swimming when you (*saw*) / *were seeing* it?

Past perfect

Form

We form the past perfect with the simple past of the verb *have* (*had*) + past participle.

Affirmative	Negative
I'd/You'd/He'd/She'd/It'd/We'd/They'd watched. ('d = had)	I/You/He/She/It/We/They hadn't watched. (hadn't = had not)

Interrogative	Short answer
Had I/you/he/she/it/we/they watched?	Yes, I/you/he/she/it/we/they had. No, I/you/he/she/it/we/they hadn't.

Use

We use the past perfect to talk about an event that took place before another event in the past that we have also related. We often use the past perfect and the simple past together.

*Jake **went** to the office yesterday after he **had met** his friends.*
Jake met his friends before he went to the office.

Jake met his friends ↓   *Jake went to the office* ↓

time ———————————————————→

We can use the following time expressions with the past perfect: *already, just, recently, before, previously, earlier, after,* and *by the time* to show the order in which the two past events happened.

*When Feng **got** to the theater, the movie **had already ended**.*
*He **had just returned** from the expedition.*
*After I **had seen** them, I went back to the hotel.*
*By the time we arrived, everyone **had left**.*

We use *because* and *so* to show that there is a reason for the later action.

*Feng was sad **because** he had missed the movie.*
*It had rained the night before, **so** he took his umbrella.*

When we relate past events in the same order they actually happened, we don't have to use the past perfect.

*I **got** up and then **went** to work.*

Practice

2 Complete the sentences with the simple past and the past perfect form of the verbs.

1 They _had used_ (use) most of their air by the time they _reached_ (reach) the wreck.
2 We _____ (pay) a deposit for the hotel before we _____ (buy) the train tickets.
3 The ship _____ (not arrive) in port by the time I _____ (wake) up.
4 The lake _____ (flood) because the snow _____ (melt).

5 Jim _____ (forget) her birthday, so his mother _____ (be) very angry.
6 The *Titanic* _____ (not reach) the US when it _____ (hit) an iceberg.
7 I _____ (sell) the yacht after I _____ (sail) around the world in it.

UNIT 4

Predictions

Form

Affirmative	Negative	Interrogative
I/you/he/she/it/we/they	I/you/he/she/it/we/they	
will	won't	will
could	couldn't	could
may	may not	may
might	might not	might
		I/you/he/she/it/we/they?

Use

We use *will, may, might, could* (*not*) + base form to make predictions about the future. We use *will* + base form to make predictions that we are certain about. The negative form is *won't*. We use *may, might,* and *could* + base form to talk about something we think is possible, but we are not certain. The negative forms are *may not, might not,* and *could not*.

*In ten years, China **will have** the world's largest economy.* (It's certain to happen.)
*In ten years, China **could have** the world's largest economy.* (China has the ability, but it's not certain that this will happen.)
*In ten years, China **may have** the world's largest economy.* (It's not clear that China has the ability so it's less certain this will happen.)
*In ten years, China **might have** the world's largest economy.* (It's possible, but far from certain.)

We can also use the adverbs *certainly, definitely, probably,* and *possibly* with *will* and *won't*. The adverbs describe whether we think something is more or less certain to happen.

certainly/definitely probably possibly
very certain ├────────────────────────────┤ not very certain
certainly not/ probably not possibly not
definitely not

When you use these adverbs with *will*, they come between *will* and the main verb. When you use the adverbs with *won't*, they come before *won't*.

*Next year, the US **will definitely have** the world's largest economy.* (I am sure it will.)

*In ten years, China **will probably have** the world's largest economy.* (I think it will, but I'm not certain.)
*Nepal **definitely won't have** the world's largest economy.* (I am sure it won't.)

Practice

1 Look at these predictions about the future. Put the word into the correct place in the sentence.

                     definitely
1   Earth's population will grow. (definitely)
2   We will pay to drive on all roads. (possibly)
3   It won't rain this afternoon. (probably)
4   People will live longer. (certainly)
5   Sea levels will rise. (definitely)
6   Life expectancy for people in the West will be 100 years. (possibly)
7   There will be more droughts. (probably)
8   Because of Internet shopping, there won't be as many stores. (definitely)

Future forms

Form

Present continuous: see also page 156
will: see also page 160

going to

Affirmative	Negative
I'm going to meet	I'm not going to meet
you're/we're/they're going to meet	you/we/they aren't going to meet
he's/she's/it's going to meet	he/she/it isn't going to meet

Interrogative	Short answer
Am I going to meet?	Yes, I am. No, I'm not.
Are you/we/they going to meet?	Yes, you/we/they are. No, you/we/they aren't.
is he/she/it going to meet?	Yes, he/she/it is. No, he/she/it isn't.

Use

We can use three different verb forms to talk about the future: present continuous, *will*, and *going to*.

Present continuous

We use the present continuous to talk about an arrangement at a specific (or understood) time in the future: *I'm traveling to Paris on Saturday morning.* (I already have my ticket.)

When we use the present continuous to talk about the future, we use a specified future time expression. If not, the present continuous refers to the present time.
We're working tomorrow. (= future)
We're working. (= present)

will

We use *will* to talk about s[...] moment of speaking.
"Would you like another piece of cake[...] have any more, thank you."
We often use *will* with *I think…*
Now that I think of it, I will apply for the job.

going to

We use *be + going to + base form* to talk about a plan or intention for the future that has been decided before the moment of speaking.
I'm going to be a lawyer.

Practice

2 Choose the correct option.

1   (We're leaving) / We'll leave / We're going to leave at three this afternoon. We've already booked a taxi.
2   *I'm buying / I'll buy / I'm going to buy* some sugar when I go into town.
3   Look at my sunburn! *I'm not spending / I won't spend / I'm not going to spend* so much time on the beach tomorrow!
4   I can't take the car on Monday. Paul *is taking / will take / is going to take* his driving test.
5   "Do you want anything to drink?" "Yes, *I'm having / I'll have / I'm going to have* fruit juice."
6   "I've got a terrible headache." "Just a minute, *I'm getting / I'll get / I'm going to get* you an aspirin."
7   "Why are you going to the supermarket?" "*I'm buying / I'll buy / I'm going to buy* some bread."
8   "When *are you flying / will you fly / are you going to fly* to Brazil?" "Next Monday."

UNIT 5

Present perfect and simple past

Form

Present perfect: see also page 157
Simple past: see also page 158

Use

We use the present perfect to talk about an experience when we don't say exactly when something happened. We use the simple past when we say, or it is clear from the context, when something happened in the past.
I've trekked through Africa. (I don't say exactly when.)
I trekked through Africa last year. (I say when.)

ent perfect
...on about an

...rtain time
..., just, yet, since, so far,
...s.
...e years.

...specific times in the past,
day, last summer, when I was

I wen... ...ld trip last year.
I saw a brow... ...I visited Canada.

Note that we can use *for* + period of time with both
the present perfect and the simple past.
I've worked here for six months. (I still work here.)
I worked in Italy for twelve years. (I don't now.)

The verb *go* has two past participles: *been* and *gone*.
We use *been* to say someone went somewhere and
came back, and *gone* to say that they are still there.
Kim has been to the US. (She's not in the US now.)
Harry has gone to the US. (He's still there.)

Practice

1 Complete the conversation with the correct form
of the verbs.

Paolo: Hi, James.[1] _____ (I / not see)
you for a while. [2] _____
(you / be) away?

James: Hello, Pablo. Yes, [3] _____
(I / just / get back) from South America.

Paolo: Really? How long [4] _____
(you / be) there?

James: [5] _____ (I / spend) about a
month there in total. You know how you
lose some days just getting there and back!

Paolo: It sounds great. How many different places
[6] _____ (you / get to)?

James: Oh, [7] _____ (I / go) to Bolivia,
Chile, Peru, Brazil, and Venezuela.

Paolo: Lucky you! What about Patagonia?
[8] _____ (I / hear) a lot about it.

James: No, that's in Argentina. [9] _____
(I / not / have) time. [10] _____
(it / be / too far).

Paolo: Well, maybe next time!

Present perfect continuous and present perfect / *How long... ?*

Form

Present perfect: see also page 157
We form the present perfect continuous with *have/has*
+ *been* + verb + *-ing*.

Affirmative	Negative
I've/You've/We've/They've **been waiting.** ('ve = have)	I/You/We/They **haven't been waiting.** (haven't = have not)
He's/She's/It's **been waiting.** ('s = has)	He/She/It **hasn't been waiting.** (hasn't = has not)

Interrogative	Short answer
Have I/you/we/they **been waiting?**	Yes, I/you/we/they **have.** No, I/you/we/they **haven't.**
Has he/she/it **been waiting?**	Yes, he/she/it **has.** No, he/she/it **hasn't.**

Use

We use the present perfect continuous to talk about
recent continuous actions. It emphasizes the duration
of an action.
I've been looking at the travel website all morning.
They haven't been traveling for long.
Has she been living here a long time?

We use the present perfect to emphasize the
completion of a recent action, rather than the duration
of the action. We also use the present perfect to talk
about a specific number of times we have done
something in the past, or the number of times we
have produced or made something.
I've worked in several different countries.
*We haven't heard from our friends in New Mexico since
January.*
She's been to Cambodia three times in the last year.
He's written five books.

We can use both the present perfect continuous and
the present perfect to talk about the present result of a
past action.
*I've been working / I've worked all morning and I'm
tired.*

We use *How long... ?* + present perfect / present
perfect continuous / simple past to ask about the
duration of an activity.
How long have you had your bike?
How long have you been waiting?
How long did you stay in Chile?

Note that we don't usually use the present perfect
continuous with stative verbs (like *be, have, know, like,*
and *understand*).
I've known him for a long time. (Not *I've been knowing
him for a long time.*)

Practice

2 Complete the conversations with the present perfect and continuous form of the verbs.

1 A: How long _have you been writing_ (you/write) for a travel magazine? *[handwritten note: done]*

B: Ten years, and I _'ve visited_ (visit) 50 different countries.

2 A: She _has raised_ (raise) $10,000 for charity.

B: I know. She _has been walking_ (walk) for six weeks.

3 A: Tourists _have been coming_ (come) here for only ten years.

B: Yes, but the number of tourists _has increased_ (increase) a lot recently. *[handwritten: Present Perfect]*

4 A: Edgar _hasn't been traveling_ (not travel) for long.

B: No, but he _has seen_ (see) lots of amazing sights already.

5 A: Did you know we _have completed_ (complete) our diving instructor's course?

B: Really? How long _have you been training_ (you/train)? *[handwritten: How long did you train?]*

UNIT 6

Modal verbs (1)

Form

Affirmative	Negative	Interrogative
I/you/we/they have to he/she/it has to	I/you/we/they don't have to he/she/it doesn't have to	Do I/you/we/they have to? Does he/she/it have to?
I/you/he/she/it/we/they can must should	I/you/he/she/it/we/they can't (= cannot) mustn't (= must not) shouldn't (= should not)	can must should I/you/he/she/it/we/they?
I'm allowed to you're/we're/they're allowed to he's/she's/it's allowed to	I'm not allowed to you/we/they aren't allowed to he/she/it isn't allowed to	am I allowed to? are you/we/they allowed to? is he/she/it allowed to?

Note these rules for modal verbs (like *can*, *must*, *should*):

- There is no third person -*s*. She **must** go. I **can** stay.
- There is no auxiliary *do*. He **can't** play.
- There is no *to* before the verb. He **should** be here.

The expression *have to* is not technically a modal verb as it does take a third person -*s*, but it is used to express obligation like the modal *must*.

Use

We use modal verbs to talk about what is allowed:

- We use *have to / has to* and *must* to say if something is obligatory.
  You **have to / must** follow the recipe.
- We use *don't/doesn't have to* to show that something is not important or necessary.
  He **doesn't have to** go to work on Saturday.
- We use *can* and *is/are allowed to* to talk about permission.
  We **can / are allowed to** eat our lunch here.
- We use *can't* and *isn't/aren't allowed to* to say if we don't have permission or it's important not to do something.
  You **can't / aren't allowed to** bring your own food.
- We use *should/shouldn't* to make a recommendation or give advice.
  You **shouldn't** eat raw seafood.

Note the difference between *have to* and *must* in the negative.
You **don't have to** eat it. (It is not obligatory.)
You **must not** be late. (It's important.)

Practice

1 Complete the sentences with the correct modal verbs.

1 You _shouldn't_ eat before you go swimming. (recommendation)

2 You _____ cook chicken thoroughly before eating it. (obligation)

3 You _____ eat in the classroom. (no permission)

4 He _____ tell anybody about our new menu. (prohibition)

5 This is an informal restaurant. You _____ wear a uniform. (no obligation)

6 You _____ eat five servings of fruit and vegetables every day. (recommendation)

7 They _____ have one small snack between meals. (permission)

8 I _____ remember to take my vitamin pills today. (obligation)

First conditional

Form

We form the first conditional using:

If + simple present, *will* + base form

If you **make** a plan, you **will succeed**.

You **won't lose** weight **if** you **eat** a lot of junk food.

We can use *if* in two positions:

- If-clause first: *If you believe in yourself, you will achieve your dream.*
- Main clause first: *You will achieve your dream if you believe in yourself.*

When the *if*-clause is at the beginning of the sentence, we use a comma to separate it from the main clause.

Use

We use the first conditional to talk about a possible future action or situation. We can also use it to talk about things that are generally true.

If you take up a new sport, you'll get in better shape.

If you eat fatty foods, you won't be healthy.

We can also use *when, as soon as, unless, until,* and *before* instead of *if* to talk about situations in the future. We use the present tense after *if, when, as soon as, unless, until,* and *before* when we refer to future events.

When the rain stops, we'll have a picnic.

You won't get thinner **unless** you give up sugar. (= You won't get thinner if you don't give up sugar.)

As soon as lunch is ready, they will eat.

We won't eat lunch **until** it's ready.

We won't pick the apples **before** they are ripe.

Practice

2 Complete the sentences with the simple present and *will* + base form.

1. I ___will make___ (make) this meal at home if they ___show___ (show) me how to cook it.
2. If you ___recommend___ (recommend) the CD, we ___will buy___ (buy) it.
3. When the sun ___comes___ (come) out again, we ___will feel___ (feel) much better.
4. You ___will get___ (get) a stomachache unless you ___eat___ (eat) more slowly.
5. We ___will not eat___ (not eat) chocolate until we ___lose___ (lose) weight.
6. As soon as we ___get___ (get) home, we ___will do___ (do) some exercise.
7. I ___will not___ (not change) my diet until I ___see___ (see) the doctor.
8. We ___will do___ (do) some warm-up exercises before we ___do___ (do) aerobics.

UNIT 7

Comparatives and superlatives

Form

Adjective/Adverb	Comparative	Superlative
short adjective/adverb		
warm	warmer (than) less warm (than) (not) as warm as	(the) warmest
fast	faster (than) less fast (than) (not) as fast as	(the) fastest
long adjective/adverb		
interesting	more interesting (than) less interesting (than) (not) as interesting as	(the) most interesting
quickly	more quickly (than) less quickly (than) (not) as quickly as	(the) most quickly
irregular adjective/adverb		
good (adj) well (adv)	better	(the) best
bad (adj) badly (adv)	worse	(the) worst

We add *-er* to regular short adjectives and adverbs to form the comparative, and we add *-est* to regular short adjectives and adverbs to form the superlative: *warm → warmer → warmest; fast → faster → fastest*

We add *more/less* and *most* to form the comparative and superlative forms with longer adjectives and adverbs: *interesting → more interesting → most interesting; quickly → more quickly → most quickly*

Note the spelling rules for comparative and superlative adjectives and adverbs:

- for adjectives and adverbs ending in *-e*, add *-r/-st*: *large → larger → largest*
- for adjectives and adverbs ending in *-y* (after a consonant), change the *-y* to *–i* and add *-er/-est*: *easy → easier → easiest*
- for adjectives and adverbs ending in consonant–vowel–consonant, double the final consonant and add *-er/-est*: *big → bigger → biggest; hot → hotter → hottest*

Use

We use comparative adjectives and adverbs to compare two things. We use *than* after a comparative adjective/adverb.

*My apartment is **smaller than** your apartment.*

*This car is **less expensive than** that car.*

*Daniel can run **more quickly than** Amelie.*

We use *as…as* to compare two things that are the same or equal. We use *not as…as* to say they aren't the same or equal.

*This tent is **as warm as** a trailer.*

*The oil stove **doesn't** work **as** efficiently **as** a gas stove.*

We use superlative adjectives and adverbs to compare three or more things. We usually use *the* before a superlative adjective.
*People say it's **the most expensive** house in the world.*
*Airplanes are **the fastest** form of transportation.*

We use modifiers such as *a bit*, *a little*, and *slightly* before comparative adjectives and adverbs to talk about small differences, and *a lot, much*, and *far* to talk about large differences.
*My car is **slightly** newer than yours.*
*Electric cars are **much** more expensive than gas cars.*

Common expressions with comparative forms are:
- *the* + comparative, *the* + comparative.
  ***The bigger** the engine, **the faster** you go.*
  ***The quicker** we leave, **the sooner** we'll get there.*
  ***The bigger** they are, **the harder** they fall.*
- *get* + comparative + *and* + comparative.
  *It's **getting easier and easier** to build your own house.*
  *They got **more and more tired** as the day went on.*

Practice

1 Choose the correct option.

1 This apartment *is bigger than / isn't as big as* that huge house.
2 Salech runs *fastest / as fast as* Abdul.
3 Their house is *the biggest / as big* I have ever seen!
4 This car is a little *most expensive / less expensive* than that one.
5 This yurt is much *more warm / warmer* than the tent we stayed in last year.
6 The weather is getting hotter and *more hot / hotter.*
7 Her kitchen is *smaller than / smallest* mine.
8 The *quickest / quicker* we get home, the sooner we'll get some news.

used to, would, and the simple past
Form

Affirmative	Negative
I/you/he/she/it/we/they **used to** **would**	I/you/he/she/it/we/they **didn't use to** **wouldn't**

Interrogative	Short answer
Did I/you/he/she/it/we/they **use to**?	Yes, I/you/he/she/it/we/they **did.** No, I/you/he/she/it/we/they **didn't.**
Would I/you/he/she/it/we/they?	Yes, I/you/he/she/it/we/they **would.** No, I/you/he/she/it/we/they **wouldn't.**

We use the base form after *used to* and *would*.
Note that the negative and question forms of *used to* do not have a final *-d*:
*Sophie **didn't use to** like opera. **Did** you **use to** like it?*

Simple past: see also page 158

Use

We use *used to* to talk about a situation, a state, or a habit in the past.
*I **used to** drive to work before they opened the subway.*
***Did you use to** go on vacation with your family?*

We can also use *would* to talk about past habits, but not about past states or situations.
Habit: *We **would** go out every Saturday evening.*
State/Situation: *We **used to** live in the country. We **didn't use to** have a car.*

We don't use *used to* or *would* with a specific time in the past. We use the simple past instead.
I used to go to college ~~in 2009~~.
I went to college in 2009.

We can only use *used to* to talk about the past. We cannot use it to talk about the present.
*I **used to go** to the park every week. (past)*
*I **usually go** to the park every week. (present)*

Practice

2 Complete the sentences with *used to* and the verbs. In which of the sentences can you also use *would*?

1 I ___used to live___ (live) in San Francisco when I was young.
2 They ___didn't use to___ (not have) their own house.
3 ___ there ___ (be) more forests and parks in the city?
4 The boys often ___used to play___ (play) tennis in the park.
5 Where ___did___ your father ___use to work___ (work) when he was younger?
6 She ___didn't use to go___ (not go) to the movies often when she was a girl.
7 He ___used to tell___ (tell) me all about his life in Australia.
8 We ___would eat___ (eat) lunch in a café near my grandparents' house.

UNIT 8
Modal verbs (2)
Form

Affirmative	Negative	Interrogative
I/you/he/she/it/we/they	I/you/he/she/it/we/they	
must	must not	must
might	might not	might
may	may not	may
could	couldn't	could
-	can't	can I/you/he/she/it/we/they?

must / might (not) / may (not) / could / can't + base form
It **must be** the original painting.
The animals **may not return** before sunset.
It **could be** a butterfly egg.
The colors **can't be** real.

must / might (not) / may (not) / could / can't + be + -ing
They **must be waiting** for spring.
The birds **could be looking** for a place to nest.
She **can't be using** that camera—it's not digital.

Rules for modal verbs: see also page 163

Use

We can use *must / might (not) / may (not) / could* and *can't* + base form or *be + -ing* to speculate and deduce things about present situations. We make the deduction based on some form of evidence.

We use *must* when we are certain something is true.
The nest **must be** somewhere nearby. (There is evidence for this, for example: *We've seen the birds.*)
She **must be telling** the truth. (We believe that she wouldn't normally lie.)

We use *might, may,* or *could* to say that we think it's possible something is true, but we aren't certain.
He **might be** right about it.
Their natural habitat **may be changing**.
Your plan **could work**.

We use *might not* and *may not* to say that we think it's possible something is not true.
We **might not find** the road before dark.
They **may not be looking** for us now.

We use *can't* when we are certain that something is not true.
That **can't be** the truth.
We **can't be going** in the right direction.

Practice
1 Complete the sentences with *must, may, might not, could,* or *can't* and the correct form of the verbs (base form or *be + -ing*).

1 It ___*must be*___ (be) a burial site. There's evidence of human remains.
2 This _____ (be) a new species, but I need more evidence.
3 This was their nest but the birds _____ (live) here any more. It's empty.
4 They _____ (have) some good photos, but I don't think so.
5 They _____ (recognize) this place; they come here every year.
6 It's only got six legs, so it _____ (be) a spider.
7 The aurora borealis is unpredictable _____ so we (see) any lights tonight.
8 The trees are turning yellow. Fall _____ (come).

Modal verbs (3)
Form

must / might (not) / may (not) / could / can't + *have* + past participle
It **must have been** amazing.
They **might have seen** this before.
It **could have been** the original painting.
The colors **can't have been** real.

Use

We can use *must / might / may / could / can't* and *could + have* + past participle to speculate and deduce things about the past. We often make the deduction based on some form of information or evidence.

We use *must have* + past participle when we are certain that something was true.
People **must have lived** in this valley for thousands of years.

We use *might / may / could have* + past participle when we think it's possible something was true, but we aren't certain.
They **might have made** boats from these trees, but we haven't found any.
These people **could have eaten** fish, but there are no rivers near here.
People **may have cooked** food, but there isn't any evidence of fires.

We use *can't/couldn't have* + past participle when we are certain that something wasn't true.
They **can't have used** carts. They hadn't been invented.
I **couldn't have gone** because I was sick.

Practice

2 Choose the correct option.

1 They *must have /can't have* lived in the trees—they couldn't climb.
2 They *can't have / may have* been able to write—these look like a kind of old pencil.
3 They *must have / couldn't have* collected fruit because there are seeds and skins here.
4 These people *can't have / might have* ridden horses, but I'm not sure.
5 The hunters *couldn't have / must have* killed elephants—they are too big.
6 They *can't have / might have* kept rabbits as pets but I think they ate them.
7 They *can't have / may have* used metal knives—they only used stone tools.
8 They *must have / could have* worn cotton clothes, but we believe they wore leather.

UNIT 9

Noun phrases

Form

a / an + singular count noun
*He got **a** credit card bill for $500.*
*I'd like to give you **an** example of a successful bank.*

the + singular and plural count nouns, noncount noun
*Have you paid **the** bill that arrived yesterday?*
*She was having difficulty making **the** mortgage payments.*
*He made **the** bed.*

zero article + plural count noun, noncount noun
*I like watching **American movies**.*
*I love **pasta**.*

possessive adjectives: *my, your, his, her, its, our, their* + noun
*I can send **my** bank emails or text messages.*
*How do you pay **your** household bills?*

Determiners

each/every + singular count noun
***Every** customer gets a free sample.*
*I always check **each** bank statement before I file it.*

all + plural noun
*They don't treat **all** customers the same way.*

all + *the* + noun (plural count and noncount) and *all* + *of* + *the* + noun.
*We interviewed **all the** people who came into the store.*
*There are sales in **all of the** stores at the moment.*

Use

Articles in noun phrases

We use *a/an* + singular count noun:
- to say that a person or thing is one of many. *He's **a** bank manager. (There are lots of them.)*
- to refer to a person or thing for the first time. *There's **a** new cell phone store in town.*
- to talk about a person or a thing in general. *I'm looking for **a** new job.*

We use *an* with singular count nouns that start with a vowel: *You will receive **an email**.*

We use *the* + singular or plural count noun or noncount noun:
- to say there is only one of this thing. *He's **the** director of the new shopping mall.*
- to refer back to the same thing or person for a second time. *Those are **the** shoes I wanted to buy.*
- with certain countries, place names, geographical regions, oceans and seas, deserts, mountain ranges, and rivers, for example: *the US, the UK, the Philippines, the Eiffel Tower, the White House, the Middle East, the Antarctic, the Pacific, the Mediterranean, the Kalahari Desert, the Alps, the Himalayas, the Amazon, the Nile.*
- with superlative adjectives, for example: *the biggest city, the newest store, the most expensive phone.*
- when there is only one, for example: *the world.*

We use zero article + plural count noun and noncount noun to refer in general to people, animals, or things.
*I don't receive **bank statements** by mail anymore.*
***Online banking** is very convenient.*
*Do you like **cats**?*

We do not use *the* with the names of people, towns, countries, continents, lakes and mountains, languages, for example: *Christopher Columbus, New York, Beijing, Australia, Poland, China, Africa, Europe, Lake Titicaca, Mount Everest, English, Spanish, Japanese.*

Determiners and possessives in noun phrases

We use determiners and possessives in front of nouns to make the information about them more specific.

We use possessive adjectives: *my, your, his, her, its, our, their* + noun to express ownership and possession.
*Where is **my** credit card? This isn't **your** mobile phone.*

We use the determiners *each* and *every* with singular count nouns to refer to individual things.
*They had to pay **every** bill before they moved out.*
***Every store** was full.*

We use the determiner *all* with plural count nouns to refer to a group of things.

*Discounts are available in **all** the local stores this week.*
*There are mortgage offers in **all** the banks right now.*

Practice

1 Complete the sentences with these words. Two sentences are already complete.

a	all	an	every	the	your

1   Do you have any money in _____ savings account?
2   There's a free gift with _____ new cell phone subscription.
3   Where is _____ money I gave you last night?
4   Do you think _____ stores are good places to work in?
5   Would _____ staff members please report to the manager after work?
6   Jan had _____ idea about how to spend the money we had won.
7   The price of _____ gas has gone up again.
8   It's _____ sunny day.

Passive voice: all tenses

Form

We form the passive with the verb *be* + past participle.

Tense	Active	Passive
Simple present	makes/make	**is/are** made
Present continuous	is/are making	**is/are being** made
Simple past	made	**was/were** made
Past continuous	was/were making	**was/were being** made
Present perfect	has/have made	**has/have been** made
can	can make	**can be** made
will	will make	**will be** made

Use

We use the passive voice when we want to focus on an action or the object of the action, rather than the person who is doing the action. The object of the active sentence becomes the subject of the passive sentence.

        subject   object
Active: *The workers **carry** the boxes.*
        subject   object
Passive: *The boxes **are carried** by the workers.*

In a passive sentence, we can say who did the action (the agent) using *by*. We use *by* + agent when it is important to know who did the action. It isn't always necessary to use *by* + agent. We don't usually mention the agent when it is obvious who has done the action, when we don't know, or when it isn't important.
Bananas are grown in Costa Rica ~~by farmers~~.

Practice

2 Rewrite the sentences in the passive form. Use *by* + agent where appropriate.

1   They will transport the goods to Asia by ship.
    The goods will be transported to Asia by ship.
2   Rashid bought a car last month.
    _____
3   Will they build a new factory to create new jobs?
    _____
4   They are producing fair-trade crafts in this village now.
    _____
5   Were they making MP3 players last year?
    _____
6   The company can't complete the project in less than two years.
    _____
7   People will not buy so many goods next year.
    _____
8   They have sold Borders Books to B&N to raise money.
    _____

UNIT 10

Defining relative clauses

Form

He is the man ***who (that)*** *invented the World Wide Web.*
This is the system ***which (that)*** *I told you about.*
That is the place ***where*** *we buy our computers.*

The relative pronouns *who, which, whose, where, when,* and *that* introduce defining relative clauses.

Relative pronoun	Gives information about	Example sentence
who	people	He's the doctor **who** treated all those children.
which	things	That's the jeep **which** can cross the desert easily.
where	places	This is the beach **where** they do extreme surfing.
whose	possessions	She's the runner **whose** leg was broken in three places.
when	time	This weekend is **when** the marathon takes place.
that	people	There's the man **that** ran 1,000 kilometers last week.
	things	These are the shoes **that** he wore to run 1,000 kilometers.

Use

We use defining relative clauses to give us essential information about a person, thing, place, possession, or time.
*That's the doctor **who** carries out the transplants.*
*Cosmetic surgery is a process **which/that** can restore faces.*
*This is the hospital **where** you go for help.*
*That's the surgeon **whose** procedure we use.*
*1992 is the year **when** Dr. Alvarez got his degree.*

We can use *that* for people or things instead of *who* or *which*. This is less formal.
*The person **that** discovered the solution was from China.*
*The factory **that** produces it employs 200 people.*

We always use *who, which,* and *that* when it is the **subject** of the defining relative clause (that is, when those relative pronouns are followed by the verb).
*He's the man **who** did the first bungee jump.*
*Is this the device **that** replaces a damaged hip?*

We can leave out *who, which,* and *that* when they are the **object** of the relative clause (that is, when they are followed by a noun or a pronoun).
*He's the man (**who**) I met in New Zealand.*
*That's the operation (**that**) she had last year.*

Practice

1 Write sentences using *who, which, where, whose,* and *when*. In which sentences can you use *that*? In which sentence can you leave out the relative pronoun?

1 this is the machine / it makes new body parts
   This is the machine which (that) makes new body parts.

2 there's the man / he flew around the world alone

3 that's the cave / four explorers slept there

4 she's the girl / her arm was operated on

5 it's the time of day / the helpline is busiest

6 here is the boat / they crossed the Atlantic in

7 this is the woman / she climbed Everest

8 we saw the device / it treats headaches

Second conditional

Form

We form the second conditional using:
If + simple past, *would* + base form
*If you **introduced** oxygen, plants **would grow**.*
*Rain **wouldn't fall if** the temperature **stayed** the same.*

We can use *if* in two positions:
- If-clause first: *If you tried, you would win.*
- Main clause first: *You would win if you tried.*
When the *if*-clause is at the beginning of the sentence, we use a comma to separate it from the main clause.

We can also form the second conditional with *could* and *might* instead of *would*:
*If there was soil, plants **could** be introduced.*
*If oxygen was introduced, forests **might** grow.*

Note that the contracted form of *would* is *'d*. Don't confuse the contracted forms of *would* (*'d*) and *had* (*'d*).
*They'**d** go on more space exploration if it was less expensive.* (= They **would** go)
*They'**d** gone to the moon years ago.* (= They **had** gone)

Use

We use the second conditional to talk about imagined situations in the present or future that are:
- possible but not probable.
   *If I **had** a lot of money, I **would** buy a Ferrari.* (I don't think it's very probable this will happen.)
- impossible.
   *If I **was** French, I'**d understand** this movie.* (But I'm not French.)
Note that when we use the simple past with *if*, it refers to the present or future, <u>not</u> the past.

We often use *If I were you* rather than *If I was you*, especially when giving advice.
If I were you, I'd train to be a scientist.

Practice

2 Complete the sentences with the simple past and *would* + base form.

1. If he ___won___ (win) the competition, he ___would be___ (be) very happy.
2. If she _____ (pass) her exams, I'm sure she _____ (go) to more concerts.
3. He _____ (not have) cosmetic surgery if he _____ (not need) it.
4. _____ you _____ (live) on Mars if you _____ (have) the chance?
5. If the boys _____ (like) music, they _____ (go) to more concerts.
6. _____ humans _____ (change) Mars if they really _____ (want) to?
7. If you _____ (have) the opportunity to travel into space, _____ you _____ (take) it?
8. If I _____ (be) you, I _____ (rest) before the journey.

UNIT 11

Reported speech

Form

When we report what someone said, we often move the tense "backwards."

Direct speech	Reported speech
Simple present Maria: "I **live** in Peru."	*Simple past* Maria said (that) she **lived** in Peru.
Present continuous James: "I **am working** at home."	*Past continuous* James said (that) he **was working** at home.
Simple past Vikram: "The interpreter **left** this morning."	*Past perfect* Vikram said (that) the interpreter **had left** that morning.
Past continuous Ali: "We **were working** here."	*Past perfect continuous* Ali said (that) they **had been working** there.
Present perfect Katy: "I **have never been** to Africa."	*Past perfect* Katy said (that) she **had never been** to Africa.
will/won't Lin: "I **won't visit** them."	*would/wouldn't* Lin said (that) he **wouldn't visit** them.
can/can't Eugenia: "I **can't do** it."	*could/couldn't* Eugenia said (that) she **couldn't do** it.

We often make other changes in reported speech:
- Pronouns: *I → he/she; we → they; my → his/her; our → their; you (object) → me*
- Time expressions: *now → then; today → that day; tomorrow → the next day; yesterday → the previous day; last night → the night before; this morning → that morning*
- Other changes: *this → that; here → there*

Reported questions

For *yes/no* questions, we form reported questions using *if* or *whether*. We do not use the auxiliary verb *do* in the reported question.
"Do you want to work on this project?" → He asked (me) ***if/whether I wanted to work*** on that project.

When we report questions with *what, why, where, who, when,* and *how,* the word order in the reported question is the same as for an affirmative statement.
"What have you been doing?" → I asked (him) ***what he had been doing***.
"Why haven't we seen this information before?" → She asked ***why they hadn't seen*** that information before.
We do not use question marks in reported questions.

Use

We use reported speech to report someone's words from the past.
Direct speech: *"The photos are on YouTube."*
Reported speech: *She said (that) the photos were on YouTube.*

Note that there is no difference whether we use or don't use the conjunction *that*.

We can also report questions in the past.
Direct speech: *"What are you doing?"*
Reported speech: *I asked what he was doing.*

Direct speech: *"Do you think this policy will work?"*
Reported speech: *He asked if I thought the policy would work.*

Common verbs for reporting what people have said are: *say, tell, explain, suggest, think, recall.*

Note that we don't follow *say* with an object.
"I think we'll go."
Sue **said** (that) she thought they would go.
However, *tell* always needs an object.
"I think we'll go."
Sue **told me** (that) she thought they would go.

Practice

1 Change the direct speech into reported speech. Remember to make changes to pronouns and time expressions where necessary.

1 Greg: "I have a new digital camera."
 Greg said that he had a new digital camera.

2 Anita: "I'll read the news report tomorrow."

3 Joe: "I visited the Amazon rain forest on my trip to South America last year."

4 Mai: "Can I give you a donation for charity?"

5 Nasrin: "I've just seen the documentary about endangered languages of the world."

6 Miguel: "I was reading the paper yesterday."

7 Simon: "Have you ever met anyone from Peru?"

8 Manuela: "We're meeting at nine tomorrow."

Reporting verbs

Form

ask / tell / remind / invite + someone + (*not*) *to* + base form
The manager **asked** *his employees* **to turn off** *their cell phones at work.*
She **told** *me* **to finish** *the report by the end of the day.*
Jaime **reminded** *his friends* **to update** *their software.*
We **invited** *our clients* **to attend** *the opening party.*

promise / offer + (*not*) *to* + base form
They **promised not to blog** *about the incident.*
She **offered to send** *a text about the party.*

The reporting verbs *realize, think, wonder,* and *know* have the same pattern as *say* and *ask* (see Reported speech on page 170).
She **realized** *(that) she had forgotten to turn off her cell.*
They **knew** *(that) she was coming to visit on the weekend.*
Feng **wondered** *if they read his blog.*

Use

Say, tell, and *think* are the most common reporting verbs, but we often use others to report speech.
"Please check your information before continuing." → *The website* **reminded** *customers to check their information before continuing.*
"Don't send me emails until my computer is fixed." → *She* **asked** *her friends not to send her emails until her computer was fixed.*

Other reporting verbs with this pattern include: *advise, convince, encourage, persuade,* and *warn.*

When we decide what reporting verb to use, we think about the purpose of the speaker's words.
"Remember to turn off your computer." = remind (*He reminded me to turn off my computer.*)
"I'll text you when I arrive." = promise (*She promised to text me when she arrived.*)

Practice

2 Change the direct speech into reported speech, using a suitable reporting verb. Remember to make changes to pronouns and time expressions where necessary.

1 David: "I wonder if your friends are coming."
 David wondered if my friends were coming.

2 Sarah: "Can I borrow your laptop tomorrow?"

3 Jhumpa: "Download these photos to my cell."

4 Martin: "Remember to take your laptop."

5 Juan: "I'll connect you to the Internet tomorrow."

6 Lin: "Come and stay with me next week."

7 Adam: "I realize that I was wrong last night."

8 Martina: "Where are you going on Saturday?"

UNIT 12

should have and *could have*

Form

should (*not*) *have* + past participle
They **should have gone** *with a guide.*
We **shouldn't have camped** *in such a remote area.*

could (*not*) *have* + past participle
We **could have had** *an accident!*
You **couldn't have run** *any faster.*

We form the passive with *been* + past participle.
They **should have been warned**.
We **could have been eaten** *alive!*

Use

We use *should have* to talk about a correct thing to do in the past, which we didn't do.
We **should have taken** *our flashlights* (But we didn't.)
I **should have brought** *the first aid kit.* (But I didn't.)

We use *could have* or *might have* to talk about something that was possible in the past, but that didn't happen.

We **could have set up** camp by the trees. (But we didn't, we set up camp somewhere else.)

We **might have had** an accident when that boy ran into the road. (But we didn't.)

We use *shouldn't have* to talk about something that was wrong to do in the past, but we did.

We **shouldn't have come** this way. (But we did.)

He **shouldn't have spoken** like that. (But he did.)

We use *couldn't have* to talk about a lack of ability in the past, something that was impossible to do, and that didn't happen.

You **couldn't have done** anything about it. (It wasn't possible for you to do anything.)

She **couldn't have avoided** riding through the river. (It wasn't possible for her to avoid it.)

Practice

1 Complete the sentences with *should (not) have* and *could (not) have* and the past participle of the verbs.

1   We ___*should have eaten*___ (eat) that fruit—I'm really hungry now.
2   You _____ (tell) anyone about it! It was supposed to be a surprise.
3   It was a very dangerous situation. They _____ (get) hurt.
4   He had a very long time to do his research. He _____ (come) up with better results.
5   Do you think we _____ (ask) a guide to come with us? Then we wouldn't be so lost.
6   He didn't travel to the area, so he _____ (take) this photo.

Third conditional

Form

We form the third conditional using:

If + past perfect, *would have* + past participle

If *we* **had planned** the trip, *we* **would have reached** our destination more quickly.

We **wouldn't have been** late if *you'd* **checked** the schedule.

We can also form the third conditional with *could* and *might* instead of *would*.

She **could have visited** Cuzco if *she'd* **gone** to Peru.

If *you'd* **eaten** that, *you* **might have gotten** sick.

We can use *if* in two positions:

- If-clause first: *If we had planned the trip, we would have reached our destination more quickly.*
- Main clause first: *We would have reached our destination more quickly if we had planned the trip.*

When the *if*-clause is at the beginning of the sentence, we use a comma to separate it from the main clause.

Use

We use the third conditional to talk about situations in the past that did not happen, and the hypothetical result. The situation described is often the opposite of what actually happened.

If I **had seen** *him, I* **would have said** *hello.* (I didn't see him and I didn't say hello.)

If I **had traveled** *abroad, I* **would have taken** *my passport.*

Note that the contracted form of both *would* and *had* is *'d*. Don't confuse the two forms. *Had* is followed by a past participle:

If I'd seen him,… = *If I* **had** *seen him,…*

Would is followed by *have* + past participle: *I'd have said hello.* = *I* **would** *have said hello.*

We can use *could/might (not) have* to speculate on a possible consequence of the imagined past situation.

If he **had asked** *for directions, he* **might not have gotten** *lost.*

Practice

2 Complete the sentences with the past perfect and *would have* + past participle.

1   If you ___*had driven*___ (drive) more slowly, you ___*wouldn't have had*___ (not have) an accident.
2   They _____ (find) the camp if they _____ (not lose) the map.
3   _____ you _____ (plan) the trip better if you _____ (know) about the problems ahead?
4   If the explorers _____ (prepare) better, they _____ (succeed).
5   The local people _____ (be) friendlier if we _____ (understand) their language.
6   What _____ you _____ (do) if they _____ (attack) you?
7   We _____ (not feel) nervous if we _____ (read) about their customs first.
8   If she _____ (want) to come with us, we _____ (welcome) her.

Unit 1

🔊 1

A: Do you want to do this quiz?
B: What's it about?
A: Colors and what they mean around the world. For example, look at this photo. Where are the women going?
B: I don't know. To a party?
A: No, they're guests at a wedding in India. The guests and the bride herself wear bright colors like these red and orange clothes. OK, here's your next question. Does red have different meanings in Eastern and Western cultures?
B: Yeah, I think it does. I always associate red with strong emotions like love, or passion or anger.
A: That's right. And in Eastern cultures it means luck and prosperity. Oh, and courage too, it says here. OK, next: Where does yellow symbolize wisdom?
B: Well, a yellow jersey means the winner of the Tour de France to me! But I don't see the connection with wisdom.
A: Well, there are two options. Is it China or India?
B: I think it's… oh, India.
A: Let's see… yes, you're right, it's India. It means both wisdom and knowledge in India, actually. And in China, it's a symbol of power.
B: Well, I didn't know that. What's the next question?
A: OK… which color means "happiness" in Japan? Orange or pink?
B: Oh, I know this. I think it's orange. It's happiness and love.
A: Yes, it is! Well done! Amazing!
B: Are there any more questions?
A: Yeah, the last one is: Who uses green as their symbol? There are two options, but I'm not going to tell you them—it's too easy.
B: Green? Something to do with nature? Oh yes, environmentalists, conservationists, that kind of thing.
A: Of course! Now, here's a quiz all about the color green. Do you want to give it a try?

🔊 2

1 Do you want to do this quiz?
2 Where are the women going?

🔊 3

1 Where does yellow symbolize wisdom?
2 Is it China?
3 What's the next question?

4 Are there any more questions?
5 Do you want to give it a try?

🔊 4

1 **P:** Good morning! Allow me to introduce myself. I'm Paola Jimenez.
   C: How do you do? My name's Colin Burke.
   P: It's a pleasure to meet you, Colin. I see you work for an advertising agency.
   C: Yes, umm… Paola. I'm the art director at Arrow Agency. I mostly work on web advertising.
   P: That sounds interesting.
   C: It is. We're developing some really new ways of advertising. Do you use the Internet much in your work?
   P: I do, actually, Colin. I'm in sales. I work for an electronics company and we're starting to sell online.
   C: Really? Well, Paola, why don't I give you my card? Here you are.
   P: Thanks. It's been good talking to you. Let's stay in touch.

2 **L:** Hi, how are you? I'm Lucy.
   Y: I'm very pleased to meet you. I'm Yuvraj Singh. I work for Get Fit. It's a chain of gyms.
   L: Oh yes, my brother goes to Get Fit.
   Y: Does he? Great. We're building a big new gym downtown. It's nearly ready to open, in fact.
   L: Is it? That's great.
   Y: Yes, we're all really excited about it. Umm, what about you?
   L: Well, I'm looking for a new job, actually.
   Y: OK, well, thanks for your time. Let me give you my card. Don't forget to check out our new gym when it opens.

🔊 5

1 **Colin:** I mostly work on web advertising.
   Paola: Do you?
2 **Paola:** I'm in sales.
   Colin: Oh, are you?
3 **Lucy:** Oh yes, my brother goes to your gym.
   Yuvraj: Does he?

Unit 2

🔊 6

M = Manny, I = Isabella
M: You've just heard a very lively and energetic track from Manu Chao and you're listening to Global Music with me, Manny Ramirez. Our studio guest today is Isabella Rey. She's an expert on world fusion—that's music

which mixes influences from several countries. Isabella, tell me about Manu Chao, because he's a very successful artist, although he hasn't been as successful in the English-speaking world yet.
I: No, indeed he hasn't. But Manu Chao is a perfect example of a truly globalized, 21st-century artist. His origins are Spanish, but he's lived in France for most of his life. He sings in six languages: French, Spanish, English, Galician, Arabic, and Portuguese.
M: That's an amazing range!
I: Yeah. It shows the influences that exist in his music. He mixes in all sorts, from punk, rock, salsa, and reggae to ska and raï. He's hugely successful in Europe and Latin America, but as you say, he hasn't had a big impact in this country yet.
M: So he's a good example of world fusion music?
I: Yeah. Paul Simon's another example. He's worked with Zulu artists Ladysmith Black Mambazo and several other African musicians. In fact, world fusion music has become better known since the 1986 release of Paul Simon's album *Graceland*.
M: That was a fabulous collaboration. We've got a track from that album coming up later in the show. And, of course, what about WOMAD?
I: WOMAD—that's World of Music and Dance—is a great example of how different musicians from around the world have been able to meet and influence each other. The British musician Peter Gabriel was the founder and he's been a big part of it for many years now—since the 1980s. These days, we've all heard of the incredible Senegalese singer, Youssou N'Dour—basically he's become popular outside of Senegal since his collaboration with Peter Gabriel. But he's not the only one, of course.
M: And what's happened since then, since the 80s, in terms of world fusion?
I: Well, we've seen younger musicians mix things like punk, new wave and hip-hop styles with non-Western styles to create dazzling new sounds. Like Manu Chao, as we've heard, and also Zap Mama, a new band from Belgium. They've already had several international hits. Their lead singer, Marie Daulne, has a beautiful and powerful singing voice.
M: Well let's listen to Zap Mama. This track is called "Show me the way."

7

L = Lesley, R = Richard

L: Do you feel like going out tonight?

R: Sure, why not? We haven't been out for ages. What's playing?

L: Well, there's a movie about climate change. Do you like the sound of that?

R: No, not really. It doesn't really appeal to me. What's it about? Just climate change?

L: I think it's about how climate change affects everyday life. I wonder how they make it entertaining.

R: Well, it sounds really awful. It's an important subject, I know, but I'm not in the mood for anything depressing. What else is playing?

L: There's a flamenco festival.

R: Oh, I love dance! That sounds really interesting.

L: Apparently it's absolutely superb. Let's see what it says in the paper: "Ana Gómez leads in a thrilling production of the great Spanish love story *Carmen*."

R: Great. What time is it at?

L: At 7:30.

R: Well, that's no good. We haven't got enough time to get there. Is there anything else?

L: There's a comedy special.

R: Where?

L: It's at the City Theater. It's a kind of comedy marathon for charity with lots of different acts. It looks pretty good. The critic in the local paper says it's the funniest thing he's ever seen. It says here: "Jackie Chan is absolutely hilarious as the embarrassing host to a night of comedy gold."

R: Hmm, I'm not crazy about him. He's not very funny.

L: Are you sure you feel like going out tonight? You're not very enthusiastic!

R: Maybe you're right. OK, let's go and see the flamenco—but tomorrow, not tonight.

A: Great. I'll go online and book the tickets.

 8

1   It sounds really awful.
2   That sounds really interesting.
3   Apparently, it's absolutely superb.
4   It looks pretty good.
5   Jackie Chan is absolutely hilarious.
6   He's not very funny.

Unit 3

 9

[Use young female voice for first paragraph and young male voice for second paragraph]

1   I live in Zambia and we have fantastic river systems here. I love rafting on the Zambezi River. It's one of the best white-water runs in the world. On my very first trip, we had a real surprise! We were coming down fast from a section of rapids and we could see calm water ahead. Then I saw a big hippo near the river bank. It's best to avoid hippos if you can! We started paddling away quickly because it was coming towards us! We were going around a small island in the middle of the river, when suddenly…

2   I began diving when I was about 12. I actually learned to dive on vacation in Mexico. My parents went there to explore the underground lakes—or cenotes. My brother and I were sitting around on the beach, getting bored, so we took a diving lesson. Then we did our first dive in the "easy" cenotes while my parents were exploring the dangerous stuff. It wasn't deep underground and the sun was shining in through an opening in the roof of the cave. It was really calm and beautiful. I felt like staying there all day! I was concentrating on doing everything right. I didn't notice that…

 10

1   We were going around a small island in the middle of the river, when suddenly we surprised an 18-foot-long crocodile. It was lying in the sun on the other bank. It jumped into the water about three feet away from our boat and soaked us all. Fortunately, he didn't catch up with us!

2   I was concentrating on doing everything right. I didn't notice that I was swimming into an area that was only for advanced divers. There were ropes and signs to stop you from going into a sort of labyrinth of tunnels where it was easy to get lost. Luckily for me, my mom realized pretty quickly that I was missing and she came after me. I still had no idea!

 11

1 **A:** Did I ever tell you about the time we had a lot of animals? Our house was a zoo.

B: No, I don't think so.

A: Well, among other things, we had these goldfish—they were really huge. And they lived in a fish tank above the kitchen sink. But these two fish were really active—they loved to jump in the air. Especially when someone was doing the dishes.

B: No way!

A: Seriously! After we saw it the first time, we put a lid across the top of the tank. So, a couple of weeks later, I came into the kitchen one morning and the tank was empty. No fish!

B: Oh, no!

A: Oh, yes! During the night, the fish had jumped out of the tank! They were lying in the sink! Fortunately, there was some water in it!

B: That's incredible!

2 **C:** I remember once, a couple of years ago, we were looking after this friend's parrot when he was on a business trip. Anyway, after a few days, I realized that this parrot knew how to open its cage.

D: Really?

C: Oh yes! It happened a couple of times. When I went out, the parrot was in its cage. And when I got back home, it had gotten out. So one day, I was at work when all of a sudden I remembered that I hadn't given the bird food and water. I immediately rushed back home and there it was: the empty cage again. I searched everywhere. I was going around the house calling "Polly! Polly, here Polly, Polly!" But I couldn't find it.

D: What happened then?

C: Well, the next thing was, I started to panic. So I went into the kitchen to make tea, and guess what? There was the bird. It was taking a bath in my teacup!

D: That's unbelievable!

 12

1   Especially when someone was doing the dishes.
2   They were lying in the sink!
3   We were looking after this friend's parrot.
4   I was going around the house calling "Polly!"

Unit 4

💿 13

1 Devi is from West Sumatra in Indonesia

D: I didn't stay in school because generally girls don't here. But then I got this job. I'm the first girl in my family to work outside the home. Since the economic crisis, more women have jobs. I feel very different about my future now. I'm not going to stay in this job forever. I want to be a nurse, so I've applied to college. I hope to get in. I'm taking the entrance exam next month. I'm very nervous about it. I haven't told my boss, but I suppose I'll tell him soon.

2 Elisabeth is from Bruges in Belgium

E: I work in a factory. It's a good job, but the company is laying people off so I'm going to take the early retirement package because it's an opportunity to start again. I got married very young and had a family, so I didn't finish my education. But I've just finished evening classes in business administration, and now I'm going to start my own business. It's something I already do as a hobby. I make specialty cheeses. Just a moment, I'll get you some… Here you are, taste this. Do you like it? Well, I'm meeting the bank manager on Wednesday to discuss my business plan. And hey, maybe I'll take some cheese for him to taste as well!

3 Sahera is from Kabul in Afghanistan

S: It's very difficult to study at the college level here. Many girls get no education at all. But I have managed to complete my degree and graduate from the department of language and literature. Now I'm thinking about the next step. Many of the graduates are going to work as teachers. My friend is going to continue her studies in the United States. I'm going to stay here in the city, because my family is here. I guess I'll take some time off and visit my parents. And I want to spend time with my friend because she's leaving next week.

💿 14

R = Raaj, M = Mani

R: This looks interesting—this research assistant job for a TV company.

M: I know. The only thing is the experience. They want two years, but I've only worked part-time for a year, really.

R: One or two years' experience it says, and anyway you meet the other requirements. You're good under pressure and with deadlines—you always hand your essays in on time at college!

M: I'm not sure that's the same thing.

R: Of course it is! And you're really well-organized, hard-working, highly motivated…

M: OK, OK, if that's what you think. Is it all right if I give you as my reference?

R: Hmm, I'm not sure about that. I don't think you can just put down your friends' names.

M: I know, too bad! But seriously, do you mind helping me with my resume? I need to make it look a little more professional.

R: Of course I will. Are you going to apply for this job, then?

M: Yeah, I think I will. But I'll need my resume anyway, whichever job I apply for.

R: OK, print it out and I'll take a look at it.

M: Will you be able to do it today?

R: Yes, I will. But what's the hurry?

M: The deadline for applications is in a couple of days. Oh, can you have a look at my cover letter too?

R: Have you already written it?

M: No, but I'll do it this afternoon and then I can send everything off tonight. Hey, they might ask me to go for an interview this week!

R: Yeah, they might.

M: But I haven't got any good clothes! Would it be OK to borrow your suit?

R: Sure, no problem.

💿 15

M: Will you be able to do it today?

R: Yes, I will.

Unit 5

💿 16

Conservationist Mike Fay is somewhere in central Africa. He's in the middle of the longest walk of his life—so far! Fay is traveling almost 2,000 miles through the dense forests of Congo and Gabon. He's lived in the area for several years and he's worked on various forest conservation projects there. Now Fay and his team are making a record of the region's ecosystems and wildlife, especially in the unexplored and unexploited areas. Traveling through untouched forest and down wild rivers to remote villages, they can only travel on foot or by boat. They've completed about half of the route. The trek will take about fifteen months to complete, through what Fay calls "the last wild place on Earth."

💿 17

1 The WCS has financed the work.
2 The trip has taken longer than expected.
3 The team members have worked hard.
4 The results have surprised us.
5 The project has been a great success.
6 The government has helped the project.

💿 18

1 L: Hi there, I'm Li.
M: Hi, I'm Matt.
L: Is this your first time here?
M: No, actually. We've been coming here for about four years now. We come every July.
L: Oh, it's strange that we haven't bumped into each other before now.
M: Really? How long have you been coming here?
L: About six years. We love it. There's so much to do here—that's why we keep coming back.
M: I know, and the nightlife's awesome!
L: I always tell everyone at home it's got everything you need for a vacation—great beaches, perfect weather, and lots to do. Are you going to the barbecue later on?
2 M: Hi, Rosa! What a surprise! How long have you been here?
R: Matt! Hi! Oh, we just got in yesterday.
M: Good to see you again!
R: Listen, we're staying at the SeaView this year—the food is absolutely fantastic there.
M: The SeaView? A few miles up the coast? Isn't that a little remote? And expensive!
R: Well, I've been working really hard recently. I needed a relaxing, peaceful break this year.
M: You're getting old!
R: I know, tell me about it. I'll be 30 next year!
3 P: OK, we're ready to go. Are you nervous?
M: A little. But I like to try something new every vacation. I always have great memories to look back at when I get home.
P: I know what you mean. Well, sky-diving is one experience you won't forget!
M: So Ping, how long have you been sky-diving?
P: Oh, for quite a few years now. I qualified as an instructor five years ago.
M: How long did that take you?
P: Well, you need to do a minimum number of jumps before you can start the training course. It took a while! But you know, it's a great job. You can travel all over the world and find work.
M: So what do you do for a vacation, then?
P: I meet up with friends. We like a little excitement—New York, Rio de Janeiro, Moscow, you name it!

💿 19

1 T= female tourist, G = tour guide
T: I wonder if you could help us. Our luggage hasn't arrived.
G: Right. Are you with ChinaTimes tours?

T: Yes. Mr. and Mrs. Wong.
G: And which flight were you on, Mrs. Wong?
T: The ChinAir flight from Beijing. I think it's CA2498. We've been talking to some of the other passengers and their luggage has come through, no problem.
G: Ah, yes. It seems some bags have gone to another airport. Flight CA2498?
T: Yes, that's right. Do you know where our bags have gone to?
G: Yes, I'm afraid the luggage has gone to Shanghai.
T: Shanghai? Well, how did that happen?
G: I'm not sure, but all the missing bags are coming on the next flight.
T: But when's the next flight?
G: It's tomorrow morning. Don't worry, we'll arrange everything. Which hotel are you staying at? Your bags will go there directly.
T: But all our summer clothes are in the suitcases…
2 T= male tourist, G = same tour guide
G: Hello, Mr. Biswas. Is anything wrong? Can I help?
T: Well, it's about my wife, actually. She hasn't been feeling well for a couple of days.
G: I'm sorry to hear that. Is it something she's eaten, do you think? Or just motion sickness?
T: I don't know. She's had a temperature all night, but she feels cold.
G: Hmm. Have you both been taking anti-malarial tablets?
T: Oh, yes. But the hotel hasn't provided mosquito nets. And they haven't been spraying the bedroom at night, either.
G: OK, how long has she been feeling like this?
T: A couple of days? Yes, since the boat trip on Tuesday. Is there anything you can do?
G: Well, it's probably nothing to worry about. But I'll ask the hotel to call a doctor, just in case.
T: That's great, thank you.

💿 20

1 Do you know which airport our bags have gone to?
2 Yes, I'm afraid the luggage has gone to Shanghai.

💿 21

1 Which hotel are you staying at?
2 Are you staying at the Ocean Hotel?
3 Where have you traveled from?
4 Why haven't we heard from the airline?

5 What have we been waiting for?
6 Are you waiting for the manager?

Unit 6

💿 22

1 A: I've never tried durian. Have you? Apparently, it tastes much better than it smells.
B: No, I haven't tried it. But I know that it smells so much that you're not allowed to take it on buses in Singapore.
2 C: I feel a little sick. I wonder if it was the mayonnaise on my salad?
D: Was it fresh mayonnaise? You should avoid using raw eggs in mayonnaise, you know. They can make you sick.
3 E: What's fugu? F–U–G–U?
F: Oh, I know what it is. It's a kind of fish they eat in Japan. It's actually poisonous, so only qualified chefs are allowed to prepare it in restaurants. If you eat the wrong part, it can kill you!
4 G: Can you eat shark meat?
H: Yes, it's popular in lots of countries. Sometimes you have to ferment it first because the fresh meat is bad for you. That's what they do in Iceland. It's called *hakarl* there.
5 I: I love eating oysters, but I can never remember when it's safe to eat them.
J: The rule is you can't eat them in the warm summer months, but I don't know why.
6 K: Are you going to boil those potatoes like that, without peeling them?
L: Yeah, why? You don't have to peel potatoes before you boil them.
K: Yes, you do. At least that's what we do in our house!
7 M: Are you making chilli con carne?
N: Yes, but the recipe says red beans must boil for fifteen minutes or they aren't safe to eat. Do you think that's true?
8 O: What's this on the menu? Steak tartare? Is that raw steak?
P: Yes, you can eat steak raw. It's cut into very thin pieces. You should try it.

💿 23

1 You're not allowed to take durian on buses in Singapore.
2 Only qualified chefs are allowed to prepare fugu.
3 You have to ferment *hakarl* first.
4 You don't have to peel potatoes before you boil them.

24

L = Lin (female), J = Jack

L: Hi, Jack. Have you read this item on imaginary eating?

J: Hi, Lin. Yes, I saw it this morning. What a bunch of garbage! I've never heard anything so ridiculous. If we think about eating food, we'll lose weight, it said.

L: Not exactly. It said if you think about eating food, you stop wanting to eat it so much. So if you don't eat it, then you might lose weight. I thought it made sense.

J: No, it's nonsense. I'll believe it when I see it! You can't "think yourself thin."

L: Well, I'm not so sure. I think willpower is really important, especially where food is concerned. Imagine you're overweight and you want to lose a few pounds. If you don't train your mind, you won't be able to lose weight. I think you can achieve anything if you believe you can do it.

J: You mean like "mind over matter"? Well, OK, mental attitude is important when you're trying to change something in your life. But I don't think that's the same as what the news item said. So are you going to do this imaginary eating thing, then? Do you really think it'll work?

L: Yeah, why not? I won't find out unless I try.

J: So what exactly are you going to do?

L: OK, let's think. I eat too many potato chips and snacks, right? So, when I want to eat a snack, I'll try just imagining that I'm eating it. Hey, you know what? This could be amazing. I'll never have to buy chocolate again if this technique works!

J: Well, I can't believe my ears!

L: Hey, as soon as it starts working, I'll let you know. Self-confidence, that's what's important.

J: I'm going to buy you some chocolate just in case. I think you'll need it.

 25

W = Waiter

W: Are you ready to order?

A: Umm, not quite.

W: No problem. Would you like something to drink while you decide?

A: Yes, please, just water's fine for now.

B: Oh, this menu looks interesting. I love trying new dishes. What are plantain fritters?

A: Well, plantain is a kind of banana and a fritter is a fried dish—in this case, fried mashed banana balls.

B: Do you mean like a sweet dessert banana?

A: No, plantain is a type of savory banana you eat as a vegetable. It's quite a bland flavor, really.

B: OK. What about akkra? What's that made from?

A: It's made from a kind of bean called blackeyed peas. They're fritters too.

B: Hmm. What do they taste like?

A: Well, akkra's usually pretty hot and spicy.

B: Sounds good! I think I'll try that. Now, what's this—ackee and saltfish?

A: Where's that?

B: In the entrees, at the top of the list.

A: Oh yes. I think ackee's a kind of fruit that's traditionally served with saltfish.

B: And saltfish?

A: That's dried salted cod. You have to soak it in water before you cook it, but then it's a bit like fresh cod. It doesn't taste salty when it's cooked.

B: OK. I might try that. What are you going to have?

A: I can't make my mind up. Oh, here comes the waiter again.

W: Can I take your order now?

A: Yes, please. I'll have the akkra to start.

B: And I'll have the same.

W: And for your entree?

A: I'd like to try the ackee and saltfish. Does it come with vegetables?

W: Yes, with plantain.

A: And how's that cooked? Is it fried?

W: No, it's boiled.

A: OK, that sounds fine.

W: And what about you, sir?

B: Can I have the goat curry, please?

W: Certainly.

A: I've never tried goat.

B: You can try some of mine when it comes. It's like lamb, but the flavor's a little stronger.

A: OK, great.

Unit 7

 26

1 As an architect, I'm interested in all aspects of house design. But we can learn so much from traditional constructions and designs. They're usually the ones that are much better in bad weather conditions, and they are much more appropriate to people's needs. If you live in a flood zone, it makes sense to build your house on stilts, doesn't it?

2 Well, a shelter is something less permanent and more basic than a house. Things like the ice igloos that people build in the Arctic region, or brush huts in tropical areas, are perfect for specific needs—like when you are hunting, for example— because you can put them up quickly. The purpose of a shelter is to protect you from the elements, whereas a home has several spaces with different functions.

3 Ah yes, a ger combines elements of both a shelter and a home. It has a fireplace and maybe a chimney or at least a smoke-hole, and separate areas for men and women. It isn't as solid as a brick or stone house but it's certainly easier to take down and put up, which is what nomadic people in Mongolia need.

4 Usually the most important thing is the local climate. You know, if you live in Turkey, why build a house under the glare of the hot sun if you can adapt a cool cave? Cave houses are some of the oldest homes known, and they're a lot less basic than you might imagine. They're the best solution in really hot climates. Of course, the colder the climate, the warmer your house needs to be. Central heating, especially when combined with energy-efficient windows, heats buildings more efficiently than open fires.

5 Well, modern homes are fairly similar wherever they are in the world, which doesn't necessarily mean that they are the best design for every situation. And in our crowded cities they're getting smaller and smaller. I think, even with a modern home, you should make sure the design is the most appropriate for your climate and your needs.

27

1 Oh, well, it's great for us because it's so much cheaper than a house. And we're all students. We don't have as much money as people who are working. Plus, renting is easier and simpler than actually buying a place.

2 Actually, it's really good because I don't have to worry when things break or go wrong. Everyone in the complex pays an amount each month for repairs and stuff.

3 We don't have anyone living right above us, so it isn't as noisy as our old place.

4 I love having a garden, don't get me wrong. But it's a little dirtier than a balcony, especially with kids and animals running in and out all day! I can't keep the place as clean as I'd like to because I have a full-time job so I don't have a lot of spare time.

28

1 We don't have as much money as people who are working.

2 I can't keep the place as clean as I'd like to because I have a full-time job.

29

A = realtor, C = female customer
A: Good morning.
C: Hi, I'm interested in any properties you have downtown.
A: OK, and is that to rent or to buy?
C: Oh, it's to rent. I've just started a new job here, so I think I'd rather rent than buy, for now anyway.
A: Sure. Well, we have quite a few apartments on our books, from studios to four-bedroom apartments.
C: I'd prefer something small, but not too small. I imagine I'll get a lot of friends staying with me. So, two bedrooms, and preferably with an elevator. I bike a lot and I don't want to carry my bike up lots of stairs!
A: Well, most of the modern buildings have elevators, but a lot of the properties downtown are quite old. Would you rather look at new places or older ones?
C: I don't mind—at this stage I'm just getting an idea of what things are like here.
A: OK... so you're new to the area?
C: Yeah, I lived in a small town near the mountains until recently.
A: Oh, that sounds lovely.
C: To be honest, I prefer cities to small towns. The problem with a small town is that everyone knows your business. Maybe I'm unfriendly, but I like the way the city is more anonymous.
A: Ah yes, I've heard a few people say that! I have to say I prefer living here. I suppose I like my privacy too. OK, umm, what about garage space? Do you need that?
C: No, I don't have a car. I prefer to walk or bike. It keeps me in shape.
A: Of course, you mentioned your bike!
C: Yeah! And anyway, in my experience, driving downtown is a nightmare!
A: I know, and it's getting worse. OK, well, the next thing to consider is your budget and the rental period.

30

Would you rather live in a town or a village?

31

1 Do you prefer playing soccer or basketball?
2 Would you rather have tea or coffee?
3 Do you prefer summer or winter?
4 Would you rather go by car or by bike?
5 Do you prefer English or French?
6 Would you rather eat fish or meat?

Unit 8

32

1 At certain times of the year in the Arctic circle, the sky looks as though it's on fire. The colors are so vivid—like neon street signs—that you think they can't be natural. You imagine that they must be man-made and that someone must be projecting disco lights into the sky. And yet they are completely natural. In the past, people thought they might have a religious significance, and more recently scientists speculated that they could be a form of radiation. So what exactly are these lights? We now know that they are the result of particles in the Earth's atmosphere colliding with each other. The colors come from different kinds of particles. When the particles are mainly oxygen, the sky looks green. If you see a lot of red, on the other hand, that comes from nitrogen.

2 This might be a painting or a work of art. There's something very composed about it. It looks as if the green spiral is holding the orange ball. Or it might be protecting the ball. But look carefully—the amount of detail is incredible. That's because it's a close-up—or macro—photograph. It shows a butterfly egg on the stem of a plant. Why do butterflies lay eggs in such places? They must have a reason. Scientists think that this species of butterfly may choose this spot to keep the eggs safe from ants and other predators.

3 Plants that eat animals? That can't be true… or is it? It may not seem logical, but there are indeed plants that catch insects—mostly flies, beetles, ants, and so on. But how do they do it? They must use a very special technique, because obviously they can't move and chase after things. Well, one way of catching food is to pretend to be something else. Take this Australian sundew plant. To an unfortunate insect, these shiny drops look like water. But the insect must get a nasty surprise when it tries to take a drink and gets caught on the sticky spikes. Then the plant's chemicals dissolve the insect so that it can "eat" it.

33

The Nazca lines are enormous drawings on the ground in the Nazca desert of southern Peru. Their scale is huge: the biggest of the drawings is about 650 feet across. Most of the lines are geometric shapes, but about 70 are animal shapes such as a spider, different types of birds, a monkey, and a dog. There are human figures, too. Altogether there are hundreds of these drawings and they cover an area of about 200 square miles. The lines date from a period starting about 2,000 years ago. Basically, the marks on the ground were made by moving the reddish brown stones that cover the desert and revealing the white ground underneath. You can still see the stones along the edges of the lines.

34

1 A: Did you hear that story about the sheep?
B: No, I don't think so. What was it about?
A: Apparently, they reflect the sun back into the atmosphere because they're so white.
B: Really?
A: Yeah, and then the heat from the sun gets trapped, so it makes everything hotter. So they think sheep cause global warming.
B: Come on!
A: Well, that's what it says in the paper today.
B: You're pulling my leg!
A: It does—here, look.
B: Hmm, that can't be right! Wait a minute… what's today's date?

2 C: Let me take a look at those twenty-euro bills for a minute.
D: Why?
C: The blue ones are no good—they're forged.
D: You're kidding me! All twenty-euro bills are blue!
C: Not the real ones.
D: Are you sure?
C: I'm absolutely positive. The girl at the travel agency told me. It was on the news last night.
D: No way! They must have made a mistake. We've just changed all this money! What are we going to do?
C: I don't know… but it is April first today…
D: Oh, honestly! I really believed you!

3 D = daughter, F = father
D: Dad, did you see the news about gas prices? They've gone down by almost half.
F: Oh, yeah? How come?
D: I don't know. But anyway, I put gas in the car.
F: Great! Wait a minute, did you say gas?
D: Yeah.
F: Are you serious? The car uses diesel, not gas!
D: I know, but gas is so much cheaper!
F: But, but…!
D: I'm sorry. Did I do something wrong?
F: Diesel engines don't work with gas. You must know that! Oh, this is going to cost me a fortune!
D: Dad?
F: Yes?
D: How do you suppose I managed to drive the car home? April Fools'!

35

Oh yeah?
Come on!

Unit 9

36

Welcome to *Money Talk*. On today's show we discuss cell phone technology and personal banking. In particular, we look at how technology allows people who have never had a bank account to manage their money using their cell phones. More and more people have cell phones these days. Did you know there are about five billion phones in the world today? But, there are a lot of people without easy access to banks, which are generally located in big towns and cities. So we are seeing lots of innovations in cell phone banking—in other words, using your cell phone to manage your bank account. An example of this is the interactive voice menu system which cell phone banking uses. Using the menu system, you can talk to your cell phone and tell it what to do with your money! Now, at its most basic, cell phone banking lets you transfer your money from one place or person to another. But now the list of things you can do from your phone is expanding into paying bills, buying goods and managing your savings account.

A new cell phone banking plan has recently begun in Afghanistan. It's a good place to see how cell phone banking works in action because the cell phone network covers every town and city. Under the new plan, the Afghan National Police has started to pay all salaries through cell phones, so the policemen don't actually receive cash. Salary payments are now made directly to each individual police officer. When a payment is made, each police officer gets a text message on his phone. He can then use his phone, via the interactive voice menus, to make payments from his salary. The new system is changing the way the economy works. The Afghan people can control their finances more easily: the cash they used to carry around is now safely in the bank.

37

1 I tried to save money to get a new phone.
2 The model I wanted cost a fortune.
3 I gave up chocolate, buying DVDs, and smoking.
4 I gave the money to my sister to take care of.
5 She told me how much I'd saved each week.
6 When I had enough, I went to buy the phone.
7 The store had a special offer.
8 I got a free upgrade with a new phone!
9 And I still had the cash I'd saved. Amazing!

38

1 I tried to save money to get a new phone.
2 The model I wanted cost a fortune.

39

1 I tried to save money to get a new phone.
2 The model I wanted cost a fortune.
3 I gave up chocolate, buying DVDs, and smoking.
4 I gave the money to my sister to take care of.
5 She told me how much I'd saved each week.
6 When I had enough, I went to buy the phone.
7 The store had a special offer.
8 I got a free upgrade with a new phone!
9 And I still had the cash I'd saved. Amazing!

40

S = salesperson, C = customer
1 **S:** Can I help you?
   C: Yes, can I look at this silver chain?
   S: This one?
   C: Yes, please.
   S: It's lovely, isn't it? Is it for you?
   C: No, for my sister.
   S: It's on sale actually; 20 percent off.
   C: Oh? I like it, but it's a little heavy. I was looking for something more delicate.
   S: How about this?

C: Yeah, that's great. That's just right, I think. Can she return it if she doesn't like it, though?
   S: Yes, she can exchange it within ten days.
   C: OK, good.
   S: That's as long as she's got the receipt, of course.
   C: I'll take it then. Can you gift-wrap it for me?
   S: Well, we don't actually do gift-wrapping, but we have some nice gift boxes for sale, over there.
   C: Thanks.
2 **C:** Excuse me, do you work here?
   S: Yes, can I help you?
   C: Well, I'm looking for a sofa that I saw on your website, but I don't see it here.
   S: OK, do you have the reference number or the model name?
   C: Yes, it's Craftmaster. The number is 00389276.
   S: OK, let me see if it's in stock.
   C: The website said "available" this morning...
   S: Yes, here we are. Do you want it in red, floral, or natural?
   C: Floral, if you've got it.
   S: Yes, there are plenty in stock. Just give them this reference number at customer pick-up.
   C: OK. What about delivery? How much do you charge for that?
   S: Can you tell me your zip code? The charges go by area.
   C: 33062.
   S: That would be $55.
   C: Wow! OK...
   S: If you go to the customer service desk, they can take your information and arrange the delivery date.
   C: And do I pay here or...?
   S: The cash registers are over by the customer pick-up. You can pay by card or in cash.
   C: Great, thanks for your help. Umm, how do I get to the cash registers again?
   S: Just follow the yellow arrows.

Unit 10

🔊 41

P = presenter, G = guest

P: Now most of us will remember TV series like *The Bionic Woman* or *The Six Million Dollar Man*, or more recently, the *Terminator* movies, in which the characters are a futuristic mixture of technology and nature. Tonight on Channel 10, there's a fascinating documentary which suggests that this bionic future is already here. Nadene, you've seen a preview of the show.

G: Yes, Owen, and it really does seem as if science fiction has become science fact. The show follows the treatment of a woman whose arm was amputated in a traffic accident, a man who has had a full face transplant and an amazing process which actually grows human organs.

P: So it's not just looking at what medical science *might* be able to achieve, but how it's changing people's lives right *now*.

G: Absolutely. Take the woman I mentioned—the lady who injured her arm—Amanda Kitts. She's been getting treatment in a hospital where they specialize in bionics. And they've developed a bionic arm which fits onto her shoulder.

P: And what kind of things can she do now?

G: Well it's still too early to tell for sure, but the doctors are confident that she'll be able to do the normal things that we take for granted, like making sandwiches or holding a cup of coffee.

P: So bionics is great news for patients who have lost the use of a limb.

G: Absolutely. And the show shows all sorts of other bionic devices, too. There will come a time when the blind can see, the deaf can hear... Right now, it seems as if the possibilities are endless. The technology, or should I say biotechnology, already exists.

P: And that's on Channel 10 tonight at 9:30.

🔊 42

1 A: What on earth happened to you? There's blood all over your leg!

B: Oh, it's nothing. I tripped over a tree branch or something when I was out running.

A: Let me see. Oh, that looks nasty! It's quite a deep cut. You'd better wash it right away.

B: Yeah, I will.

A: You know, if I were you, I'd go down to the emergency room and have it looked at.

B: It doesn't hurt. It's just a cut, really. I'm not going all the way to the hospital for a cut on my leg.

A: Hmm, it might need stitches, though. I would keep an eye on it if I were you.

B: OK, if it doesn't stop bleeding, I'll call the doctor's office and see if the nurse is there.

A: Good, because I don't think we've got any bandages big enough!

2 C: Is my neck red? I think I've been stung or something.

D: A little, yeah. It looks a little swollen. Is it itchy?

C: Not exactly. It's painful rather than really itchy. How funny, I don't usually react to insect bites and stuff. Oooh, I'm feeling a little sick.

D: You should put some antihistamine lotion on it and see if it gets better.

C: Have you got any?

D: Yes, I'm sure I've got some somewhere. You'll have to check the date on the tube, though. I'm not sure how long I've had it.

3 E: Ow!

F: Is your wrist still hurting you?

E: Yeah, actually it is. It hurts when I move it.

F: It might be worth getting it X-rayed. It's been, what, three days now? I wouldn't just ignore it—you might have broken something.

E: No, you're probably right. But I'm sure it's just a sprain, from when I fell against the table...

F: Even so, you should get it looked at.

E: Hmm.

F: Why don't you go and see Rosana in reception? She's the first-aid person. She'll know.

E: Good idea.

🔊 43

A and E

cuts and bruises

sprains and breaks

wasp and bee stings

bites and stuff

go and see Rosana

Unit 11

44

1 **A:** I like this Twitter travel idea.
  B: What's that?
  A: It's this travel journalist, Zi Chen. She goes to different places and asks her Twitter followers to suggest things to do. You know, "I've just gotten off the train in Bogota and I'm hungry. Where can I get a good breakfast?" That kind of thing.
  B: OK. And then what happens?
  A: And then she writes about it. It's like a travel guide by local people—they're the ones who really know what's good. It's a great idea to use Twitter for something like that.
  B: I didn't realize Twitter could be useful for anything!

2 **C:** It says here there's an eclipse tomorrow. Did you know?
  D: Tomorrow? I thought it was today.
  C: No, tomorrow. We should be able to see it from here. I'm just looking at this weather blog. It's reminding people not to look at it with telescopes.
  D: Yeah, I know.
  C: It's really a good blog. It tells you all kinds of things.
  D: I know. I've got it bookmarked.
  C: Oh, I wondered if you had.

3 **E:** Wow, that's terrible. Have you seen this? It's bad enough to lose your job, but finding out by text!
  F: I saw that story. The company sent about 200 employees a text message. They told them not to show up for work on Monday.
  E: I didn't think that you could do that.
  F: Me neither, but there you go…

4 **G:** Oh, that's hilarious!

H: Hmm?
G: You know that weird politician, the one who believes in UFOs?
H: Oh yeah, I can't remember his name, but I know who you mean.
G: He's posted a video on YouTube. He's invited "all friendly aliens" to a meeting at the Capitol.
H: No way! Have you seen it?
G: No, but there's an article about it in the paper. Look!

45

1 **A:** It's a great idea to use Twitter for something like that.
  B: I didn't realize Twitter could be useful for anything!

2 **C:** It says here there's an eclipse tomorrow, did you know?
  D: Tomorrow? I thought it was today.

46

1 **A:** How much did the coffee cost?
  B: What? You asked me to get tea.

2 **A:** We need to send a text about this.
  B: What? I thought you said send an email.

3 **A:** I'm going home now.
  B: Really? You said you were staying.

4 **A:** I heard that story on the news yesterday.
  B: You did? It wasn't in the papers.

47

A = answerphone, R = Roger, S = secretary

1 **A:** The person you are calling is not available. Please leave a message after the tone.
  R: Hi, this is a message for Raj Singh. It's about the apartment for rent, the one advertised in Town Hall. OK, uh, my name is Roger, I'm at 617-555-1212.

I'll try and call you later if I don't hear from you first. Thanks.

2 **S:** P and Q Associates, good morning.
  R: Oh, hello. Could I speak to Jess Parker, please?
  S: I'm afraid she's not in the office at the moment. Can I take a message?
  R: Actually I'm returning her call. She left me a message this morning.
  S: OK, I'll let her know that you called. Who's calling?
  R: It's Roger Li. She has my number.
  S: Well, I'm sure she'll get back to you as soon as she comes in, Mr Li.
  R: OK, thanks.

48

R = Raj, N = Naomi, J = Jess, S = secretary

1 **R:** Hi, any messages?
  N: Oh, hi Raj. Yes, there were some messages for you. Umm, let's see… Anam called about the party tonight. She wants you to call her back. A woman from the bank called. She says she can't make it to the meeting tomorrow. And someone called about the apartment. He left his name, but he didn't leave his number.
  T: OK, thanks.

2 **J:** Hi, I'm back.
  S: Hi, Jess. Just a moment, there were a couple of calls for you while you were out. Suzy… she said she would call back… and a guy called Simon said he was returning your call.
  J: OK, thanks. Any more?
  S: No, that's all.

49

1 Could I speak to Jess Parker, please?
2 Can I take a message?

Unit 12

🔊 50

E = Emma, B = Beth

E: The first real eye-opener I had of what life was like in the African forest was on my first-ever expedition. It was the first day and we ended up making camp early that evening. I was exhausted and I fell fast asleep immediately. About four hours later, I was awakened by a lot of screaming and shouting and the words NJOKO, NJOKO! It was the local trackers shouting. Then I heard loud trumpeting and sounds of heavy steps. Basically, we'd put our tent in the middle of a giant elephant path. We couldn't have picked a more inappropriate place! By the time I'd managed to get all my gear and get out of the tent, all of the trackers and all of the local guides had already disappeared into the night. When we came back, three of the tents were completely flattened. That was my first taste of camping in the forest.

B: A couple of summers ago we went to Siberia. We were looking for mammoth bones and tusks, and even hoping to find some mammoth mummies. We flew in on a small plane. It's pretty remote and deserted. When you land and get out of the plane, you look around and there's nothing there. And you set up your camp and there's still nothing there. And you're sitting there, relaxing, in total silence and there's nothing… Then all of a sudden, you're joined by ten million mosquitoes. I remember we made this kind of rice and fish dish for dinner, and we were sitting there, trying to enjoy it while being eaten alive by mosquitoes. We had nets over our heads, but they were totally inadequate. The mosquitoes could still bite you. And you had to take the net off in order to eat. Every time you did that, hundreds of mosquitoes landed all over your face. They got in the food as well. It was just one part rice, one part fish and one part mosquito! You could go crazy after just a few days of that!

🔊 51

1 I ate something I shouldn't have eaten.
2 I couldn't have felt any worse.
3 I should have had some medicine with me.
4 I should have taken it immediately.
5 I could have died without it.

🔊 52

1 **A:** Is everything OK with your food?
   B: Yes, yes, it's wonderful. But, umm, I should have told you that I don't eat meat.
   A: Oh! Oh, dear!
   B: I'm really sorry you've gone to all this trouble.
   A: There's no need to apologize—it's not a problem.
   B: No, I should have said something earlier.
   A: It's OK. I should have asked you if there was anything you couldn't eat. It's my fault. I'll make you something else.
   B: No, please don't. The vegetables are delicious and there's plenty to eat.
   A: Are you sure?
   B: Yes, really. I'm enjoying this. I'll just leave the meat if that's OK with you.
   A: Of course!

2 **C:** Oh, my goodness! What was that?
   D: I dropped the tray of glasses!
   C: Oh, those nice glasses from Italy?
   D: I couldn't help it—I slipped.
   C: Are you OK? Let me help you up. You are clumsy, though.
   D: Don't blame me—this floor is slippery.
   C: Yes, but if you'd been more careful…
   D: Look, it was an accident! It could have happened to anyone.
   C: I know, I know. It's not your fault. Sorry I got upset.
   D: It is a shame about those glasses, though. We haven't had them for long.

3 **E:** I'm so sorry to keep you waiting. The bus didn't come!
   F: Were you waiting for the number 46?
   E: Yes, it was supposed to come at five thirty.
   F: Don't worry about it—that service is terrible. It's always late.
   E: I tried to call you, but I couldn't get through.
   F: Ah, I think my phone is off! Sorry about that!
   E: Wow, I'm almost an hour late!
   F: It's OK. It's just one of those things—buses are unreliable! Anyway, you're here now and that's what matters.